THE EVERYTHING.
Human Resource Management
Book

Dear Reader,

Working in the human resources field for thirteen years has made me a better person. I have learned that it is rewarding to see great things happen to good people. I have also learned that there are two sides to every story, and people will be willing to talk if someone is there to listen.

I wrote this book because I have always enjoyed writing, and I like human resources too, so it made sense to put them together. During the course of my career, I have been able to work full time, part time, and flex time in order to cater to the ever-changing needs of my growing family. When your supervisors allow you to do things like that, it makes work a nice place to be. Then, in turn, you want to be able to do the same thing for someone else, which I have been fortunate to be able to do.

What I like most about working in human resources are the people, because after all, that's what the job is all about.

Sharon Anne Waldrop

Welcome to the EVERYTHING® Series!

These handy, accessible books give you all you need to tackle a difficult project, gain a new hobby, comprehend a fascinating topic, prepare for an exam, or even brush up on something you learned back in school but have since forgotten.

You can choose to read an *Everything*® book from cover to cover or just pick out the information you want from our four useful boxes: e-questions, e-facts, e-alerts, e-ssentials. We give you everything you need to know on the subject, but throw in a lot of fun stuff along the way, too.

We now have more than 400 *Everything*® books in print, spanning such wide-ranging categories as weddings, pregnancy, cooking, music instruction, foreign language, crafts, pets, New Age, and so much more. When you're done reading them all, you can finally say you know *Everything*®!

QUESTIONS?
Answers to
common questions

FACTS
Important snippets
of information

ALERTS!
Urgent
warnings

ESSENTIALS
Quick
handy tips

DIRECTOR OF INNOVATION Paula Munier

EDITORIAL DIRECTOR Laura M. Daly

EXECUTIVE EDITOR, SERIES BOOKS Brielle K. Matson

ASSOCIATE COPY CHIEF Sheila Zwiebel

ACQUISITIONS EDITOR Lisa Laing

DEVELOPMENT EDITOR Brett Palana-Shanahan

PRODUCTION EDITOR Casey Ebert

Visit the entire Everything® series at *www.everything.com*

THE
EVERYTHING®
HUMAN RESOURCE MANAGEMENT BOOK

Attract and keep the people who will
drive your company's success

Sharon Anne Waldrop

avon, massachusetts

Dedicated to Bill, Amber, Rachel, Ian, and Kymberlie

An Everything® Series Book.
Everything® and everything.com® are registered trademarks of F+W Publications, Inc.

Published by Adams Media, an F+W Publications Company
57 Littlefield Street, Avon, MA 02322 U.S.A.
www.adamsmedia.com

ISBN 10: 1-59869-624-6
ISBN 13: 978-1-59869-624-0

Printed in the United States of America.

J   I   H   G   F   E   D   C   B   A

Library of Congress Cataloging-in-Publication Data

This publication is designed to provide accurate and authoritative information with regard to the subject matter covered. It is sold with the understanding that the publisher is not engaged in rendering legal, accounting, or other professional advice. If legal advice or other expert assistance is required, the services of a competent professional person should be sought.

—From a *Declaration of Principles* jointly adopted by a Committee of the American Bar Association and a Committee of Publishers and Associations

Many of the designations used by manufacturers and sellers to distinguish their products are claimed as trademarks. Where those designations appear in this book and Adams Media was aware of a trademark claim, the designations have been printed with initial capital letters.

This book is available at quantity discounts for bulk purchases.
For information, please call 1-800-289-0963.

Contents

Acknowledgments

I would like to thank the following individuals for generously offering their expertise:

Dr. John Fuller, Diversity & EEO Officer at Johns Hopkins Hospital, for reviewing the section about ADA reasonable accommodations.

David Lewis, President/CEO and Founder of OperationsInc, a human resources consulting and outsourcing firm based in Stamford, Connecticut. Mr. Lewis showed me the ways an insurance broker can help a business choose and manage a medical insurance plan.

John Curtis, Ph.D., President of IOD, Inc., a full-service organizational-development consulting firm. Dr. Curtis reviewed the section about employee development. Integrated Organizational Developmental, Inc., has offices in Florida and North Carolina.

Top Ten Essential Functions of Human Resource Management

1. Ensure that all hiring and employment practices are in compliance with federal, state, and local labor laws.

2. Provide a work environment that recognizes diversity and encourages employee development.

3. Maintain a pay and benefits package that is competitive with the local industry.

4. Realize the need of employees to balance work and family life.

5. Recognize that a company's most valuable assets are its employees.

6. Provide a safe work environment that is free from discrimination.

7. Administer constructive feedback and progressive discipline to resolve performance issues.

8. Acknowledge employee privacy laws and keep confidential information secure.

9. Ensure fair treatment of all employees by regulating consistency in policies and procedures.

10. Maintain filing and record-keeping requirements mandated by federal, state, and local regulations.

Introduction

▶ RIGHTS TO PROTECT employees have come a long way since the 1960s, and it's a good thing. There is now the Equal Pay Act of 1963, Title VII of the Civil Rights Act of 1964, the Age Discrimination Act of 1967, the Americans with Disabilities Act of 1990, and the Family and Medical Leave Act of 1993, to name a few. As a human resource manager, you need to keep all of your Acts in place, not only because it's the right thing to do, but because it will keep you out of trouble, too.

Staying in compliance with Federal antidiscrimination laws is just one piece of the human resource puzzle, because the state is watching you, too! By the time you finish reading this book, you will see that there is a lot to learn about in this field.

In order to have a need for human resources, you need people in the workplace. You will learn where to find them and how to (hopefully) select the candidate most qualified for the essential functions of the job. Getting them to stay is another added challenge. Once they decide to stick around, you'll need to learn how to pay them because they are not keeping you company all day for free. No paycheck is complete without a benefits package to go with it, and some employers go a step beyond that and offer really great things like tuition reimbursement, personal concierge service, and retreats.

That's the fun stuff in this job. The not-so-fun stuff is disciplinary action and processing an employee's final paycheck due to an involuntary separation. And no matter what you may hear on television, it's not proper to say that you are going to "fire" an employee. Instead, you "release" or "separate" them from employment. You can even say that you are going to terminate employment, but don't get any more harsh than that.

Along with everything you need to know about getting people in the front door, you'll learn how to set-up personnel and confidential files, develop employees, and the importance of recognizing a job well done. This book recognizes the need to balance work and family life and discusses pregnancy in the workplace, the Family and Medical Leave Act (FMLA), and alternative workschedules. Keep in mind that pregnancy applies to only some members of the female workforce, but FMLA and alternative work schedules can be a part of anyone's life at one point or another. There is much more to the FMLA than providing protected leave for a woman who has had a baby; it allows you to take care of yourself or a sick family member, too.

If you are a new business owner and need to build your human resource department, this book is for you, too. After all, you may actually be the only human resource (HR) department employee and you'll need some guidance to get organized. This book will arm you with the ammunition you need to get started. It's up to you to utilize the resources shared to take it all a step further.

You will find everything you need in *The Everything® Human Resource Management Book*. In addition to great information, you'll also find fun HR acronyms you can memorize and use to impress all of your friends (and other HR people), sign up for free electronic newsletters, and view samples of forms and templates that no human resource office should be without.

CHAPTER 1

Finding the Best Applicants

The people that you employ in your business represent both you and the company. They may be the first contact when a customer walks in the door, the friendly voice on the telephone, or the person trusted to complete a transaction from start to finish. Regardless of what they do, they set the image of the company and will have a lasting impact on your customers. It's important to pick the right people for the job and there are several resources to help you find them.

Employment Ads That Get Attention

The first step in attracting a pool of candidates for a position is to prepare an advertisement for employment to be placed in your local newspaper or one of the other resources mentioned later in this chapter. An ad that simply states the position, rate of pay, and how to apply will not excite anyone. Chances are that the people who respond will be those who are simply looking for a paycheck with no concern for a rewarding career opportunity. They are the ones applying for any job that is available, regardless of whether it's something that they would enjoy doing. People who are not happy at work will not impress your customers. Customers who are not impressed are unlikely to come back because they will patronize the competition instead.

A catchy advertisement will grab the attention of the best applicants. If the job is fast paced, mention this in your ad because many people thrive on being busy. Flexible scheduling options are a hot item right now as many people struggle to balance work, family, and continuing education. A person who works well independently is likely to respond to an ad seeking a self-starter. Is there an opportunity for growth? Let people know. Adding these extra perks turns a dry announcement into an exciting venture.

Newspaper advertisements are most successful if they appear in the Sunday edition of the paper. When you place an ad, you will have the option of running it for Sunday only, weekends only (Friday, Saturday, or Sunday), or in increments of a few days or a week or two. As long as Sunday is covered in the timeframe you choose, you will get the best exposure possible.

An advertisement for employment may be used to determine if someone pays attention to detail and follows instructions. For example, if your ad instructs applicants to send a salary history along with their resume and they don't do this, assume that this person will not be meticulous at work.

Before placing your ad, decide how you want people to apply, and let it be known. You may want them to request an application in person at specific times. For positions that are beyond entry level, you may want to see a resume by mail, fax, or e-mail as the first step. If you need someone with prior experience, stating this in your ad will save time for everyone involved. Use bold print or a bigger font for the name of the position to make it stand out. Short ads are likely to be skimmed quickly and over-looked. Invest in the space you need to draw attention to your ad.

Before placing an ad or taking advantage of one of the other resources for finding people in this chapter, make sure you have an ample supply of employment applications. Most importantly, ensure that the applications ask questions that are legal in your state! The laws may change from year to year. Your state employment or labor-relations agency can help you verify if your applications are in compliance if you are not sure. Most likely, if you order your applications from a reputable source and they are current, you will be in compliance. Beware of outdated applications that may ask questions that were legal a few years ago, but that you are no longer allowed to ask.

If the applications you use ask job seekers for their social security number, verify if this is allowed in your state. If it is, keep completed applications in a secure place for the sake of the applicant. Some states have strict laws about who in the company has access to this information.

Online Job Boards

It's an Internet world and the Web is where many people go for everything, including a job search. If you place an ad in the classified section of your local newspaper, inquire if a listing on the paper's Web site is included in the price. If not, it's worth the extra expense to make it happen. Here are some online job boards to consider:

- Monster.com
- CareerBuilder.com
- HotJobs.com
- Jobing.com
- craigslist.org

Prices vary substantially amongst these Web sites. Some things to check out before making a decision are if they offer the flexibility to make changes to your ad before it expires; how much traffic the Web site receives (other-wise known as how many "hits" it gets); and if the board is the best match for the position that you have available. Some job boards have a higher concentration of entry-level, technical, supervisory, or managerial positions.

Applicants who check online job boards for employment opportunities can perform a search by position, status (part time or full time), location, or duration (temporary or permanent). On some boards, they can even search by company name.

Career Fairs

Whether it's called a career fair, employment expo, or job extravaganza, this is a resource that offers a good value for the dollar. Career fairs are usually sponsored by a school or university, government entity, or local chamber of commerce. Conduct a Google search to find the next one in your area. Early spring and late summer are popular seasons for job expos, when people are looking for employment after graduating or relocating. If you are hiring for a position that requires a college degree, attending an event at a university is your best bet. There isn't a better place to find a large room filled with college graduates eager and ready to work.

A career fair may focus on a specific discipline such as food and beverage, construction, or positions that require college degrees. Make sure that the theme of the event is consistent with your needs. Most fairs cater to an array of positions, but if it's not clear in the advertising, ask.

There are several benefits to these events. You are able to meet job seekers in person immediately, thus eliminating instances of someone who is impressive on paper but disappoints you when you call them in for an interview. Also, recruitment efforts can be accomplished in one day instead of sporadically over the course of a week. You'll be able to talk to job candidates away from the workplace and the distractions that go along with it. You may also meet other business owners in the community and share your recruitment ideas.

What to Bring

When you sign up to participate in a job fair, you should be told whether or not tables and chairs will be provided. If you are planning to have brief interviews, it's best if both you and the applicant are seated, but if you'll simply be manning a booth, it's most courteous if you stand. Wear comfortable shoes, especially if the ground is concrete. Here is a list of supplies that are handy to have at a job fair:

- Employment applications
- Tablecloths
- Stapler or paperclips
- Pens
- Flyers about the company
- Business cards
- Sign-in sheets
- Notepads

Some people may want to take an application home and drop it off or mail it the next day, so provide the company address on your flyers or bring a stack of business cards. Use the stapler or paperclips to attach resumes to applications. If you plan to conduct interviews, have a sign-in sheet available so that you can greet people on a first-come first-served basis, and use your notepad to take notes. Look ahead to Chapter 2 for a list of questions that you may not ask during an interview.

You can stay a step ahead of the other exhibitors and purchase a banner to hang from the front of your table. Keep it generic, with your company name and logo, so you can use it for other occasions, too. Many office supply stores sell customized banners or you can do an Internet search for companies and local print shops that specialize in these products.

Bring someone with you to help at the job fair. If the person you bring is a current employee, he is to be paid his normal wages for his time, or overtime if it applies. Ask him to take a walk around and look at the other tables for creative ideas for your next job fair.

Allow yourself ample time to set up your area prior to the start of the fair. For your comfort, bring some drinking water and inquire if there will be options for purchasing lunch. If you will be alone, bring a "Will Return at __" sign to place on the table when you leave for a break or lunch. If you brought a laptop computer or any other valuables, take them with you anytime you leave your assigned area.

It is a nice touch to provide a bowl of candy, tray of cookies, or attention-grabbing tokens to give away at your table. You can find inexpensive doodads by visiting *www.orientaltrading.com*. Seasonal items and pens go over well with an adult crowd.

People Watching

The environment at a career expo is usually casual and it's a great way to observe applicants when they are likely to let their guard down and be themselves. Once someone is comfortable at work, this is what you get, and it's good to see it before the hiring is done. Look for people who are courteous, respectful, and mature. If you are seeking "front line" employees—those who will have direct contact with your customers—look for people who appear to be friendly and approachable. If they'll be working in the back of the house, these issues aren't as important.

Although the atmosphere at these events can be somewhat relaxed, attendees should still take the experience seriously. Proper job-searching attire is expected, cell phones should be turned off, and this is not the time to be socializing with friends and family members. Beware of recent high school graduates who are being led by a parent or a person being pressured by their spouse; a job applicant who isn't there of her own free will is unlikely to be an enthusiastic employee.

Have Your Own Job Fair

You may also plan your own job fair. Schedule a few employees to answer questions about the positions that are available and pass out applications. You can briefly interview attendees while they are there, then follow up at a later date with more in-depth interviews with the candidates who may be a good fit for the job.

Government and Nonprofit Resources

Look to your state employment agency when you are in need of hiring people. It is likely that you can place an advertisement on their job board for free, and many offer referral programs where they screen applicants first to verify that they have the job skills you are looking for. Search the Internet or the government section of your phone book for the agency in your area or refer to Appendix C.

FACT

Some of the people referred to you by your state employment agency are those who were laid off from work or have left a government assistance program. In some cases, the applicants have received state-sponsored vocational training to assist with their qualifications to find employment. A trained employee is a benefit to your company.

Many nonprofit organizations that assist the disabled offer programs that train an employee for you. The programs generally work like this: You tell them what your needs are. If they have someone able to perform the job, you train the organization's caseworker, who then trains the person being considered for the job at no expense to you. The reason for this is that the prospective employee may take longer than most people to train in the position or get up to speed. When the employee and the caseworker both feel that the worker is ready to perform on her own, she is put on your payroll. Search your local telephone directory for listings under Vocational Schools for the Mentally Challenged or Developmental Disabilities Information and Services.

You can find military veterans looking for work at the HireVetsFirst Web site. Disabled veterans and those who have recently left the military are available for positions from entry level to management. You will also find instructions for applying for grants to offset the costs of hiring, training, and employing qualified veterans.

Applicants Who Qualify for Tax Credits

The Work Opportunity Tax Credit (WOTC) provides a federal tax credit to employers who hire a qualifying person in at least one of eight target areas. There is a minimum amount of time that the qualified employee must work, and like many things in life, this is subject to change. The eight qualifying target areas are:

- A person receiving Supplemental Security Income (SSI)
- A veteran who is a member of a family that is receiving or recently received food stamps
- An eighteen- to forty-year-old member of a family that is receiving or recently received food stamps
- An ex-felon
- A member of a family that is receiving or recently received Temporary Assistance to Needy Families (TANF) or Aid to Families with Dependant Children (AFDC)
- An eighteen- to twenty-four-year-old resident of a Federally designated Empowerment Zone (EZ), Enterprise Community (EC), or Renewal Community (RC)
- A sixteen- to seventeen-year-old EZ, EC, or RC resident hired to work as a Summer Youth Employee between May 1 and September 15
- A disabled person who completed or is completing rehabilitative services from a state or the U.S. Department of Veterans Affairs

The tax credit for the first year is equal to 40 percent of the first $10,000 in wages. The credit for the second year is 50 percent of the first $10,000 in wages for a total of $9,000 over a two-year period, provided the employee works that long. There is no tax benefit for the third year of employment. If employment ends during either year before the $10,000 cap is reached, the tax credit is based on the actual amount earned.

To participate in the program, complete IRS Form 8850 on the day the job offer is made. Within twenty-eight days of the employee's first day of work, complete and mail ETA Form 9061 or Form 9062 to your state's workforce agency, together with IRS Form 8850. Form 9061 is used if the new employee has not yet been conditionally certified as belonging to one of the eight target groups. Form 9062 is used if the new employee has already been conditionally certified. You can print a copy of Form 8850 and its instructions from the IRS Web site. ETA forms 9061 and 9062 are available from your regional or state WOTC coordinator, who you can find on the U.S. Department of Labor Web site at *www.uses.doleta.gov/wotcdata.cfm*. Your envelope with the Form 9061 or Form 9062 and IRS Form 8850 must be postmarked no later than twenty-eight days after the employee's first day of work. These procedures may change at any time, so check with your local WOTC coordinator before getting started.

ALERT!

In the past, there have been several instances of the WOTC program expiring, then being reinstated with retroactive benefits in effect. At press time, the current WOTC program was scheduled to expire on December 31, 2007. If history repeats itself, the program will be extended again after that date.

You may not ask an applicant if their status will qualify your company for the WOTC when they are being considered for employment. However, in some instances when a state employment office refers an applicant to you, WOTC eligibility may be disclosed. Although the tax credit will not benefit your company until your year-end or fiscal year-end taxes are filed, many business owners find the credit to be a benefit and worth the time to process the paperwork.

Employment Agencies

If you are short on time or want the opinion of a trained employment expert before offering a job to someone, an employment agency may be a good fit for you. There are other benefits, most notably the fact that prospective employees have been prescreened and tested for job skills. In addition, they have had their references checked before walking through your door. Once you have worked with an agency to place an employee, they will know enough about your business and the kind of work you do to find people for you quickly.

Most agencies offer a temp-to-hire option. This means that for a designated time, the employee is a staff member of the agency, but physically works at your location performing tasks that you assign. The benefit of this is that you can gauge the person's performance, work ethics, and dependability before making a job offer. Just because someone interviews well doesn't mean that he is a good fit for the job.

Temp-to-hire workers receive their paychecks from the agency and your company pays the agency for this service. They are employees of the employment agency, not your company. Generally, you pay the agency a per-hour rate for the worker. In return, the agency pays the employee a lower per-hour rate. The difference in the two rates covers employer taxes, workers' compensation insurance, benefits, and a service fee to the agency.

FACT

Fees paid to employment agencies can be costly. Most guarantee the placement of the people they represent. In this case, if you hire someone from an employment agency and the person doesn't work out within a designated period, the agency will find you a replacement.

Business owners who are fans of employment agencies appreciate the quick accessibility to a pool of qualified job candidates ready to be interviewed. The time saved by not having to place employment ads and check references is a benefit. Take the amount of money you would have spent placing an employment ad and consider the value of your time spent in the recruitment efforts. Calculate this into the expense an agency charges and you may see that it is money well spent.

College Recruitment

Contact the career center at your local college or university and inquire about listing your job openings there. This is a student resource at no cost to you. If your opening is a Monday through Friday job during the day, don't let this deter you because some students attend school in the evening. You may need to adjust work hours to accommodate someone's school schedule. Many students are available only for part-time work in order to keep up with their studies.

Hiring an intern is another option at the college level. An intern works for you at no charge in exchange for college units. Since it's a vocational educational opportunity, the school will have to approve of the job duties before an internship agreement can be made. The duration of the internship usually runs in conjunction with the semester, and part-time work hours apply. Prior to hiring an intern, it's best to interview them just as you would any other employee, and you may ask their professors for a letter of reference.

High schools and adult continuing-education facilities often offer vocational programs similar to internships at no cost to you. The purpose of these programs is to teach job skills in preparation of venturing out into the workforce. Like internships, these programs usually provide only part-time workers.

Before entering into an internship program, ask yourself about your needs. It takes time to train a new employee, whether or not they are paid, and time is money. Can the duties of the job be learned quickly enough to justify the short time that someone will be working?

Just because someone is an unpaid intern does not mean that poor work performance is acceptable or should be tolerated. They are being graded to work for you. Look at this as their compensation, and expect as much out of them as you would a paid employee. Also, be prepared to show proof of workers' compensation insurance to the high school or university you are corresponding with. Whether a work-related injury will be the responsibility of your company or the school is another issue.

Networking

The perfect employee for your company may be just a neighborhood away. Hiring friends is something that many business owners stay away from because a working relationship may ruin a personal one if there is ever conflict in the workplace. But your friends, neighbors, or family members may know a good person looking for a great job. Ask around at your church or fitness center, and check with people that you currently do business with for a reference.

If you are involved in your local Chamber of Commerce, you will be surrounded by other professionals who can help you out, and you can return the favor when the moment arises. They may know someone seeking a job or be on the lookout themselves.

FACT

As a business owner, you should always be on the lookout for people who will make a positive impact on your company. If you receive excellent service from someone while they are at work, give them your business card and ask them to keep you in mind if they are ever looking for a job.

Being visible in the community will help you attract the best applicants when you need them. Sponsor a sports team, participate in community fundraisers, and patronize local businesses whenever possible. Spend your advertising dollars in areas that will give you the best exposure. Become a household name in the neighborhood and when you're looking for people to help your business succeed, they'll want to work for you.

Set up an employee referral program at your company. Who could be better at selling someone on the idea that your company is a great place to work better than the people who are already there? Offer a program that works something like this: Refer a friend or family member for a job opening. If they are hired and pass the introductory period, receive a $100 bonus on your next paycheck.

Get in touch with former employees who left on good terms and ask if they know anyone looking for work. Since they were once employees at the company themselves, they can describe the job to someone who may be interested and send them to you for an application. If you hire them, send a thank-you card to the person who sent them, along with a gift certificate to a local store or restaurant.

CHAPTER 2

Interview Tactics

Now that you know how to find people who want to work for your company, it's time to meet some of them. There will be days when the applications that impress you far outnumber the positions you have available. This is a good dilemma to have! You will have a tough choice to make, and it's important to give all qualified applicants an equal chance. This is to your own benefit because it will give you more people to choose from and help avoid discrimination suits.

Deciding Who to Interview

Unless you are in dire need of hiring someone quickly, wait a few days to collect an ample number of applications and resumes before you start calling people in for interviews. This way you'll be able to sort through and compare resumes you have received and make a solid decision about which candidates should be called in for a face-to-face meeting. Interviewing people who are unlikely to meet your needs is a waste of your time and gives a false hope to the applicant. You want to give everyone a fair chance, but not at someone else's expense, including yours.

FACT

To be on the safe side, check with your state labor board and inquire whether you are required to keep a position open for a specific period of time before making an offer. Some states do have laws about this. Filling a position too quickly may be seen as not giving enough people a fair opportunity to apply.

Once you have a stack of completed applications, give each one your undivided attention. Sloppy and incomplete applications may be a sign that the person does sloppy and incomplete work as well. Applicants are expected to act their very best when trying to impress a prospective employer; if this is their best work, then anything less may be a disappointment down the road once they are hired. Here are some things to ask yourself when reviewing applications and resumes, but keep in mind that some of these apply only to applications:

- Is the writing legible, with correct spelling and grammar?
- Does the previous-employment section show signs of stability?
- If previous experience is required, does the applicant have it?
- Are all of the questions answered?
- Is the application signed?
- Does anything look questionable?

Consider the position you have open and whether or not you can over-look some of the questions above. For instance, if there is no writing involved in the job, penmanship and spelling skills may not be a prerequisite, and you may decide to overlook this and give the person a chance. The applicant may have never won a spelling bee at school, but based on his experience with other things, he may be able to make your customers happy.

If an applicant has the experience you are looking for but appears to be a job hopper (works at places for short periods of time), you may find it worthwhile to call the person in for an interview and find out what was up; she may have a good explanation. However, beware of people who don't stay at a job very long without a valid reason—the cost to recruit and train a new employee is costly. Most employers find employee retention to be a big issue for them and are looking for people who are likely to stay with the company for a few years or longer.

Read the part of the application or resume carefully that shows what the person's job duties were at their last position. These may be quite different from their job title. For instance, if someone worked as a receptionist their job duties could have been much more than just answering the phone, greeting customers, and sorting mail. They could also have been responsible for ordering office supplies, making travel arrangements, and typing business correspondence.

Duties performed during volunteer work carry as much weight as paid work, which is why most applications instruct job seekers to include it in the employment-background section.

You will be viewed as a fair business owner if you give a chance to as many people as possible who meet the minimum requirements for the job. It may not be possible to interview everyone who qualifies, but it is to your advantage to meet with as many as you can. If several applicants have the same level of qualifications, interview each one.

Keep all of the applications that you receive, whether or not you interview the person. Have a file for the people you will be interviewing and one for those you will not be interviewing. You may end up with a third pile of applicants—those who you aren't sure you want to interview at this time. This is your "maybe" pile. Hold on to these so that you have them handy if you need to call in more people. You may interview everyone in your first-choice pile, still not be in a position to make a job offer, and want to interview another round of applicants.

Scheduling Interviews

In a perfect world, as you call applicants to set up appointments for interviews, each one will answer the phone and set a date and time to meet with you. In the real world, this never happens; you will end up playing phone tag with a few of them. Keep track of when you called and what form of message you left (e.g., left a voicemail message, spoke with someone named Joe and asked that the message be forwarded, etc.). It's a rare thing to call someone in our high-tech times and hear a busy signal or a phone that simply rings and rings, but it does occur, so keep track of this as well. If the applicant calls to inquire about the status of his application, you can let him know that you tried to contact him and were unsuccessful. Your obligation is to make a reasonable effort to schedule interviews; if someone is too hard to reach, he needs to re-evaluate his availability.

Once you have reached an applicant, give them a description of the job duties and verify that they are interested and can perform the job. Have two or three dates you are available to interview them so that you don't have to juggle dates and times while you're on the phone. Give directions to your company and let them know which door to enter, how to find you, and an estimate of how much time to allow for the interview. If you have only a resume from the applicant, ask them to arrive fifteen minutes early to fill out an application before your appointment.

If an applicant lives far away and is hesitant to spend the time and gas to meet with you without the guarantee of a job, let them make the decision whether or not to come. There are expenses involved with looking for a job and this is something that you are not expected to absorb.

Some employers prefer to do a preliminary interview over the telephone, then narrow it down from there, and call people in for appointments. If you do this, first ask the applicant if they are still looking for employment. If they are, tell them how long you expect the phone call to last and ask them if they are available now, or would like to set a time for you to call back later.

ALERT!

If you call someone to schedule an interview and they tell you that they have already found a job, thank them for their interest in working for your company and wish them well in their new position. Indicate on the application that they are no longer available for work and start a separate file for applications with this status.

If you set an appointment with a candidate who does not show up, make note of this on the application. You made an attempt to give this person a fair chance and she didn't follow through with her end of the arrangement. She may call later to say that there was an emergency and ask to reschedule the interview. If this happens, try your best to reschedule with her because everyone has a legitimate crisis at one time or another. Whether or not you are able to schedule another interview, indicate on the application that she called you to let you know why she did not show up. You can never be too careful about documenting the contact you have with people who make an attempt to get a job at your company.

When scheduling an interview with someone based only on a resume, she must fill out and sign an employment application before you meet with her to discuss the job in person. Her signature on the application finalizes her intent to apply for the position and it holds her responsible for the information stated on the application. See Chapter 3 to read about applicants who are not truthful.

Some of the questions asked on an application may be answered with "please see resume" if it is covered on the resume. One of the most common areas where this falls is the section of the application that asks for the duties of the jobs the applicant has had in the past. Resumes don't usually include the phone number and address of previous employers. If this is the case with your applicant's resume, then she should put the contact information on the application so that you have it handy if you do a reference check.

Setting Your Candidate's Comfort Zone

The person scheduled to interview with you may be a little nervous, or very nervous. Job seekers may have a lot at stake if they have been out of work for a while and really need a job or they may want to work for your company so badly that this alone will cause anxiety to build up. If you can make them feel comfortable from the start, the experience will be better for both of you.

Try to be ready for the interview at the appointed time. Sometimes business gets in the way, and you may have to troubleshoot something or your biggest customer may call two minutes before the interview is scheduled to begin. The longer someone sits and waits for you, the more time there is for apprehension to build up. If something comes up and you are running late, ask an employee to offer the applicant a drink of water or coffee and check in with him again in a few minutes to let him know that you'll be with him as soon as you can.

To start the interview, introduce yourself, shake hands, and thank the interviewee for coming. Proceed to wherever the interview will take place, preferably in a quiet private area where nobody can overhear. Send your phone calls to voicemail, turn off the ringer on your cell phone, and set your computer to mute so that it does not make noise when you receive e-mail.

FACT

Allowing interruptions during an interview will disrupt the interviewee's thought process while answering your questions and sends the message that the meeting is not a priority in your day. Ask your staff to hold all questions unless there is an emergency.

The first step to help the applicant feel at ease is to initiate conversation. Do not ask any personal questions during an interview or reveal too much about yourself. Talking about current events may spark a comment about political, religious, or moral views, so these topics should be avoided. Instead, tell the applicant some things about the company, such as how long you have been in business, the focus of your productivity, and any upcoming goals that have been set.

Body language will come in to the mix as the talking begins. Both parties should be facing the other person and sitting up tall or leaning slightly inward. Eye contact should be direct when speaking and listening. There should be no fidgeting or other distractions. A truthful, sincere, interested job candidate is likely to show positive body language.

Questions That Get Answers

A "yes" or "no" response during an interview isn't going to adequately answer your questions. Some applicants will go ahead and elaborate, yet others will not. Here are some samples of open-ended questions that will get results:

- What are two things about you that your last supervisor raved about?
- Tell me about a time when a customer wasn't happy and you turned the situation around.
- Please let me know what you have done in the past when you had a conflict with two things that needed to be done at once.
- Why are you the best person for this job?
- Everyone has at least one weakness. What is one of yours and how are you working to overcome it?
- I want to hear about your strengths, too. Please tell me about them.
- What is it about this job opening that brings you here today?
- What do you think a person can learn from constructive feedback?

If someone doesn't have an answer to one of the questions, offer a moment to think about it. Don't stare him in the eyes while you are waiting. If he still doesn't have an answer after a minute, ask him if he would like to go on to the next question. Take notes during the interview and keep them in your files along with the application.

Challenging Candidates

It doesn't happen often, but you may encounter an applicant who is difficult to deal with. This person may try to monopolize the interview, be unable to answer most of your questions, make snide remarks about the questions you ask, or beg you to give her a job.

Turn the situation around at the first sign of an interviewee trying to lead the conversation. If you ask about the things at her last job that she enjoyed most and she spins off into a story about a coworker who throws a great Super Bowl party each year, it's time to take control. Say that you would like to hear more about the party, but it's time to focus on the interview, then quickly ask the next question. An interview is a two-way conversation, and doesn't mean that you do all the talking and the applicant speaks only when asked a question. But when the discussion strays off topic and is unproductive, it's hard to properly evaluate the candidate.

If an interviewee has no answers to most of your questions, you may wonder why she is there in the first place. She may not really want the job and was pressured to apply by a parent or spouse, her work history may not really be what it appears to be on paper, or she may simply not know what to say. You can help her out by answering one of the questions yourself to give her an idea of what you are looking for. If this doesn't help, finish the interview as best as you can.

ALERT!

It is a good idea to ask identical questions of each person who applies for the same position. This gives everyone an equal opportunity to sell him or herself and will protect you if you are accused of being discriminatory. Prepare a template of your questions and print one for each interview, writing the applicant's answers below each question.

When you receive a snide remark about a question that you ask, ensure the applicant that you are asking all applicants the same questions, others have answered it, and you feel that it is a fair question. Give the person the opportunity to skip the question and go on to the next, and indicate his response in your interview notes.

It's hard to avoid being pulled into someone's story about how much they need a job. There can be a personal or financial hardship that places the candidate in a tough situation, but this should not be brought up in an interview, though it does happen. When it does, a simple, "I am sorry to hear that you are going through a tough time right now. Looking for a job is a wise choice," and proceed with the interview.

Illegal Interview Questions

As much as you may want to know if an applicant has children, thus the possibility of missing work when the kids are sick, or if he owns his house, which means that he's not very likely to move away, you cannot ask these questions. Here are a few others to avoid:

- Are you married?
- Do you have plans to get pregnant in the future?
- Have you ever taken a leave of absence from a job?
- What does your spouse do for a living?
- Do you go to church?
- Will you have to hire a babysitter if you get this job?
- How old are you?
- From what country does your family originate?
- What year did you graduate from school?
- How will you get yourself to work?

If the job requires occasional overtime, you may ask the applicant if he is available and how much advance notice he needs to work extra hours. It's permissible to ask him if he speaks a foreign language, as long as you do not inquire if he is a native speaker. If the job involves overnight travel, you may ask the candidate if he is able to leave town and again, how much notice he will need. You may ask an applicant if he owns a car and has insurance only if driving his own vehicle while on company time is part of the job. Otherwise, questions about transportation are limited to asking if he has reliable transportation to get to work. If he considers the bus, his bicycle, or a neighbor willing to give him a ride to work reliable transportation, then this is reliable transportation.

May I ask an applicant if he has a disability?
No, you may not ask an applicant if he has a disability. You may ask if he is able to perform the job—every applicant should be asked this. For example, you could say, "This job requires you to stand on your feet and walk without assistance for two hours before taking a break. Are you able to do this?"

During an interview, a job seeker may voluntarily bring up something that falls under the category of questions that you should not ask. When this happens, change the subject quickly and do not write the information down in your interview notes. If, for instance, someone accused you of not hiring them because they have four children, and your interview notes indicate that they have four kids, you may have a hard time proving your contrary argument if the candidate otherwise meets the criteria for the job.

Applicants with Criminal Backgrounds

Depending on the state in which you operate your business, there may be questions about criminal convictions on the employment application. There may also be questions asking the applicant if she is awaiting trial. Don't be too quick to bypass a candidate with a conviction or pending trial for two reasons: One is that many employers feel that if someone admits to a mistake, makes no excuses for what they did, is remorseful, and is making a true effort to turn her life around, she deserves a second chance. Second, the behavior that resulted in the conviction may have nothing to do with the job duties and may not affect your other employees. This isn't meant to advocate the hiring of convicted criminals; it's just a reminder that every circumstance is unique and a good candidate is worth the inquiry.

If you interview an applicant who indicated "yes" to questions about trials or convictions, do not ask about it just yet. If she brings it up first, then you may discuss it. Otherwise, if this person is one of your top choices and you are considering hiring her, call her in again and say that you need more information about the conviction. At this point, she is a top contender for the job and you do need to know the details about a conviction. It's best to get this in writing by preparing a form that asks for their name, the place and date of the conviction, a brief description of what happened, and a place to sign. Don't make any promises afterward, just thank them for filling out the form and let them know that you will be making a decision soon.

It is important to know how to handle applicants with criminal convictions because it will come up. Chapter 3 goes into more detail about pre-employment screening and when a conviction should mean refraining from making a job offer.

The details of an applicant's conviction should not be revealed to anyone at the company. Just like any other personal matter, it's not open for discussion unless the person involved brings it up if she is hired. You do have an obligation to provide a safe work environment for your employees and make a reasonable effort to staff it accordingly. Have confidence in the hiring decisions that you make.

Closing the Interview

Give the applicant a chance to ask questions before ending the interview. A candidate who has questions about the job or company is displaying an interest in ensuring that the job is right for her. It's a two-way street; both you and the candidate want the match to be a good fit. You are looking for a new employee who wants to come on board and stay for the long haul. Applicants are seeking a job that they will find rewarding in a positive environment.

Your candidates will appreciate it if you let them know what the next step will be. You may want to narrow the selection down to two or three applicants then do a follow-up interview with each one, or have a manager that works with you conduct a second round of interviews. You don't have to interview your top choices a second time, but some business owners find it helpful at the end if there is more than one likely candidate. As with the first round of interviews, ask each person the same questions and take notes for your files.

It is always a pleasant surprise when an applicant follows up with a handwritten note thanking you for the interview. This is a display of gracious social skills and a continued interest in securing the job. If you receive such a note, clip it to the person's application. Some people may ask you if they can call to follow up in a few days to see if a decision has been made. Once you have opened your door to invite someone for an interview, she deserves this courtesy.

How Long to Keep Applications Active

Some employers keep applications active for as little as sixty days, or as long as six months. This means that as other positions become available, they re-evaluate the applications that they already have on hand during the hiring process. The person who was second choice for the last position you filled may still be looking for a job and you may now have the opportunity to hire him.

There may be provisions in your state that require you to post an ad or announcement each time you have an opening. If this is the case, you can still go back to the applications that you already have on file as long as they are considered active. It's important to maintain a consistent policy. If you keep applications active for ninety days, maintain this until you formally change your policy. Once an application becomes inactive, repeat job seekers should be asked to fill out a new one for subsequent positions.

You may find it helpful to set up an applicant log in Excel or a similar program. Indicate the person's name, the date they applied, and for which position they applied. Next time you have an opening, you'll have quick access to the names of the people who were recently interested in the position. Keep the applications filed in alphabetical order and you can pull them out by name instead of going through each one and looking for people interested in that particular position.

An applicant log will also let you see if someone is showing a continued interest in your company by applying every few months. It will give you an idea of peak months when people are most likely to apply for jobs, and which positions most people are looking for.

CHAPTER 3

After the Interview

By now you probably realize that quite a bit of time and expense is involved in selecting new employees to join your company. But your job isn't finished once you have narrowed it down to the person you are considering hiring. It's a good idea to speak with professional references and you may even want to do a background check. You might hit an obstacle along the way and decide that your top candidate isn't the right person after all. This chapter examines the procedures and steps prior to making the job offer.

Reference Checks

Some people do a wonderful job at selling themselves. They have the right answers to the toughest questions. They carry themselves well and look you right in the eye when talking. You are impressed, and after an hour of interviewing them you think that your decision has been made. But these things don't always add up to the person who is right for the job and your company. Talking to former employers may help you realize this before you bring the person on board.

Unfortunately, companies are afraid of litigation from former employees if they share unfavorable facts. As a result, you're unlikely to find out if someone has an anger-management problem, excessive unexcused absences, or was convicted of stealing from the company. During a reference check, a former employer may volunteer to tell you only the good things about the applicant and leave out other things. Or, the current employer of an undesirable employee may say great things about the employee so that you will take him away.

Most companies these days have a policy to reveal only a former employee's start date, separation date, and the position they held. In some states, this is the only information that employers are legally allowed to share. Yet others may answer the question of whether or not a person is eligible for rehire with a simple "yes" or "no" answer. Some companies have gone as far as to have a "no reference check" policy. What's interesting about this is that it is common for these companies to call on others for references and expect an answer!

More Than a Phone Call

Checking references may sound like a quick task, but this isn't always the case. There may be only one person at the applicant's former employer authorized to give references and she may be hard to track down. You may call a company and be told that they will only verify information with the signed consent of the applicant. This means calling the applicant back in to sign a consent form, sending it to the company via fax or mail, and waiting for a response. It can be frustrating when you need someone to start working right away and have a delay in finalizing the hire.

Before the end of an interview with someone you are likely to hire, ask him to sign a consent form for reference checks addressed to his last two or three employers. It will save you a step if you are asked to provide one when you call to check references.

A consent form to check references should include the employee's name, social security number, dates of employment, position, and a statement giving permission to verify the information. Include a signature line with the date for the employee to sign. You may prepare a checkbox option for the employer to indicate whether or not the information is correct. If the information is incorrect, provide a space for the employer to explain. You may also include questions about the applicant's work habits and behavior, but employers with strict policies about what they will share may not answer them. It is reasonable to ask to have the completed form returned to you within twenty-four hours. Some employers prefer to respond over the telephone and will do so once they have signed consent.

You may also ask an applicant for written consent to view past performance appraisals and inquire about disciplinary action that may be in the personnel file. Your state labor board may prohibit you from asking for this information, so find out first if it's legal. There is a listing of each state's labor board in Appendix C and you will read more about reference checks in Chapter 10.

Easy Reference Checks and Automated Systems

Applicants who are proactive will contact previous employers, tell them that they are looking for a job, and ask them to be available as a professional reference. You'll be presented with a list of former supervisors pleased to help the applicant. These people are usually the ones likely to answer specific questions about the applicant. Again, the company may have strict policies about offering information and a manager who wants to answer the questions may not be able to. They may volunteer a comment about wishing that the employee still worked there or something else to let you know that the employment period was a positive one.

Many large companies have moved toward an automated employee verification system. Some companies charge a fee for the use of the service. If there is a cost associated with checking the reference, it is worth it. These systems usually work by keying in the applicant's social security number, followed by a computerized voice giving you the information that the company is allowed to share. There is no live person to talk to and no chance to ask additional questions.

Reference-Check Questions

During a reference check, focus on questions about the demonstrated ability to perform specific tasks, work ethics, teamwork, and behavior. Here are some examples:

- Tell me about a time when he became frustrated about something. How did he handle it?
- How would you describe the individual's ability to get along with others?
- Does he adapt well to change? Please give me an example.
- He says that he was responsible for payroll processing from start to finish. What were the tasks he accomplished to get the job done?
- Does he need a lot of supervision?
- Please tell me about a time when he displayed loyalty toward the company.

If you are doing reference checks on two runners up for a position, ask the same questions for both applicants. This will give both a fair opportunity to get the job, provided you have cooperative former employers for both. In the event of two equally qualified applicants, it's the reference check that may put one person ahead of the other.

ALERT!

If you are considering hiring someone who is employed by another company, be almost certain that you will be offering a position before starting a reference check. Get permission from the applicant before verifying employment with his current employer. Most job applications include a section that asks this question.

An employer who gives a reference check is offering you a valuable service. Thank them for their time and document the conversation along with your other notes gathered during the recruitment process. Keep everything attached to the employment application whether or not you make a job offer. Applications, interview notes, and reference-check information for all applicants not hired should be kept for at least one year. Your state labor board may suggest a different timeframe for retention.

Background Check

The three most common pre-employment screenings are background checks, drug testing, and physical exams. You are not required to do any of them. Some companies do one, two, or all three. If you choose to pre-screen, decide if all positions will require it, or if only select positions will require screenings based on the duties of the job. There may be a position that requires a physical and drug test, but another that requires only a background check. It is important that you remain consistent and screen all applicants according to your policy. Let's start with the basics on background checks.

Hiring a reputable company to conduct a background check on people you are considering hiring is a wise business choice. The number of companies starting this practice increases each year, and for good reason. One motive is that conducting a background check will increase your efforts to provide a safe work environment and decrease the likelihood of theft. Another is to catch people who lied on their application or resume, which is where the highest number of inconsistencies occur. Most resume bluffs consist of stretching the truth about dates of employment, positions held, and education completed.

FACT

Criminal, driving, employment, education, residence, identity, credit, and workers' compensation are the most common background items to check. It is worth the extra expense to screen nationally. You must have written consent from the applicant before the check, and she must be informed of what areas will be screened and that a job offer is contingent on the results.

An applicant trying to hide an extended period of unemployment, time in prison, or a job from which they were fired tend to stretch the employment dates of positions before and after the event. For instance, if they were fired from a job they held for two years and do not want to list it on their resume, they'll add a year to the positions they held before and after that job.

Education is another area on an application where people may lie. A fake diploma may be purchased from a degree mill, but no matter how authentic it looks for the $400 the applicant paid for it, you won't be fooled if you conduct a background check that includes education credits. Applicants have even been known to go as far as to falsify a Ph.D.

ESSENTIAL

Do not try to save money and conduct your own background investigation by doing an Internet search. It is unreliable for positive identification purposes and will not deliver a fair assessment. Infolink and ADP Screening and Selection Services are two of the biggest companies available to help you.

Criminal background checks are important because you may not want to give someone control of your company's petty cash account if they have been convicted of fraud. If your business caters to children, you have an obligation to keep pedophiles away. Employees who drive vehicles on the job should have a good driving record and a background check can spot out-of-state violations. A person with bad credit could have experienced an unfortunate hardship, which you may choose to overlook, or she may have uncontrollable spending habits that may be a red flag. I-9 verifications will tell you if the person is honest about her identity and eligibility to work in the United States. All of these things can be discovered during a background check. A basic check costs about $20. More extensive checks run $100 or more.

Drug Screening

People who use illegal substances are not only breaking the law, they can be a liability to your company. The U.S. Department of Labor reports that drug use costs employers an estimated $75–$100 billion per year. And since about 73 percent of drug users are employed, you may have one in your workplace. You can expect attendance, performance, and behavior to be poor from drug users. The best deterrent is to implement a policy to drug screen every new employee. Once you earn the reputation of being an employer who drug-screens applicants, the users won't even apply.

Contact an occupational health facility in your area and ask the office manager for a tour and an explanation of their pre-employment drug-testing program. Urine testing is the most commonly used practice and the least expensive, but blood and hair testing are also available. Inquire about the chain of custody that is used for the handling of the urine, how long it takes to receive results, and how you will be notified. You can expect to receive results within twenty-four to forty-eight business hours. The facility should be clean and make you feel comfortable. Look for a staff that is friendly and responsive. Think of it as a reflection on your company and what the perception will be from your applicants.

ALERT!

Before scheduling an applicant for a drug screen, have him sign a consent form that states that he understands that an offer of employment is contingent upon passing the test. A sample employment-offer letter that doubles as a consent form may be found in Appendix A.

A drug screening is paid for by you, the employer. For your convenience, find an occupational medical facility that is willing to bill you for services. When you send an applicant for a drug screen, he is not yet an employee and you are under no obligation to reimburse him for mileage expenses.

To ensure that only approved job candidates are screened, there should be a procedure set in place between you and the screening facility. Normally, you will need to call in and let the facility know that an applicant is coming. Additionally, the job candidate may need to bring in something signed by you to authorize the visit and give permission to bill the company for the charges.

Inform applicants that they will need to bring proof of identification with them to the appointment. In most states, anyone under the age of eighteen is required to have a parent with them to give consent. Find out from the testing facility what the applicant needs to do to prepare himself for the test. If it is a urine test, they may have to have a full bladder. Blood or hair tests may also have preliminary requirements.

You should receive test results in writing. If an applicant fails the drug screen, you may be informed of which drug was found in his system, but you do not need to give him the details. This is news that they should hear directly from the drug-screening facility. Your role is to simply arrange for the screening and determine whether or not the candidate is eligible for employment after receiving the results. Simply let the applicant know that he failed the drug test and you are pursuing other candidates.

A written drug-screen policy should clearly state who will be drug tested and when. You may choose to screen new hires only, or you may also screen employees before returning from a leave of absence, immediately after a work-related injury, at random, annually, or for probable cause. Valid reasons for probable cause could include witnessed participation of drug or alcohol use, slurred speech or staggered walking, or a noticeable negative change in work performance. As always, check with your state labor laws to ensure that you are not breaking any rules.

An employee who will be drug and alcohol screened for probable cause should not be allowed to drive herself to the testing facility. Call a taxi or have a manager or human resource representative transport the employee.

ESSENTIAL

Post-accident drug and alcohol testing may reduce your overall workers' compensation expenses. If a policy is in effect to drug screen all employees who are injured on the job, those who test positive for drugs or alcohol in their system may be ineligible for workers' compensation benefits. Check with your state workers' compensation board for the legalities.

There may be strict guidelines for random drug testing, and a written policy must be in effect prior to testing anyone. Before considering this, check and see if it is allowed in your state and follow the legal procedures carefully. See Chapter 17 for procedures on implementing a drug-free policy.

If random drug testing will take place, set the criteria for how often it will occur—monthly, quarterly, biannually, yearly, etc. The employees selected at random should be picked by the drug-testing facility. This will encourage workers to remain drug free all year and will catch those who stayed away from drugs only during the period they were seeking employment.

Recovering alcoholics and drug addicts may be protected under the Americans with Disabilities Act (ADA) and eligible for the Federal Family Medical Leave Act (FMLA). The ADA applies to employers with a staff of fifteen or more. Find out if the FMLA applies to your company in Chapter 12. If a worker comes to you to report that he is an alcoholic or recovered drug addict, he may be protected and may not be disciplined or released from his job because of his situation. However, employers may still take action if the employee reports to work under the influence or hung over. Having an addiction to drugs or alcohol is by no means permission to break company drug or alcohol policies and normal disciplinary actions still apply. Check into the legal guidelines in your state to ensure that you handle the situation properly.

Pre-Employment Physicals

Regardless of how healthy or physically competent someone may appear, do not assume that they will be able to perform the job for which they applied. Although it is legal to ask someone if they are able to perform the duties of a job, they could be mistaken or untruthful. A post-offer physical exam before an applicant starts working will help protect both you and the applicant. You may not randomly choose who will receive a physical; for every position in which you feel a physical is necessary, every single applicant must be examined.

FACT

If finalizing a job offer is contingent on passing a physical, you must have written consent and understanding from the applicant. If you have a policy in place that requires a physical exam, applicants should not fill out new-hire paperwork or start working until after they have passed the exam.

Choose one physician to perform all of your post-offer exams to ensure consistency. For the most effective program, inform the doctor of the job duties and the frequency of the following:

- Repetitive movements
- Prolonged standing or sitting
- Kneeling
- Bending
- Lifting
- Stooping
- Driving
- Exposure to heat or cold

As an employer, you do not have the right to ask applicants about their medical history or any prescription drugs that they take. This stays between the physician and the job candidate. The doctor's role is to determine if the applicant can safely perform the job. Here is one example: If a job requires someone to frequently lift ten-pound boxes over her head but she has a shoulder injury with permanent 20 percent disability, she may not be able to perform the job safely. If necessary, the physician performing the exam will consult with the doctor who treated the injury. What is important is that a worker is never put into a position where they could further aggravate a pre-existing condition or perform job duties beyond their capabilities.

When an Applicant Is Untruthful

You may find this out during a reference check that you do yourself, or through a background check, but it's going to happen. You'll meet someone that you want to hire and discover that he lied on his application. Sometimes it's something minor, such as being a month or two off on the start or end date of a job. In this case, you can always call the applicant and say something like, "I checked your reference at the hotel job you had last year. The dates they gave me are different than what you put on your application. Will you double check the dates and get back to me?" Something like this could have just been an error. Occasionally, someone will consider their last date at a job as the last day he worked, but the employer may refer to the day they were taken off the payroll records, which could be weeks later due to lack of follow up on the company's behalf.

However, some people will stretch out the dates of one job to cover up another one in which they worked a short time or feel that they will receive an unfavorable reference. Sometimes they will exaggerate a title they had or job skill that they learned. Lying on an application is a very valid reason not to hire someone and may be valid grounds for termination if you hire the person then find out later.

If an applicant is untruthful about something that does not endanger themselves, coworkers, or the company, you may not have legal recourse to terminate the employment in some states. Make sure that you have proper documentation to prove the lie before checking into whether or not you may end the employment.

If you have already interviewed someone for a job and started a reference check, you may contact him for another interview in person or by phone if you receive conflicting information. Keep in mind that the person you speak with to verify employment may not be the person who directly supervised the applicant. For instance, someone in the payroll or human resources department may verify dates of employment and the job description, but may not know much about the person's capabilities. In order to fairly evaluate someone, it's important to get the facts straight. For instance, if an applicant states that he used PeopleSoft at his last job, but it's not one of the usual duties for the position, this doesn't mean that the applicant was untruthful on the skills section of their application. It could simply be that the person you spoke with was not fully informed of the job duties. This is why it is helpful to speak directly with an applicant's former supervisor whenever possible.

If you suspect that someone may be stretching the truth, say something like, "Since you'll be working with Excel for several hours a day, I'd like to learn more about your skills. Tell me step by step how you set up formulas to calculate columns." If the candidate claims to be proficient in Excel but can't explain how to do this, then he may be stretching the truth about his abilities.

Beware of people who forget to sign an application. They may be hoping that it will be overlooked and that the lack of a signature will give you no legal grounds to reverse a job offer if they are caught lying. In addition, check applications for completion and beware of people who skip the sections about felony convictions, the reason for leaving a previous employer, or other areas that may leave a negative impression. To protect your company, check an application for completion and a signature before starting an interview. If something is missing, ask the applicant to finish it.

ALERT!

It is to your benefit that your employment applications include a line that states that falsification may result in employment ineligibility or grounds for termination. You may make it a policy to avoid interviewing people with incomplete applications as long as this is a consistent rule for all applicants.

If an applicant is reluctant to sign a consent form for a background check, but then admits to lying about something on the application or claims that they forgot about it earlier, you may have saved yourself the cost of a background check. Think very carefully about whether or not this person is someone you want to hire. People who come clean only after they think they may get caught are holding a red flag.

It's inevitable—you'll extend a job offer to someone based on the contingency of a background check and run into a conflict. A job that he held for three out of the past five years is not listed on the application. The degree is an associate's degree from a two-year community college and not a bachelor's degree from a university. When this happens, tell him that you have decided to pursue other candidates.

Employing Minors

The U.S. Department of Labor has set forth child labor regulations in the Fair Labor Standards Act. Your company must abide by these federal standards if there are no state laws in effect that overrule them. Generally, only state laws that have stricter guidelines for minors will overrule federal law.

There are regulations regarding the types of jobs that minors can perform, the industries in which they may work, and the equipment and machinery that they are allowed to operate. The hours that teenagers under the age of eighteen are allowed to work vary based on whether or not school is in session. There are daily and weekly limitations and they may not work between specific hours.

A work permit may be required before you can offer a job to a minor. If you do not know if one is required in your state, contact the counseling office of your local high school or your state employment board. A school will issue an application for a work permit to students in good standing. Generally, the application must be signed by both the parent and the prospective employer. It will advise you of the hours in which the student will be allowed to work and your signature confirms that you will stay within these guidelines. The application may also state that you will maintain workers' compensation insurance. In lieu of a work permit, some states require a proof-of-age certificate to ensure that the minor is old enough to be employed.

Handling Telephone Inquiries

Some applicants may call you after an interview to inquire whether you have made a decision. You may not have decided who to hire yet because you have only one position open and several qualified applicants. It could take a day just to review the applications and interview notes and determine who is best qualified for the job. Additionally, there is the issue of conducting reference checks or waiting for background or screening results to come back. The whole process can take a few days. To help alleviate the waiting period for applicants, let them know how long you expect it to take to make a decision.

It is likely that the people you interview have also applied at other companies. The most qualified candidates will be hired quickly. An efficient, timely hiring process will help you get the applicants you want before the competition gets them. Reference checks are usually the hold up. Be proactive and start calling previous employers right away.

You may meet an applicant who has crossed the line between showing an interest in working for you and being annoying or aggressive. Someone who calls too often to see if you have made a decision is showing a lack of patience. When this happens, tell her when you will be in touch and ask her to wait for you to contact her, or say something like, "If you don't hear from me by Wednesday at 2:00, feel free to call again." Then see if she is able to follow instructions.

Offer of Employment

Success! You are finally ready to offer a job to someone. Call him on the telephone, share the good news, and ask if he is still interested in working for your company. Remind him of the name of the position he applied for, the salary, and how many hours per week he will be working. If he accepts, schedule his first day of work to come in and fill out new-hire paperwork and receive an orientation, as discussed in the next chapter.

If the applicant asks to give you an answer later, he may be waiting to hear about a job offer from another company or may have changed his mind about working for your company. It could also be because he knows that accepting a job isn't something to take lightly, and he simply wants to be sure that this job is one that he really wants. Give him the time he has requested, as long as it is not too long. Twenty-four hours is reasonable, and ask him to contact you with his answer regardless of whether it is yes or no. If you do not receive a response by the deadline, offer the job to the runner-up candidate. For this reason, do not tell an applicant that a position has been filled once you have decided to hire; wait until you have made an offer and it has been accepted.

Notifying Unsuccessful Candidates

Job applicants that you interviewed but have not selected deserve to know if the position has been offered and accepted by someone else. You may notify them by telephone, which is a common courtesy for anyone who has been called in for a second interview or was a top candidate, or you may notify them by mail. A sample letter for unsuccessful candidates is included in Appendix A.

Someone may ask you why she was not chosen for a position, but you are under no obligations to give details. Simply explain to her that you chose the candidate you felt was best qualified for the job and that it was a tough decision.

CHAPTER 4

First Day of Work

It took a lot of time and effort to find the new person you have chosen to join your team, but the longest part of the journey is about to begin. You need to get the employee on board, trained, and feeling confident that he knows the job well. If the first day starts out as a good one, the rest are bound to follow the same note. This chapter discusses the paperwork involved with entering into an employment agreement and ways to make your new coworker feel welcome.

New-Hire Paperwork

You already have a signed application, your interview notes, and documentation from reference checks to start the personnel file. The actual file will be explained in more detail in Chapter 5, but getting it started involves some forms required by law before a person starts working. Some states require that employees are "on the clock" when they fill-out employment papers, so check the laws in your state. Contact your state labor board (see Appendix C), or to save time and be on the safe side, go ahead and have the employee clock in when they start the papers. It is a nice gesture to pay someone for his time getting set up as an employee, whether or not it is required.

If the new employee qualifies for the WOTC mentioned in Chapter 1, remember to fill out the paperwork that is required on the employee's first day of work. It would be a shame to loose a tax credit over a sheet of paper that was forgotten.

When you set up the day and time for a new employee to get started, let him know when the workday will end as well. Tell him where to park, what entrance to use, a recap of the dress code, and if there are facilities for storing and heating-up lunch. Also, let him know how long the lunch break is so he can determine if there is enough time to go out and buy lunch if he wishes. Taking a new employee out for lunch on his first day is something to consider, too, but only if it is something that you do for everyone.

Try to have a timecard ready for the employee on the first day and show him how to use the time clock when you're ready to get started. Let him know what is expected regarding the use and care of the timecard.

Form W-4 and State Tax Withholding Form

Federal Form W-4 is filled out by the employee to determine the amount of taxes that will be withheld from her check. You can download a copy of this form from the IRS Web site. For each state that requires state withholding, there will be a state form to use for that purpose. You can get a copy of this form by contacting your state taxation office. You may order one by telephone or print one from the Web site listed in Appendix C. State income tax withholdings do not apply to people employed in the seven states listed below. Therefore, there is no separate state form for the employee to fill out.

- Alaska
- Florida
- Nevada
- South Dakota
- Texas
- Washington
- Wyoming

The tax withholding form will ask if the employee is married or single. The tax rate for single people is higher than it is for married people; however, some people who are married prefer to have their taxes withheld at the higher single rate to help decrease their chances of not having enough taxes taken out during the year and having to pay on April 15th. Then, the number of exemptions is chosen based on the number of dependants the employee has or other criteria of her own choosing. Employees also have the right to file "exempt" and have no federal or state taxes withheld from their check.

Unless you are a CPA or other tax professional, you should not give your employees advice about the marital status or exemptions they should claim on their tax withholding forms. Even if you are a tax professional, this is not a good idea unless you are already the person's tax preparer because you don't know her financial situation. If she wants you to do her taxes in the future, then that's fine and she can adjust her tax withholding forms then. Employees can change their exemptions at any time.

It's easy to transpose numbers. Ask your employee to double-check the accuracy of her social security number on the W-4 form. Also, look at it and verify that you are reading the numbers correctly. A "3" may look like a "5," and changing a social security number error for payroll purposes is difficult.

There is some generic advice about the tax withholding forms that you can give. If the employee asks, you may let her know that the higher the number of exemptions, the lower the rate of tax that will be taken out. Leave it at that, and let her know that she can update the form any time she needs to.

Form I-9 and Corresponding Documents

The United States Citizenship and Immigration Services Form I-9 Employment Eligibility Verification is perhaps the most important form that both you and your new employee will prepare. In addition to verifying eligibility to work in the United States, it confirms identity. You may download and print the form and instructions from the USCIS Web site listed in Appendix C, or call 800-870-3676 to order the forms and instructions.

It is your responsibility as the employer to ensure that the employee fills out Section 1 of Form I-9 on his date of hire, which should be the first day of work. The form must be accompanied by the instructions, which are on a separate piece of paper. If an error is made on the I-9 form, give the employee a new form and shred the old one. The employee may also cross out the incorrect information with a single line and correct it above. Follow the same procedure if you make an error on your section. There cannot be anything on either the employee or employer section of the I-9 form that has been scribbled out or is illegible.

All employees who were hired after November 7, 1986 are required to fill out an I-9 form. If the employee previously worked for you and it has been less than three years since an I-9 form was filled out, you may verify and update that form instead of issuing a new one.

Acceptable Documentation

The instructions on the Form I-9 include a list of acceptable documentation that confirms identity and verifies the eligibility to work in the United States. Within three days of starting work, the employee must present you with the original documents for your personal review. You may not accept copies of the documents from the employee. With the original documents in your hand, fill-out section 2 of Form I-9, then return them to the employee. You may not have another employee or even a manager sign the form unless they are also the person personally reviewing the documentation.

FACT

Employers may make a copy of the employee's documents to keep on file with Form I-9 as long as both the front and back of the documents are copied, they are used for I-9 purposes only, and copies of every employee's documents are kept on file. You may not pick and choose whose documents to keep—it's everybody's or nobody's.

If the employee has not presented you with his I-9 documents within three days of starting work, you may not continue his employment. Employing undocumented workers is not something that you want to do. It is illegal and the consequences are costly.

The documents that you may accept are either one from List A, or one item from both lists B and C on the instructions. You may not tell employees which documents to bring in or which list or lists to choose from. Do not review or make copies of more documents than you need. Employees sometimes bring in too many things because they do not read the instructions carefully or are not sure what is expected of them. The A, B, and C lists can be confusing to someone who is not familiar with the procedure.

In a few instances, you may accept a receipt in lieu of an original document. A receipt for a replacement document that was stolen, lost, or damaged may be accepted as long as the replacement is shown to you within ninety days. Receipts for Forms I-94 and I-551 may also be accepted, but the procedures are complex and instructions should be obtained directly from the USCIS. The M-279 handbook for employers and "The I-9 Process in a Nutshell" publication are good places to find this information.

Form I-9 Retention

Retain a copy of the Form I-9 for three years after employment begins or one year after it terminates—they can be retained electronically. If an employee presented you with an unexpired foreign passport containing a temporary I-551 ADIT stamp, it is subject to reverification upon the expiration date. Set up a system to notify you at least ninety days in advance of the expiration date of these documentations so that you can remind the employee that it's time for a renewal. It takes about ninety days for the USCIS to process work authorization applications. If the I-551 ADIT stamp expires, the employee can no longer work for you.

There are several documents that qualify for I-9 verification that may be unfamiliar to you. You can look them up on the "For Employers" section of the USCIS Web site. You are not expected to be a document authenticity expert, but are expected to make a reasonable judgment whether a document is valid. If you are in doubt, check with the USCIS.

Some good ways to notify yourself when a I-551 ADIT stamp is about to expire are to utilize the reminder function in Microsoft Outlook, use a manual index-card system, or log the information in a computer database. If you choose the last two systems, make it a habit to check the sources every Monday to look for expiration dates coming up within the next ninety days. Although it is the employee's responsibility to ensure that his work authorization doesn't expire, it's a lose-lose situation if it does. It's worth your investment in the employee to help make sure that it doesn't happen.

New-Hire Orientation

After the new-hire paperwork is completed, the following hour or two should consist of an orientation to help the new employee feel welcome and begin a smooth transition into the company. The orientation may be lead by either you or an employee who has been trained to handle the task. It is important that consistent information be given to all new hires, and that as policies change the staff is notified accordingly. With this practice, new staff members, as well as the not-so-new ones, will have the same information. Many managers find it helpful to develop an orientation checklist to ensure that all pertinent information is covered on an employee's first day.

There is a lot for a new employee to absorb on the first day of work. The orientation should not be rushed, and the employee should get your undivided attention. This is an important day for her and will set the tone on how accessible you will be when she needs something, as well as how thorough you are in keeping employees up to date. Following are some things to cover during the orientation.

Attendance Issues

Let the employee know what time work starts each day and when she is expected to clock in and out (for example, if work starts at 8:00 A.M., you may not clock in earlier than 7:55 A.M.). If the work schedule varies each week, let her know where and when the schedule is posted, the procedure for switching days with another employee, and how to request a day off. Discuss what to do if she is ever going to be late for work or is sick and cannot come in.

If employees are not allowed on company property during nonwork hours, let new employees know. Your workers' compensation insurance may not cover them if they are injured on the property while off the clock. This is the most common reason why employers do not allow hourly employees to be on the premises.

ALERT!

Many companies put into effect an "introductory period" for the first thirty to ninety days after a new employee is hired. This time is used to determine if the person is indeed a good match for the job. Benefits usually do not go into effect during this period. If you designate an introductory period, let the employee know.

Personal Property at Work

Employees who bring a purse to work should be advised how to keep it safe and where to put it. If radios are allowed, set a limit on volume and let it be known. In this high-tech age, many people like to bring a cell phone to work or even a laptop to tinker with while on a break. Employees will need to know if the ringer on their cell phone is to be turned off during working hours and if it is okay to plug into the company's electricity or Internet access when using their laptop.

Breaks and Lunch

When are breaks, how long are they, and where should they be taken? Designated smoking areas should be pointed out to all employees, whether or not they smoke. If loitering in the parking lot is not allowed, now is the time to share that information, but let employees know if it is okay to sit in their cars on company property during break or lunch. Some people like to do this to read, use their cell phone in privacy, or just have some peace and quiet. Sitting in a car isn't usually considered loitering, since the employee is off the clock and owns the car, so it should be allowed as long as they are not disruptive.

Employees are unlikely to make personal phone calls on the first day of work, but this is the perfect day to bring up your policy to avoid having it abused later.

Pay and Benefits

This is why people work, and their pay and benefits are of the utmost importance. Salary was discussed when the job offer was made, but the employee will now want to be familiar with the payroll calendar. Let her know how often she will be paid and on what days (every Friday, alternate Wednesdays, or the first and fifteenth of the month). Employees will also want to know when they will receive their first paycheck and how many days of pay they will receive. If they started midcycle in the payroll period, their check may be for three days of work instead of five, or seven days of work instead of ten if payday is biweekly.

Show the employee how the pay periods work. On a calendar, point out the first and last days of the current pay period, when payroll is processed, and on what day the checks arrive. This will give her a better understanding of how many days she will have on her first check.

Inform the employee where and when paychecks are distributed and what the procedures are for having a family member pick up their paycheck should the need arise. Also, advise them to look at their check stub carefully to ensure accuracy; people and computers are not perfect. If there is an error on the employee's paycheck, you want to know about it promptly so that you can have it fixed.

People will want to know when they can expect a pay raise. Some companies give one at the end of successfully passing the introductory period. Others give them once an employee has worked for six or twelve months, or a combination of both or all three. Raises may also be given to everyone across the board at the end of the year or the company's fiscal year. If a performance evaluation is tied to the percentage of increase someone will receive, let them know this. It's a great incentive for a person to work harder. A lot of people expect at least an annual cost-of-living raise. If this applies, let them know.

If there are any benefits that are included in the compensation, give the employee the enrollment materials and the procedures for signing up. Explain who qualifies as an eligible dependent on the insurance plans.

ALERT!

If the employee needs to sign up for insurance plans by a specific date to avoid a delay or denial in coverage, give her this statement in writing and ask her to sign it. Make a copy for the employee and put the original in the personnel file. It is the employee's responsibility to turn in the paperwork on time.

If you offer paid time off such as holiday, vacation, or sick leave, let the employee know which holidays are covered, how many sick and vacation days are earned each year, when these benefits go into effect, and what the policies are to request the time off.

At the end of the orientation, ask the employee if she has any questions and let her know that you are available to answer them as they come up, whether it's now or in the future. It's a good idea to encourage employees to ask you or their supervisor the most important questions to make sure that they receive a correct answer. If they ask an employee who unknowingly has incorrect information or has their own opinion about something, the employee could end up breaking a rule or procedure.

Tour of Facility and Introductions

Chances are your new employee knows the room where you interviewed him and gave the orientation, but that's about it. He shouldn't be left to fend for himself on the first day, so give him a tour of the building, or have another employee do it so that he can get to know one of his coworkers better. The person who does this should be someone who knows the scoop on everything and likes to talk.

He'll want to know where the restrooms are, who sits where, the functions of each department, and where the drinking fountain and supply room are located. Let him know if he is free to take supplies as he needs them, or if there is a procedure. Speaking of supplies, he should know who to ask if there is something he needs to do his job better or be more comfortable.

As you walk a new employee around the building, introduce him to everyone you can find, being sure to pronounce his name correctly. Help him get to know coworkers by saying things like, "This is Sally. She has worked here for ten years," or "Ben was awarded 'Employee of the Year' in 2006."

The company tour is also a good time to discuss safety issues. Tell him that spills on the floor should be cleaned up or brought to the right person's attention immediately, and to close any drawers or cabinets that are left open. Explain that a buddy system is used for lifting heavy items and point out the MSDS sheets if this applies. MSDS sheets are discussed in Chapter 11. Point out all possible exits in the event there is an emergency, and where the telephones and fire extinguishers are located. If safety compliance training is something that the company practices, let him know when the next session will be.

Walk around the outside of the building, too, showing where all of the entrances are and letting him know what is in the neighborhood if he is not familiar with it.

Training

Your company will only be as successful as the people who do the work with you. How well they are trained sets the tone for their productivity and job satisfaction. In a recent survey, lack of proper training rated high on the list of things that frustrate people at work. Training your staff well is worth the time and investment. Unfortunately, there are no shortcuts, but there are ways you can make the training more effective.

Have patience and realize that some people catch on to tasks quicker than others. This has to do with how quickly they process and retain things that are shown to them. Some people learn better by watching first for several minutes. Others do best if they are shown once and given the opportunity to jump right in. Everyone will thrive if they are given the opportunity to learn in the way that suits their abilities best.

FACT

Don't just show how to do something, show why. Explain the reasoning for getting from Point A to Point B the way that it is done. Talk about what can go wrong by going through the what-ifs. Most people will understand something better with this logic.

Wouldn't it be nice to have a detailed training manual with steps for performing every job in the company? Think of how much easier it would make training a new employee. It would promote consistency and ensure that nothing is left out in the training process. This doesn't mean that the training manual would take the place of a human being. Handing someone a manual and telling her to figure out the job isn't very effective. The manual is to be used as a tool to assist both the trainer and trainee.

Prepare a training manual on the computer and print copies as you need them. Use staples, a report folder, or a three-ring binder to keep the pages intact. The cover page should state the position and have a space for the trainee's name. Next, pick the first thing a new employee should learn on the job and type out detailed instructions, then continue with the next thing. Each page should have two columns next to each task with the headers "Trainee" and "Trainer." Once the trainee has mastered each task, both the trainee and trainer sign off on the column. For added fun, include a True or False quiz at the end of each task.

ALERT!

You can always count on procedures changing on occasion as you and your staff discover better ways to do things. When this happens, update the training manual so that the next person hired learns how to do the job correctly from the start.

Utilizing a formal training program with consistency from one employee to the next will back you up in the event you have to release a new hire from employment because they are unable to learn how to do the job efficiently. You will have proof that you developed a program that gives everyone the same chance at success. This will help you if you are ever accused of issuing an unfair employment termination.

It is sometimes possible to have the training seminar or workshop come to you. This depends on how many people will be attending and if computers are needed for the class. The dollars that you spend on training are an investment in the people who work for you.

CHAPTER 5

Personnel Files

Where there are employees there is paperwork, and you'll need a secure and effective filing system to keep everything intact. You'll want to stay in compliance with federal and state laws, too. Access to the files should be given to a minimal number of people, and there are privacy laws to consider for everyone. This chapter talks about how these files get started and how to maintain them like a pro.

The Contents

You should have a personnel file for each employee. First, you'll have the employment application, resume, notes from the interview, and reference checks that accumulated during the selection process. Tax withholding and I-9 forms will be filled out on an employee's first day of work, but only the tax withholding form is placed in the personnel file. You'll find out what to do with the I-9 form in the next section of this chapter. Here are some other documents that are found in a well-prepared personnel file:

- Pre-employment skills testing
- Emergency contact information
- Awards and commendations
- Training documentation and certificates
- Job descriptions
- Job title and salary records
- Benefit enrollment forms
- Performance appraisals
- Disciplinary action
- Exit interview

Folders with index tabs work great for personnel files. Arrange your files in alphabetical order for quick retrieval when you need one. You may write the employee's name on the tab, or use a computer or label maker for a neater, more professional look. Folders with metal fasteners will help keep the contents intact. Use a hole puncher on the paperwork, but make sure that you do not punch out critical information before you fasten papers into the file.

Place the papers in chronological order, with the oldest documents on the bottom. You can also purchase sectional folders and divide the contents by category. As months and years pass, the contents of the personnel file will multiply. Sectional files come in handy for long-term employees.

Once a person is hired and starts working, you may call the Social Security Administration at 800-772-6270 to verify if a social security number is valid. You will be asked for the name that is on the card and the number. The representative will tell you whether or not it is a match. If it is not a match, they cannot tell you what the discrepancy is, but you can assume that the card is a fake. Employees without a valid social security number may not work in the United States. You are allowed to verify up to five records per phone call.

Personnel files should be kept in a locked cabinet with a key carried by only a few people—preferably someone in human resources and a member of upper management. Under no circumstances should an employee's file be left in an area that other employees can access. Files should be locked away when not in use.

The items kept in an employee's personnel file are those that are directly related to the person's employment and compensation. You should be able to look through the file and identify the employee, know his address and phone number, the date employment started, the position he holds, pay and benefits, his level of performance, and dates of promotions or transfers. Only the files of employees who have left will have an exit interview form if you conduct them upon separation, as mentioned in Chapter 10.

Implement a policy to conduct a personnel file audit at least once a year. During a self-audit, look through each file for items improperly filed, incomplete paperwork, missing documentation or signatures, and other things that could cause problems down the road. The person assigned to do the audit should be someone who normally has access to the files. It is important to keep your files safe, especially if the contents are not stored electronically. Check that the files are safe from theft or natural disasters.

What to Keep in a Separate File

I-9 forms are not to be kept in personnel files. Make a separate binder for the forms and file in alphabetical order. If you are visited by the U.S. Citizenship and Immigration Services or the U.S. Department of Labor for an I-9 audit, you are expected to immediately turn over the documents to the officials. If you have an I-9 binder ready, all you have to do is present it to them when requested.

There are other things that do not belong in personnel files, and you may be prohibited from federal or state law from keeping them there. If you receive a wage garnishment for one of your employees, do not put it in the personnel file. You may keep it with the payroll records, in a file specifically for garnishments, or in a confidential file on behalf of the employee. If a background check was done, it doesn't belong in the personnel file either. Equal Opportunity Employer questioners that reveal gender, race, veteran, or disability status are private and should be treated as such. The key is that any personal information that is not directly related to the person's employment should not be in the personnel file. Each employee should have a confidential or medical file, but some will not for the simple reason that there are no contents. These files may be kept directly behind the respective employee's personnel file in the filing cabinet, or in a separate area. Again, keep the files under lock and key; never leave them unattended on a desk.

The Americans with Disabilities Act (ADA) and federal Health Insurance Portability and Accountability Act (HIPAA) require that all medical documents be filed separately from personnel records. Medical information should be kept confidential and away from personnel records even if your company does not fall under ADA or HIPAA regulations. Many states have their own laws about employee medical information, too, and it is important to be familiar with them. Medical paperwork that should be filed separately includes the following:

- Reports from pre-employment physicals
- Drug- and alcohol-testing results
- Workers' compensation paperwork
- Medical leave of absence forms
- Disability paperwork
- Insurance applications that reveal pre-existing conditions
- Anything that identifies a medical issue

Insurance-enrollment paperwork that does not inquire about medical background should be filed in the regular personnel file. Insurance is part of the employee's compensation package and this is a normal part of the personnel file.

A medical, personal, or confidential file is what many companies refer to as the file that holds nonemployment information. You can prepare a medical file and a personal or confidential file for the employee, or just one file and combine everything. What is important is that contents that contain personal non-job-related information are not in the personnel file. Medical information is known as PHI—Protected Health Information.

ALERT!

If you receive a summons to provide a copy of an employee's records for a hearing, be sure you're clear on what to send. If it's a labor relations issue, only the personnel file may be needed. If it's for a workers' compensation or ADA matter, the medical file may be the one to send. Clarify what is needed before proceeding.

A supervisor's file is just that—a supervisor's file. She may have one of her own for each employee, or just one general file to document all notes and observations about the staff. Generally, incidents that fall below the need to issue a warning or discipline are documented in this file. For example, if an employee starts to show a pattern of tardiness, the dates and times of clocking in will be recorded. Then, if tardiness becomes a problem, the supervisor will have the documentation she needs to address the issue. Supervisor files should be kept secure in a locked cabinet in the supervisor's office, and are in no way related to a personnel file; it's simply a place for supervisors to document and keep notes about events and conversations that occur in the workplace.

Health Information Portability and Accountability Act (HIPAA)

HIPAA is a complex set of federal rules that applies to most businesses and everyone in the healthcare industry—insurance providers, hospitals, medical offices, laboratories, etc. Privacy, mainly about Protected Health

Information (PHI), is critical and you will stay in compliance if your company keeps medical information confidential and secure. This applies to both verbal and written health updates.

Find out if your company must comply with HIPAA regulations by contacting the U.S. Department of Health and Human Services. The size of your company and health insurance plan are the main criteria. If HIPAA provisions do not affect you, employee medical privacy should still be considered out of respect and to avoid litigation.

With this in mind, supervisors are not to tell other employees when a coworker has a doctor appointment, a test at the hospital, or will be going on medical leave. The employee is free to share this info if he chooses, but it is not the place of an employer representative. If someone asks about the whereabouts of a coworker with a doctor appointment, a response from the supervisor of "He has an appointment" or better yet, "He will be here in about two hours" is all that should be shared. If an employee will be off work for six weeks due to surgery, anyone who inquires or needs to be informed about the absence should be told that the employee is on a leave of absence. Do not say that they are on medical leave. If the employee chooses to tell his coworkers that he is having surgery, that's fine.

An employee's pregnancy is news that should be shared only by the woman who is expecting. Although it is not an illness, it is a medical condition that will result in a temporary disability period after giving birth. Most pregnant women will notify human resources or their supervisor prior to the condition being obvious.

Posted work schedules should never indicate when an employee is out sick or on medical leave. Outgoing voicemail messages and e-mail out of the office auto-responders set up by someone other than the employee should simply announce that the person is out of the office and who should be contacted in their absence.

HIPAA regulations will affect you when an employee is excused from work by his physician or put on modified duty due to a medical reason. Without written consent from the employee (most doctor offices won't accept a faxed signature), physicians can't give employers too much information. In some instances, the employee's physical or health issue may be something that employers are not privileged to know anyway.

If a doctor's office will be faxing off-work notes, drug- and alcohol-test results, physical-exam reports, or similar documents to your office, it is crucial that the fax machine is not in a public employee area. If it is, have the medical office call you before the document is sent and wait by the fax machine for it to arrive.

If your company offers a self-funded or flexible spending account for medical expenses, make sure that anyone handling the billing has been trained about the importance of PHI issues. For example, an accountant or accounts payable clerk may have access to medical bills and must adhere to the confidentiality of employee medical conditions and expenses. Managers and human resource professionals are accustomed to being discreet about personal issues, but this can be new to other people on staff. Regardless of how well one employee knows another, personal issues that are brought to someone's attention during the process of paying medical or insurance bills should never be shared.

Further respect employee privacy by having a policy prohibiting the distribution of employee addresses in a company directory without permission. A company directory has its benefits and can be a fun tool; however, some people will not want their private information available for all employees to see. If your company distributes an address book that may include the name of family members, birthdates, and anniversary dates, get written permission before adding someone's name and information.

Employee's Right to Copy of File

Whether or not an employee has the right to review or request a copy of her personnel file depends on the state where your company is located. Also, what is allowed varies from state to state.

First, confirm what employees are entitled to review in your state and if they can make copies or request a copy made by you. Next, implement a written policy with the procedures for obtaining access to the file. In most states, the employee is to make a request in writing and the employer is obligated to comply within a reasonable period of time. This may or may not occur during the normal course of the employee's workday. Your company should have a policy regarding where access to the file will be granted, such as in the human resource office where the file is kept.

FACT

Personnel files are the property of the company and consist of legal documents. When employees are given access to their file, it should be done under the direct supervision of a person who is the custodian of the files. This is to ensure that the file remains intact.

When employees receive a performance review, commendation, disciplinary action, or other event that generates paperwork, give them a copy. They are entitled to it, and doing so will decrease the number of requests you receive from employees who want something from their file because they already have some of the contents. When you give copies to employees, treat the documents with confidentiality, even if they are of a positive nature. Hand it directly to the employee, or leave it in a sealed envelope on the employee's desk, in-box, or bulletin board. You can also deliver it via the U.S. Postal Service.

Employee Handbook

A receipt from an employee that proves he was given a copy of an employee handbook is one of the wisest things to require in your personnel files. Employees have a lot to absorb during their orientation on the first day of work. A handbook that outlines company policies reminds employees of the rules and lets them know that the company is doing its part to help them succeed. The book shouldn't be just a posting of rules and regulations. It tells the employee everything they need to know about working for the company.

Prepare a receipt for employees to sign the day they are given the handbook. A sample is included in Appendix A. You may include it as the last page of the booklet, then ask the employee to tear it out after it is signed. Put it in the personnel file as soon as it is signed.

Some managers ask employees to read the handbook from start to finish before they start working. An hour on their first day can be set aside for this. Others send it home with the employee and advise them that they are expected to read it and ask about anything they don't understand. Employees should be told that failure to comply with one of the policies or procedures because they didn't read the handbook is unacceptable.

How to Write a Handbook

You can prepare a handbook yourself by using a word processor or custom publishing program or you may hire a professional writer or human resources consultant to do it for you. The booklet will be a lot of work, but worth the effort. Be sure to save the document in two places. You'll want to have a backup if one file is destroyed.

Number the pages like this: 1 of 35, 2 of 35, etc. so that you and employees will both know that the booklets are complete when distributed. This will make it easy to identify a missing page.

What to Include

Start out with a welcome message. Let the employees know that you're happy to have them on board and give the history of the company. If there is a mission statement, include it toward the front of the booklet. A mission statement spells out a company's purpose and future goals.

Here are some of the policies to include in the handbook. Once in the handbook, they are considered the company's written policies.

- Attendance and tardiness
- Calling-in sick
- Personal relationships with customers

- Personal calls
- E-mail and Internet
- Dress code
- Being on property during nonwork hours
- Sexual harassment
- Discipline procedures
- Complaint process

Chapter 17 explains how to develop company policies. You may have ideas for policies not mentioned above. Talk with other business owners or HR professionals for ideas. There may be rules to set that are specific to your line of business.

Keep It Updated

The employee handbook should be reviewed twice a year to make sure there have not been any changes or additions that didn't make it into the book. When there is a change, update the original document on the computer and reprint the respective page for any handbooks that are yet to be distributed to employees. Toss the page with the old information and add the updated one. Send an amendment to the handbook to everyone on staff.

ALERT!

When there is a change to the employee handbook, ask each employee to sign a receipt acknowledging the change. This is for the employee's benefit as well as the company's. If an employee is not aware of a policy change, he could break one of the rules as a result of the lack of communication or understanding.

An annual handbook review during an all-staff meeting will help keep everyone in compliance and the lines of communication open. For fun, have a quiz with prizes for the people with the most correct answers.

Job Descriptions

Every employee should have a signed job description in his file and a copy at home. The benefit to the company is that it will help avoid misunderstandings by the employee about what is expected of her. It will establish a collaborative and effective workplace overall if each position has its own assigned duties. The employee benefits because salary should be in alignment with the job description. If new duties are added on a continual basis or they get more technical, she will have the backup she needs to ask for an increase in salary or promotion.

There will always be a few discrepancies between what is listed on a job description and the actual duties. Just because something isn't on the job description doesn't mean that an employee can say, "It's not my job" if she is asked to do something. The last item on the job description should indicate that reasonable requests by management are valid job assignments.

Have job descriptions available when you interview applicants so that there won't be any surprises for them after they are hired. It's better for someone to find out that the duties of a job do not interest him before he actually starts working. Current employees who want to transfer into another position can benefit from them, too.

A job description should list the most essential duties of the job first. You can also have a section of primary and secondary duties as well as ones that are infrequent. List skills needed to perform the job—these are skills that the employee should possess before they are hired or have the ability to learn.

Review job descriptions at least once a year for accuracy. Keep a computer copy for easy updates. Each department head should have a copy of the job descriptions for everyone that works in that area.

Emergency Contact Information

Nobody wants to think of an employee being so injured or sick at work that they are unable to notify a family member by telephone. Unfortunately, it happens, so you need to be proactive. You have each employee's telephone number, but this doesn't mean that it's the best number to call in case of emergency.

Each employee should have a red "In Case of Emergency" form in their file. The form should ask for the names and telephone numbers of people who should be notified in case of an emergency. Ask for work numbers, cell numbers, pager numbers, any number where someone may be reached.

ALERT!

For purposes of privacy, do not ask about the relationship of the people on an employee's emergency contact list. All you need is the first and last name and a few phone numbers. It is okay to inquire if a number is home, work, or cell.

Ask employees to review their emergency contact form twice a year to catch outdated information and add new names or numbers. This can be done at the first of the year and the first day of summer, or each time the clocks are set back or ahead.

Employee Name Changes

If an employee changes her last name, you'll need more than just a request from her to revise her personnel records and the name on her paycheck. First, you'll need to update her I-9 form. There is a section on the Form I-9 specifically for updates. You will need to see the original corresponding documentation that reflects the name change before you sign Form I-9 and make the official change in company records.

Additionally, wages are attached to social security numbers, and the name on the paycheck should match the name on the social security card filed with the Social Security Administration (SSA). If the employee doesn't use a social security card as one form of ID for I-9 purposes, verify that the name on the card has been changed. When you report end-of-the-quarter wages, the names of the employees should match the social security numbers.

Once a name change has been properly processed, update the employee's file, timecard, name badge, directory listing, benefit enrollments, and everywhere else the name appears.

Purging and Retention

Personnel files and medical files must be kept during the duration of a person's employment and thereafter. The amount of time you keep the file is referred to as the retention. There are federal retention requirements for the Americans with Disabilities Act, the Family Medical Leave Act, and the Age Discrimination in Employment Act, and each state has its own retention schedule, too. Both federal and state laws may vary according to the number of employees a company has. You may find that you're not sure exactly how long to keep personnel files after an employee has left. Err on the side of caution and keep the files longer than you think you are required just to be safe. If a discrimination suit is brought against the company, it is important to be prepared by having the correct records. This is the basis for some of the retention requirements.

FACT

Personnel files and medical files for released employees should be kept under lock and key in the same way that current employee files are kept. For your convenience, keep them in a different drawer. Privacy issues are still in effect and forms that you no longer need, like direct deposit authorizations, should be shredded.

If the company has fifteen or more employees, ADA and Title VII of the 1964 Civil Rights Act requirements apply, and files must be kept for one year after separation. If there are twenty or more employees, ADEA regulations come into effect, and there is also a one-year retention requirement. The FMLA requires that all medical documentation and other paperwork related to the leave are kept for three years. These are just federal laws; your state discrimination laws may supersede the federal requirements. In the event of a workers' compensation claim or litigation, the files may need to be kept indefinitely.

To purge a file means to remove it from your inventory. Once it has been determined that it's safe to purge a file, it should be shredded. You can shred it yourself with a high-quality paper shredder or hire a shredding company to do the job for you.

CHAPTER 6

Payday!

Your company may be the best place in the city to work, but your employees are there for one reason— to receive a paycheck. They will trust you to pay them in accordance with federal and state labor laws. Paycheck stubs should show how many hours they are being paid for and the amount of each deduction. Payroll may be prepared on site or contracted out to a third party. Where there are earnings, there are taxes, so be prepared to calculate and pay these, too.

Wage and Hour Laws

One of the most important things to be aware of are federal and state wage and hour laws. Employers are fined or sued more often for violating these laws than discrimination violations. There is a two-year statute of limitations for an employee to file a claim, and in some cases it is three years. Recent class action lawsuits filed against mega companies have resulted in multimillion-dollar payouts. On a smaller level, noncompliance can hurt your company, too. This is not an area in which to be careless or take chances. Negligence can multiply into substantial monetary damage, diminish the trust of employees, and harm your company's reputation.

The Department of Labor's Fair Labor Standards Act (FLSA) is something that you should become very familiar with. It regulates laws about minimum wages, youth employment, overtime, and payroll record keeping. There are a few exemptions to overtime and minimum wage eligibility to find out about, too. Keep in mind that there may be state regulations that are more generous toward the employee and overrule FLSA regulations. Contact your state labor board located in Appendix C to find out.

ALERT!

You may be required to pay an employee for a minimum amount of hours each time they clock in. For example, if there is a two-hour minimum of time in which an employee must be paid and you need him for only ninety minutes, he must be paid for two hours. Find out what the rule is in your state.

Hourly and salaried nonexempt employees may be called in to report to work if needed, but they cannot be put on "on call" status without being paid for the time they are on call, whether or not they work. If someone is scheduled to be on call, this usually means that they have to stay close to home and make no plans. The purpose is to guarantee their availability to come in to work if called. The employee has to remain in a position where he is able to work, such as avoiding alcoholic beverages and getting enough sleep, as they would before a normal workday.

There are laws in regards to paying hourly employees for travel time to and from a destination other than the usual workplace. If they are participating in off-site training or going somewhere that includes air travel, it is important to find out when you are, and are not, responsible for wages.

Overtime

Employees who are paid by the hour are entitled to overtime pay. Generally, overtime pay is paid at time and a half of the employee's usual wages (e.g., an employee who earns $6.00 per hour will be paid an overtime rate of $9.00 per hour). In some states, overtime is paid to employees who work more than forty hours in a work week, regardless of how many hours are worked per day. However, in others, overtime is paid for any hours over eight in a day, even if the total hours for the week are less than forty. For example, if an employee worked three ten-hour days during the week for a total of thirty hours, six hours would be paid at time and a half. This represents two hours for each of the three days.

For payroll purposes, your company's work week may start on Monday and end on Sunday, begin Saturday and end on Friday, etc. It may begin on any day of the week, must have a designated starting and ending time, and remain in place unless a formal notice is distributed to employees announcing a change in policy. The designated work week is important in determining overtime pay and it may not be changed for the purpose of avoiding overtime payments.

The company's specified work week must include seven consecutive days, even if your business operates only Monday through Friday. This is the law, and will be needed for payroll purposes if employees are ever required to work a Saturday or Sunday. The days of the work week should be spelled out in the employee handbook.

Your company's typical work week will also determine when overtime is due if your state has regulations about paying overtime to employees who work more than five days in a row. Laws about consistent days of work may or may not carry over from one pay period to the next. If there are no state laws regulating this type of overtime, there may be a company policy in place that does.

There may be laws in your state that prohibit employees from working too many consecutive days (i.e., you may be required to give workers a specific number of days off per week or month). The nature of the job duties can be a determining factor, too. For instance, there are rules about how many hours a truck driver can be on the road per day.

Minimum Wage

The federal minimum wage was $5.15 per hour for ten years until President Bush approved an increase in mid-2007. The increase will take effect in three increments of seventy cents per hour, with the minimum wage reaching $7.25 per hour by summer 2009.

Your state's minimum wage may be higher than the federal minimum wage. If this is the case, the state wage supersedes the federal minimum wage.

In some states, employees who receive tips may be paid a lower salary by employers if the wages and tips combined meet or exceed the minimum wage. In 2006, this rate was $2.13 per hour but is expected to rise along with the minimum wage increase mentioned above. For any pay period that the wages and tips do not meet the minimum wage, the employer must make up the difference.

FACT

Federal rules that allow employers to pay below the minimum wage for tipped employees or workers under the age of twenty may be illegal in your state. As always, if a state law is more generous to an employee than federal law, the state law overrules the federal law.

Workers under the age of twenty may be paid a lower wage for their first ninety days of employment in some states, as long as their employment doesn't displace another worker (i.e., you release a higher-paid worker from her job for the purpose of hiring someone else to do the same job at a lower rate).

Hourly, Non-Exempt, and Exempt Status

Most employees are paid by the hour and overtime rules apply as stated above. They punch a time clock or swipe a timecard each day and usually follow a schedule, unless they are on one of the alternative work arrangements highlighted in Chapter 19. They are paid overtime based on federal or state law, but some employees have a salaried status and are considered salaried non-exempt or salaried exempt. The exempt part refers to whether or not they are exempt from overtime.

Salaried Non-Exempt

According to U.S. Department of Labor provisions, a salaried non-exempt employee is one who is paid a weekly salary to perform a job. The salary remains the same if the employee works under forty hours during the work week. However, if he works more than forty hours, he is subject to overtime. This arrangement is an advantage to the employee because they do not need to work a minimum amount of hours each week to receive their full pay. However, if they work over eight hours in a day or forty hours in a week, they are entitled to overtime (based on which overtime law the state recognizes). Perhaps the only advantage to this status for the employer is that it makes payroll processing easier because the employee is paid the same salary each month. As long as the employer eliminates overtime, there is no added expense.

ALERT!

Time cannot be docked from salaried non-exempt employees for working a partial day. If you are going to designate this status to workers, find out the federal and state requirements for handling full days off of work and the proper use of paid leave. There are only a few instances when pay may be docked for missed work.

Salaried Exempt

A salaried exempt employee is not eligible for overtime wages. Workers with this employment status are paid to do a job in whatever time it takes, whether it's thirty hours in the workweek or seventy. Be extremely careful before giving an employee this pay status because improperly classifying an employee may result in stiff penalties.

An exempt employee is usually an executive, manager, or professional. Some people who work in outside sales or computer technology may be eligible for this classification, too. But it's not the job title that determines if the employment status is exempt from overtime; there is a "duties test" for the position that determines whether or not the position is eligible.

Contact the U.S. Department of Labor to determine if an employee's job duties qualify for salaried exempt status. Generally, the employee will need to supervise at least two people, have the ability to make important business decisions, perform management duties during the majority of the workday, or a combination thereof, among other things.

Employers need to beware that scheduling managers to work shifts normally assigned to hourly employees on a regular basis can have stiff consequences. There was a recent class action lawsuit brought against a fast food chain because managers spent too much time running the cash register and cooking food. As exempt employees, the majority of their working hours should have been spent in administrative work.

There are also salary requirements that must be met before an employee can be classified as salaried exempt. Currently, employees must be paid at least $455 per week in order to qualify. With the federal minimum wage increasing, there is a chance that this figure will rise as well.

ALERT!

The rules for deducting pay for time not worked by salaried exempt employees is similar to that of the salaried non-exempt employees mentioned above. If a full day of work is missed due to a personal reason that does not include an illness, you may be able to deduct the wages for the day.

It is customary and reasonable to offer a different benefit package to salaried exempt employees. This may include benefits that are offered only to this classification, or an earlier eligibility date for benefits to begin. It's one of the perks of the additional work hours and the added responsibility required of an exempt position.

Tracking Hours Worked

Employers may require exempt employees to keep track of any day in which they perform work. This may be done by swiping a timecard anytime during the day or recording days worked on a time sheet. Since a full day of wages is earned if any work is performed (regardless of the number of hours worked), there is no need to keep track of actual hours worked. This is also due to the fact that exempt employees are not paid overtime wages.

Timekeeping for hourly and salaried non-exempt employees must be more detailed. Most companies use a time clock for hourly employees. Paper timecards that are punched by a time clock are soon to be obsolete. The newer timekeeping systems work with a plastic card that an employee swipes anytime he starts or stops work, including before and after meal breaks. Other versions have employees enter the last few digits of their social security number or other identifying information.

Minutes, Quarters, or Tenths

Recorded time may be tracked by the exact number of hours and minutes worked (for example, 11:15 A.M.–3:35 P.M. would be a total of four hours and twenty minutes), or time may be recorded by the quarter hour, in which case the hours above would total 4.25 (four hours and fifteen minutes). Time recorded this way will sometimes round down, as in this example, and sometimes round up. For instance, if the same employee clocked in early at 11:07 A.M., she would be paid for an extra quarter hour of work (e.g., 11:07 A.M.–3:35 P.M. = 4.50 hours of work instead of 4.25).

ESSENTIAL

If your timekeeping system records time in quarter-hour increments, employees who clock in more than seven minutes early or late will have an extra quarter hour added or deleted from their time worked. Although all employees should be encouraged to report to work on time, it is especially important to do so when paid by the quarter hour.

Hours worked may also be tracked by tenths, with ten increments of six minutes within an hour. A person working from 11:15 A.M.–3:35 P.M. would be paid for 4.5 hours. If they worked an additional minute until 3:35 P.M., time reported would be 4.6 hours.

Timekeeping records are mandated by both federal and state laws. Employers are required to keep a timecard, time sheet, or electronic record for every hourly and salaried non-exempt employee. These records should clearly indicate the hours worked each day and whenever sick, holiday, or vacation pay is used. Contact your state employment or labor office to become familiar with specific requirements in your state.

The Total Package

Anyone who picks up one of your payroll files should be able to easily determine the following information:

- The start and ending dates of the payroll period
- The name of each employee paid
- Daily number of hours each person worked each day
- Total number of hours each employee worked during the period
- The hours paid at straight time and the hours paid at overtime
- Scheduled days missed and unpaid to the employee
- Paid time off used by the employee
- Any bonuses, tips, or incentives paid to the employee

Some things may be stored electronically, such as the gross earnings, tax deductions, insurance premiums, retirement plan contributions, etc. It is wise to do periodic audits of your payroll files to ensure that the company is, and remains, in compliance. This includes reviewing the duties of employees to make sure that anyone classified as exempt qualifies for the status, and ensuring the payroll records are complete. Spot check a few timecards, versus the paycheck received by the employee, at random to verify accuracy. Consider any changes in federal or state law that may change your payroll processing or records requirements.

Keep detailed records for wage garnishments. When processing a garnishment, be aware of the federal Wage Garnishment Law that limits the percentage of income that may be legally garnished from an employee's paycheck. Wage garnishment and making payments to the court or creditor to repay a debt results in extra work for an employer. However, there are federal laws that protect employees from employment termination when employers are served with a wage-garnishment order.

Unpaid Meal Breaks

Employees must clock out for a thirty-minute meal period as mandated by state law. In most states, a meal period is required during a shift of five or more hours of work. Therefore, an employee who works 4.75 hours would not need to clock out for a meal break, but if he works 5.0 hours, he does. Someone scheduled to work from 1:00 P.M.–6:00 P.M. would actually work only 4.5 hours since they are required to take a break for thirty minutes; they would have to be scheduled from 1:00 P.M.–6:30 P.M. in order to be paid for five full hours of work. The rules in your state may vary, and there is no federal mandate on when meal breaks are required.

ALERT!

There is a difference between unpaid meal breaks and on-the-clock rest breaks. Chapter 17 explains what may be required and includes tips to help stay in compliance. If an employee complains to the state labor board that breaks are handled incorrectly, your company may be subject to an audit and investigation.

If a state requires an employee to take a thirty-minute meal break after five or more hours of work, but he works only 4.75 hours, he does not need to clock out for a meal break, but if he works 5.0 hours or more, he does. Keep this in mind when scheduling full-time employees who work forty hours per week—you'll need to schedule them for five 8.5 hour workdays in order to earn their forty hours (8.5 hours on the schedule = 8.0 hours of work). If an employee works more than eight, nine, or ten hours (check the rules in your state), she may be required to clock out for two thirty-minute meal breaks during the course of the workday. There is more to read about meal and rest breaks in Chapter 17.

Correcting Time-Clock Errors

If a timecard or time-sheet method of reporting is used, employees should be required to sign the documents to confirm that they worked the hours posted. Also, their signature confirms that the time reported is correct. Signatures and recorded times should be written in pen.

Employers may not change anything on a timecard. If something is incorrect or missing, a change may be made by the employer or employee and must be accompanied by the employee's signature. One of the most common timecard errors occurs when an employee forgets to clock in before they start working, or leaves for the day without clocking out. They may also clock out for their meal break, but forget to clock back in, thus causing incorrect time to be reported for the entire day. When this happens, the employee should write a manual correction on the timecard and sign it.

FACT

An employee's timekeeping record is a legal document and should be treated with extreme care. Under no circumstances should one employee be allowed to punch in or out for another. Failure to comply may be grounds for discipline, usually in the case of a verbal warning for the first offense. This policy should be included in your employee handbook.

When an employee takes an off-the-clock meal break but forgets to clock out, employers may not deduct the time from the employee's pay without a proper adjustment to the timecard by the employee. If the employee doesn't take a break, her pay cannot be deducted for the time that she should have taken off. The same rule applies to employees who record their time manually on a time sheet. Workers who are continually careless with their timecards or time sheets or do not abide by the requirements to take an off-the-clock meal break are subject to progressive discipline to correct the problem. Timekeeping documents are legal records and should be treated seriously.

Time off the clock for mandatory meal breaks can cause headaches because some employees don't want to take them. They would rather earn the extra thirty minutes of pay, which can be over two hours per week for a full-time employee. They may want to work through the break and go home thirty minutes early. However, meal breaks, or the lack of meal breaks, are not subject to the approval of the company; it is federal law that employers comply.

Payroll Processing

Now that you know that your employees are classified properly as hourly, non-exempt, or exempt, and you know how to track their hours worked, it's time to decide how you are going to pay them. Payroll is a job that is never complete. As soon as one payroll period is over, checks are processed and distributed, then it is time to start on the next cycle.

There are dozens of manual, computer, and electronic resources available to assist you with processing your own payroll. The American Payroll Association (APA) provides a wealth of information on their Web site and offers training. You can also look to office supply stores and business services Web sites like Business.com and Paycycle.com to see what is available. Most time and attendance systems (time clocks) are compatible with a paycheck processing system. With these programs, the employee's timekeeping records are uploaded into a program that also computes the paychecks, including tax deductions.

Decide if paychecks will be processed weekly or biweekly. Salaried employees are usually paid biweekly or monthly. A biweekly payday (i.e., checks are distributed on alternate Fridays) will add two paydays to the year, for a total of twenty-six. Payday can also be on the first and fifteenth of each month, which will result in twenty-four paydays per year.

Direct Deposit

A recent APA survey found that in 2006, almost 94 percent of employees were paid by direct deposit. Direct deposit is an Automatic Clearing House (ACH) transaction that works in a way similar to that of debit cards. It's an automated transfer of funds from one place to the other. This is a popular option for paying employees with several benefits to employees:

- Immediate access to wages
- No waiting in line at the bank
- Free checking account at participating banks
- No delay in pay if there is an emergency
- Access to earnings when out of town on payday

A payroll card is available through some companies and banks for employees who do not have a bank account for direct deposit. The card works like a debit card for purchases. If the employee needs to pay a bill by paper processing, they can use the payroll card to purchase a money order.

Outsourcing Payroll

Obviously, the more employees you have, the bigger a task processing paychecks will be. Outsourcing payroll to an accounting office, human resource consultant, or paycheck processing company is an option for employers who do not want the extra responsibility. Small- and medium-sized employers are most likely to utilize paycheck services because they do not have the staffing or funds to operate a payroll department. Another benefit to outsourcing payroll is that it delivers a level of expertise from a third party that may be valuable to the company, especially in the area of payroll laws and taxes.

Here are a few questions to ask when interviewing payroll outsourcing companies:

- How will hours worked by the employees be transmitted to your company?
- What types of reports will I receive for each pay cycle?
- If the vendor makes a tax error, will fines and penalties be paid by the vendor?
- Is direct deposit available?
- How is paycheck accuracy verified?
- Can off-cycle payroll checks be processed quickly?
- Are quarterly and year-end payroll tax forms processed?
- Are W-2 forms mailed to the company or the employees?

Employers can outsource all or partial payroll duties. You may want to collect time data and coordinate paid sick, vacation, and holiday leaves, but have another company calculate tax withholdings, process the paychecks and ACH transactions, file tax returns, and distribute W-2 forms.

Tax Withholdings

Employer payroll taxes are one of the things that makes outsourcing payroll attractive to many companies. Tax withholdings need to be deducted from pay and distributed to the correct taxation agency. Errors can be costly in fines and penalties, but many companies successfully process payroll from start to finish in-house.

All employers are required to match employee OASDI (Old-Age, Survivors, and Disability Insurance, i.e., Social Security) and Medicare contributions. Federal taxes are deducted from qualified employees and state taxes apply in most states. In addition, employers pay quarterly Federal Unemployment Tax Act (FUTA) taxes. Other taxes may apply in some states.

Quarterly and Year-End Tax Forms

There are quarterly and year-end tax forms to be filed, and the distribution of W-2 forms no later than January 31 after the year end (W-2 forms for the tax year ending December 31, 2008 must be postmarked or given to employees by January 31, 2009).

There are state and federal quarterly and year-end tax forms that must be submitted. Employers located in the states listed in Chapter 4 that are not liable for payroll taxes may still need to file a state employer tax return. Check with your local employment office for tax forms and instructions. You can file the taxes yourself or hire an accountant. If payroll services are outsourced, the company you contract with should provide this service.

Salary Surveys

One way to find out if your salaries are competitive with other employers in your industry is to conduct a salary survey. Contact similar businesses in your area and offer to share salary information if they will reciprocate. In exchange, compile a report and distribute it to the companies that participate. The report should have a column of the positions available at the top. The left side of the report will list the participating businesses. There will be some positions that not all companies will have and some businesses may not want to reveal how much money managers make. If this happens, leave this section out on the copy of the report for nonparticipating companies.

ESSENTIAL

Don't feel awkward asking other companies to participate in a salary survey. It is likely that they would also like to know if their pay is competitive in the industry. You are more likely to find businesses willing to participate than ones who turn down your request. For next year, ask another participant to prepare the report.

Another way to track salaries is to purchase a salary report. There are also some free resources that reveal salaries in your area, but you will receive the most detailed information by purchasing a report. Prices start at under $100. If you are a member of the Society for Human Resource Management, you are entitled to a directory of salary resources for your specific industry. Otherwise, you can look to these Web sites:

- PayScale—*www.payscale.com*
- CareerJournal—*www.careerjournal.com*
- WageAccess—*www.wageaccess.com*
- Watson Wyatt Data Services—*www.wwds.com*
- SalariesReview—*www.salariesreview.com*

Paycheck Delivery

Paychecks should be treated with care and confidentiality. The paycheck is the main reason that employees are working for your company, with benefits being the second most sought-after reward. There should be a system in place for employees to sign a checklist upon receipt of their paycheck. This is to protect the company's interest and prove that a check was issued and distributed. Employees with direct deposit will receive just a paycheck stub showing what they were paid and the deductions withheld. These should be distributed to employees in the same manner as checks.

Checks should not be left on desks or in open mailboxes, even if they are concealed in an envelope. A stolen paycheck causes hardship for the employee and extra work for you when a stop payment needs to be processed on the missing check and a new one issued. If a duplicate check needs to be issued to an employee, the reason should be because it was lost or damaged by the employee or stolen from the workplace.

There is no law against employees showing their paychecks or paycheck stubs to other employees and comparing wages. Most workers do not wish to share this information and understand the importance of confidentiality; however, there will be some who view the situation differently. Two employees who make the same salary and worked the same number of hours may wonder why one received more money than the other. This will usually be due to a difference in deductions based on tax status.

CHAPTER 7

Standard Benefits

You will learn about strategies for employee retention in Chapter 18, but you can start planning your efforts now as you read up on the benefits that will keep your employees satisfied. Insurance and paid time off are an important element in the compensation package. Even younger workers have their eye on retirement plans. Your company will be viewed as a premier employer if you offer more than just a paycheck as compensation for a job well done. Here are the most common benefits that employers choose to offer.

Medical Insurance

Your highest employee-benefit expense will be medical insurance, and it's also the top choice among employees. Recent surveys have concluded that it plays an important role in employee satisfaction. There are several choices when it comes to choosing a plan, but the two most widely used are a Health Maintenance Organization (HMO) or a Preferred Provider Organization (PPO).

Health Maintenance Organization (HMO)

An HMO is one of the most popular options for employees. There is no deductible and copayments for office visits, prescriptions, emergency room visits, and laboratory tests are low. There is usually no cost for hospital admissions. Participants are assigned to a primary care physician (PCP) who manages the care of the patient, including referrals to specialists. All services are performed by providers in the HMO's approved network.

FACT

A network is a group of physicians, hospitals, medical providers, and laboratories that have a contract with the insurance company to provide services for a negotiated fee. In turn, beneficiaries with an HMO option have low copayments. PPO patients have lower out-of-pocket expenses if they choose a network provider over an out-of-network provider.

The benefit to employees is that the out-of-pocket expenses are lowest with this type of plan. Copayments for prescriptions average about $5–$15, and may be less for generic drugs. Office visits and laboratory work is usually around $10–$25. These costs are low to the patient because the HMO contracts negotiated rates with area physicians and facilities. The disadvantage is that the employee can never go out of the HMO's network. Well, he can, but he will have to pay full price for it out of his pocket. Another disadvantage is that if the employee wants to see a specialist, he can do so only if he is referred to one by his PCP. The PCP will submit paperwork to the HMO's administrative offices to ask for an approval. If it is approved, the patient can then make an appointment. This results in an additional waiting period to get in for an appointment with the specialist. Also, the number of specialists is limited. If, for example, the employee has a heart condition and wants to see a cardiologist who was recommended to him by a friend, he can't see that doctor if he is not part of the HMO's network.

Preferred Provider Organization (PPO)

A PPO is the other common choice. This type of plan gives the patient the flexibility to save money by seeing an in-network provider, but unlike an HMO, he also has the option to see a doctor who is not in the plan's network. Services from out-of-network physicians and hospitals are paid at a lower level of benefit coverage, resulting in higher out-of-pocket expenses. There is usually a deductible for each plan year in addition to copayments. Premiums for a PPO are higher than an HMO, but to many, the cost is worth the benefit of having a larger selection of physicians to see. The flexibility to self-refer to a specialist is another added bonus. Overall, you can receive quicker medical care with the physician or facility of your choice. There are more doctors in private practice as part of PPO plans than HMOs. Most HMO physicians are part of medical groups and many have a clinical atmosphere.

Know How the Plan Works

If you purchase an HMO or PPO health plan, educate your employees about the importance of following the plan instructions. Employees with an HMO may not see a doctor other than their PCP. Otherwise, benefits will not be paid and the employee will be left with the bill. Changing a PCP can be as easy as a phone call or a click away. Some plans may have a waiting period from the time a new doctor is selected until it goes into effect, such as the first of the month or the next billing cycle. If an employee sees the new doctor before the change goes into effect, the HMO may not pay the bill.

ALERT!

HMO network directories are not always up to date, and this includes directories available on the Internet. When you choose a PCP from the list of providers, call the physician's office and ask if they are part of the HMO network. There is also a chance that the doctor is no longer accepting new patients. Ask about that, too.

Another thing that employees with an HMO need to monitor carefully is the procedures for seeing a specialist or receiving outpatient services. When a PCP processes a referral for a patient to see a specialist or have an outpatient procedure, the insurance company will not pay for the visit if it occurs before the date the service is authorized. Employees should have an authorization number on hand before seeing the specialist or having the procedure done. Otherwise, there is a risk of having an office visit or procedure deemed unauthorized and the insurance company will not pay for it.

Insurance Broker Services

Small- and medium-sized businesses can benefit from the services of an insurance broker to assist with medical, dental, and life-insurance plans. This does not add to your costs for the insurance; the price you would pay for the same policy is the same whether or not you purchase it from a broker. Insurance brokers are paid a 4 percent commission by the medical-insurance companies that they represent. You would not get that 4 percent back by purchasing the policy directly from the insurance company, so there is nothing for you to lose.

An advantage to working with a broker is that they represent several different plans from various companies, giving you a broader selection. A broker will help you design a plan for your company that will meet the needs of the employees while staying within your budget guidelines. For instance, coverage for pre-existing conditions is something that will be very important to your employees. A broker can help you search for a plan with this benefit that you can afford.

The service and support that you'll receive from an insurance broker may be that of a classic benefits administrator. Look for one that will be available to answer questions from employees about the policies and help with enrolling new employees, open enrollment, and COBRA administration.

Part of deciding how much the company can afford to pay for insurance will be reflected by the percentage of the premiums that will be paid by the employee. Very few companies can afford to pay 100 percent of the cost. Most companies pay the majority of the premium and the rest is paid by the employee via payroll deductions. Another option is for the company to pay 100 percent of the coverage for the employee only and for the employee to pay a full or partial amount of the difference for added dependents.

Alternative Medical Insurance Options

Self-funding a medical-insurance plan can keep costs down, but there is a financial risk if an employee has a catastrophic medical expense. You can choose to be partially self-funded by purchasing stop-loss coverage to limit your risk. A benefit to self-funding is that employers are exempt from state regulations and taxations because companies are exempt from the Employee Retirement Income Security Act (ERISA). Employers are not regarded as insurance companies under the law. However, companies with self-funded insurance plans must comply with the Health Insurance Portability and Accountability Act (HIPAA).

> The cost of medical insurance is expected to continue to rise. Before choosing a plan that differs from the traditional HMO or PPO plan, educate yourself about the plan thoroughly and talk to people from other companies who have chosen the plan. Ask about the benefits and disadvantages to help you make an informed decision.

Other options that have been increasing in popularity due to their ability to keep costs down are Consumer Driven Health Plans (CDHP), Health Savings Accounts (HSA), Health Reimbursement Accounts (HRA), and High Deductible Health Plans (HDHP).

Dental Insurance

You can shop for dental insurance rates on your own or through a broker. Some dental plans will be part of a network to help keep costs down, similar to the procedures of a medical HMO. Others will have no network, or give employees the option to see a dentist in or out of network. With some plans, employees have to select a dentist and the insurance company will pay for services from that dentist only. Employees can change the dentist assigned to them by making a phone call or going online.

Some plans will not pay for major expenses like braces, crowns, or root canals until a waiting period of six months to one year. Others will pay all expenses right away. Generally, most plans will cover X-rays once a year and an exam and cleaning every six months.

Life Insurance

Employees who have trouble getting life insurance or are charged inflated rates due to health problems will appreciate the benefits of a group plan that will insure everyone. Look for a group plan that will not turn anyone away. Generally, employees have to sign up within a specific timeframe, known as the period of initial eligibility (PIE), in order to avoid an application process in which they can be denied coverage. If an employee wants to increase his coverage after the PIE, she will have to go through the questionnaire process, her medical records will be examined, and she may be denied an increase in coverage.

QUESTION?

Can employees purchase life insurance for a spouse?
Most group life insurance plans provide employees the option to purchase life insurance for their spouse. Some will include the employee's children in a plan. Most plans require that the employee is enrolled, and the value and price of the spouse's insurance will be half of the employee's insured amount.

Most life insurance companies charge higher rates for people who have smoked cigarettes in the past twelve months. The rate can be as high as twice the rate for a nonsmoker.

If paying for life insurance coverage isn't something you are able to provide for your employees, giving them access to group rates is still a benefit that they cannot get on their own. In some cases, plans are portable, which means that if the employee leaves the company, they can continue the coverage. It may be at a higher rate, but it will be guaranteed coverage that they may not be able to get on their own.

Disability Insurance

If your company is in an area that does not have a state disability plan, this is a great benefit to provide for your employees. As with life insurance, if funding the policies is not in your budget, getting a group rate for your employees is still a big help to them. Disability plans never cover pre-existing conditions, even in a group plan. If your area does have a mandatory state disability plan, you can purchase a supplemental plan that will coordinate with the state plan to pay the employee a higher percentage of her wages in the event of a disability.

Disability plans come in short-term or long-term options, although both options may not be available in all states. States that provide disability insurance to employees through tax deductions may result in eligibility for short-term plans.

Vacation

Vacation pay will be the favorite benefit for some of your employees. Your vacation policy should be in writing so that there is no misunderstanding about how much vacation pay employees will receive. You can give as much vacation time as you want, but the standard appears to be from five to ten days after the first year of employment. From there, most companies raise the vacation rate based on the length of service. For instance, after five years it may increase by another week, and so on.

If vacation is earned on an accrual basis, make this clear in your written policy. An accrual basis means that the hours add up over time. For instance, if employees earn forty hours of vacation during their first year of employment, by the time they reach their six-month anniversary, they will have twenty hours accrued. When this happens, the employees usually own these hours, whether or not they are eligible to take them as paid time off. If they leave the company, they are paid for unused leave. Also, you should be clear on when accrued leave is available for use, such as whether an employee is eligible to request vacation leave after they have passed the ninety-day introductory period or reached their six-month anniversary. Most companies pay out unused vacation leave to employees who leave the company. Also, unused leave at the end of the year can be carried over to the next. You can put a cap on how much leave an employee can keep on the books. Employees who are not taking enough time off should be encouraged to do so; everyone needs time away from work to rejuvenate.

ESSENTIAL

Employers are catching on to the concept that the ability to balance work and family life is important to many employees. Offering a generous vacation-leave package will help with your employee-retention efforts. For many people, vacation-leave ranks high on their priority list.

A written procedure should be in place for requesting vacation leave. Your policy should state how much advance notice is needed before requesting time off. Let the employees know that vacation leave will be approved at the discretion of the company. If another employee has already requested the same time off and it's been approved, you may not be able to honor the request from the second person. Also, you may choose to approve time off during the holidays in order of seniority, giving the person who has been there (or in one department) the longest the first opportunity to request time off, then go from there. You can do this as long as it is in a written policy. Vacation time taken during the holidays may also be granted on a first-come, first-served basis.

Sick Leave

A sick-leave policy may vary a bit from your vacation-leave policy. Most companies offer sick leave on a "take it or leave it" option, which means that employees who separate from the company are not paid for unused leave. As always, the way in which sick leave will be earned and paid out should be spelled out in a written policy. Disability insurance plans may have a requirement about unused sick leave being used before disability payments will kick in. This is something to find out so that employees can be told what to expect if they are scheduled for surgery or have an illness or injury that results in temporary disability.

FACT

An increasing number of companies no longer separate vacation leave from sick leave. They offer what is called Paid Time Off (PTO). It combines vacation and sick leave into one paid leave. Employees who separate from the company are generally paid for unused leave on the books at the time of departure.

If it appears that an employee is abusing the sick-leave policy (e.g., calling-off sick then being seen shopping at the mall or dancing at a club), you may require that he bring in a doctor's note excusing him from work next time he claims to be ill. Before you do this, make sure that you have a valid, documented reason to make an exception. Better yet, have more than one documented instance of possible sick-leave policy abuse. And, as always, a policy about asking for a doctor's note from employees who may be abusing the policy must be consistent. Other signs that the sick-leave policy is being abused are if an employee routinely calls off sick right before or after the weekend—especially a long weekend that includes a holiday.

Holiday Pay

There are six holidays observed by most companies in the private sector, although many honor some of the holidays not on this list.

- New Year's Day
- Memorial Day
- Independence Day
- Labor Day
- Thanksgiving
- Christmas

An increasing number of companies are beginning to observe President's Day and Martin Luther King Jr. Day. Both are honored by government entities in addition to Columbus Day and Veteran's Day. Also, the day after Thanksgiving, Christmas Eve, and New Year's Eve are paid holidays for most companies. However, some identify Christmas Eve and New Year's Eve as days to take off early with full pay. Chapter 13 discusses options for reasonable accommodations for employees with religious beliefs that observe holidays not mentioned above.

Retirement Plans

A retirement plan generally works like this: The employee chooses a percentage of his salary (of which there may be a cap) to be deducted and deposited into a retirement plan. The deductions are taken from gross income (taxable income) and the funds multiply in the retirement account. Employers may match contributions, if they so choose. There are caps and limits to how much an employer can match. If the company does not match any part of the employee's contributions, the plan is still a benefit to employees. Retirement plans are highly desirable and something that many people look for in a benefits package.

The three most commonly defined contribution pension plans are the 401(k), 403(b), and 457(b) of the Internal Revenue Code (IRC). The 401(k) plan is a deferred contribution (DC) plan. These plans are also known as cash or deferred arrangements (CODA). The 403(b) plan is also known as tax-sheltered annuity (TSA) and 457(b) plans are referred to as deferred compensation plans (DCP).

Setting up a retirement plan can be a complex project. Contact the Profit Sharing Council of America at *www.psca.org* to find a vendor to set up a plan for your company.

CHAPTER 8

Enhanced Benefits

Your compensation package may be competitive with other businesses in your industry and area, so now is the time to offer benefits that the others don't. Employee retention is likely to skyrocket and the savings from that will offset what you spend on additional benefits. The reward of working is more than just a paycheck to many people. Hire a personal concierge for your employees, take them on an annual retreat, and encourage them to further their education—at the company's expense. It's a win-win situation for everyone.

Flexible Spending Accounts

A tax-sheltered flexible spending account is also known as an Internal Revenue Code Section 125 cafeteria plan. It allows employees to pay for dependant care, medical, and dental expenses with pretax dollars. The result is that employees get more money in their pocket on payday and have less income to report to the IRS at the end of the year. The company sets it up through the payroll system and all the employee does is keep track of receipts. It's an easy way for them to lower their taxable income.

There is a maximum deduction set each year, and a cap on salary eligibility also. The IRS Web site at *www.irs.gov* has instructions for setting up a plan. Your accountant or payroll company can assist you, too.

Order or download a copy of IRS Publication 15-B Employer's Tax Guide to Fringe Benefits for information about flexible spending accounts, tuition reimbursement, and some of the other fringe benefits in this chapter. Publication 15-B will point you in the right direction to get started.

Employees with childcare expenses are eligible for the tax credit provided they receive a tax identification number from the daycare operation, preschool facility, nanny, or babysitter who provides the care. Daycare and preschool businesses should give you a federal tax ID number. Ask individual child-care providers for their social security number.

If a daycare provider is paid with cash, they may not give you their social security number so that they don't have to claim the income. Without their social security number, you cannot participate in a flexible spending account plan. You can make an attempt to get it by giving them a W-9 form from the IRS Web site.

Children under the age of thirteen are eligible dependents under a plan. Paid care for older children qualifies only if the child is physically or mentally disabled or unable to care for himself for another reason. If there are two parents in the household, both must work in order for one of them to claim the credit. Workers caring for elderly parents can receive the tax credit for adult dependent-care assistance. Again, a taxpayer ID number is required.

Eligible medical expenses for a flexible spending account plan include but are not limited to insurance copays, prescription lenses, uncovered dental expenses, and out-of-pocket prescription costs. Over–the-counter medications do not qualify.

Here is how the plan works: At the beginning of the plan year, employees are asked to elect how much they are going to spend on qualified expenses. Employees should be warned that they could lose money if their receipts do not equal the amount elected. Therefore, it is important that they do not overestimate. Monthly expenses are deducted from wages up front. Once a receipt is submitted, the employee receives a nontaxable reimbursement. If there were no expenses and no receipt, there is no reimbursement.

Company Parties and Picnics

Show your employees how much you value their hard work by throwing a big bash at the end of the year or a summer picnic—or both. If your company is large enough, have a volunteer committee come up with a party or picnic plan for your approval. You may offer your suggestions, but these parties are for the employees and should be planned by them. Be sure to tell them what the budget is for expenses.

End-of-the-Year Gala

If there is one night of the year when everyone gets dressed up and gets out of the office together, it's the night of the company party. If you plan it during the holidays, it's the busy season for corporate parties, so reservations should be made early. Hotels offer package deals that will include a discount on overnight rooms in case people want to spend the night. Generally, these events are adult-only parties where each employee is allowed to bring one guest.

FACT

Hourly employees should be on the clock when they are planning the party. It is a company-sponsored event and although participation on the planning committee should be on a volunteer basis, this doesn't mean that they volunteer their time. There are strict labor laws against hourly employees conducting company business while off the clock.

Employees will enjoy dinner and live music with dancing. A minimum amount of alcohol should be served, generally no more than two drinks per person. Don't assume that everyone attending will be twenty-one or older. Younger employees may have an underage spouse or someone may bring an adult child who is not yet twenty-one. There should be a system in place for verifying that everyone drinking alcohol is over twenty-one years of age.

Most people don't have the opportunity to have their portrait taken too often. For an added touch, hire a professional photographer with a backdrop to take portraits of couples or individuals. The photographer can also go around to the dinner tables as they do at weddings. This may be done at no cost to the company by having the employees purchase prints if they are interested. Or, you can provide everyone with one picture as a gift and give employees the option to purchase additional prints.

If the company has an employee-of-the-year award, the end-of-year party is a good time to make the announcement. Have a raffle. You'll be surprised at how easy it is to get prize donations. Have the party committee contact area restaurants, hotels, and businesses that offer services that people will enjoy. Tell them that you're collecting prizes for a raffle and their company name will be announced at the party, included in the monthly newsletter, posted in the employee break room, or whatever publicity you may offer. If your company offers a service to the general public, offer to reciprocate. Or you can purchase raffle prizes. Either way, the people with the winning tickets get a prize and it makes the evening more fun.

Summer Picnic

The picnic committee is responsible for choosing the venue for the bash of the summer. Consider a regional park or a water park. If the picnic is at a water park, this doesn't mean that everyone has to wear a swimsuit! Choose a water park with a large picnic facility and there will be plenty of room for socializing. It's a misconception that everyone will be going down waterslides all day.

A water park can offer one-stop shopping. They'll provide everything from food to entertainment. Ask if you will be allowed to bring in your own desserts and beverages and make sure that the area assigned to your group will be large enough to accommodate everyone and has enough shade. Visit the park for a site tour before making a commitment.

At a regional park, you'll have more flexibility on food and entertainment. Plan a talent show or scavenger hunt; rent Karaoke equipment; pick your own live band; hire a clown, jump house, petting zoo, or pony rides for the kids. Check with the park rangers first to verify that what you have in mind will be allowed. For food, consider a catered chuck-wagon–style BBQ with an alternate menu for vegetarians.

No matter where your picnic is held, ask the committee to have some fun and design T-shirts with the company logo. Have a supply printed in adult and children's sizes to distribute at the picnic. The employees will leave with something to wear all year long. Put the date on the shirts and do it each year. Have a contest in a few years to see who has held on to the most shirts.

Jury-Duty Pay

Some states require that employers pay employees for jury-duty service. In the states with the requirement, the number of days to be paid varies by state. Also, some states do not allow employers to discharge employees from employment if they participate in long trials. The employer does not have to pay the employee for the duration of the trial if the time exceeds the state requirement. Fees paid to jurors by the court are minimal, and it is up to the employee whether or not they act as a juror in lieu of earning their usual wages. Juror fees are usually not paid on the day of jury selection. When fees are paid, the company may deduct the fee from the wages paid to the employee if it is written in the jury-duty policy that the employer will do so.

FACT

Your company should have a written jury-duty policy that explains whether or not employees are paid to serve and for how long. As a service to the community, many companies pay employees their usual wages while on jury-duty service, even if it is not required by the state.

If an employee who works nights is summoned to jury duty, they should be excused from work that evening, just as a daytime employee would be during the day. To expect an employee to report to jury duty for the day and then work at night is unreasonable. An employee who works nights should not be denied jury-duty pay benefits. Their workday is the time spent at the courthouse. To receive pay for days spent on jury duty, employees should bring in proof from the courthouse that they appeared. All jurors, whether or not they work, should be given proof of attendance when they are excused.

Personal Concierge Service

Nothing says, "Let me help you balance your work and family life" better than hiring a personal-concierge service for your employees.

Paid for by the employer, the personal concierge comes to the office to help employees with their personal business. Some of the things he may do include printing birthday-party invitations, addressing thank-you cards, picking-up dry cleaning, purchasing birthday presents, or shopping around for lower auto-insurance rates.

What makes a personal concierge such an appealing benefit?
It's something that a lot of people would like to have, but is a luxury that they may not spend on themselves. They may hire a housekeeping or lawn service, but they don't think to hire a service for themselves. People think that they have to stay in a fancy hotel to use a concierge.

You'll need a system to make sure that the availability of the concierge is fair to everyone. How often he comes to the office depends on how much money the company wants to spend on this benefit. Employees will need to give money to the concierge in advance for errands that involve paying stores or services. Look for a personal concierge or errand service in the telephone directory or classified section of your newspaper, on the Internet, or advertised with your local Chamber of Commerce.

Tuition Reimbursement

Tuition-reimbursement programs are generally offered to employees with at least one year of service. It is considered a fringe benefit by the IRS and is usually taxable income for the employee. Before implementing a program, consider these questions:

- Do the classes have to be job related?
- How many classes are eligible for reimbursement each semester?
- Does the employee need to receive a specific grade to qualify for reimbursement?
- Will reimbursement be at 100 percent?
- Will paid time off to attend classes be offered?
- Is there a cap on how many semesters an employee may participate?
- Will the benefit be offered to employees earning higher than a bachelor's degree?

Classes are paid for by the employee, not the employer. If the employee qualifies for reimbursement, it is processed after the class has ended and a final grade has been received. Verify with the IRS whether the reimbursement is tax deductible and how to properly reimburse the employee.

Personal Days Off with Pay

A personal day off with pay is not a vacation day with advance notice, and not a sick day when the employee is too ill to enjoy the day off—it's a day off just because. It's because the employee needs a mental-health day from life to do nothing or a friend from out of town showed up at the front door and wants to do something tomorrow. It's really just a way to add to an employee's vacation bank, and you're giving them permission to take the day off for themselves. A personal day off is an employee's "day for me."

You can give employees the option to preplan the day off like a vacation day, but by calling it a personal day, it sends the message to the employee that it is a benefit above and beyond the vacation time that they earn and deserve. It's an extra thank-you for doing a good job. They can use it to do weekday shopping during the holidays when the mall isn't so busy, or to chaperone a field trip at their child's school.

ALERT!

Your written policy on personal days should indicate what happens to unused personal days at the end of the year. May they be carried over to the next year? Also, if more than one personal day is given per year, may two days be taken consecutively?

Give as many personal days as you wish, but two per year is the standard for a lot of companies. There should be discretion when requesting a personal day off. Unless it is an emergency, a day off should not be taken when it is an important day for the employee to report to work.

Retreats

There are many kinds of corporate retreats—management retreats, staff retreats, couples retreats, overnight retreats, and day retreats (which are usually called outings). A retreat can be at a busy hotel or at a quiet, relaxing resort. There is one important criteria—it must be away from the office!

Management Retreats

Managers spend fifty to sixty hours per week managing people. Give them a break and some time away from the staff to relate to the other managers in a relaxed atmosphere without any interruptions. The purpose of a retreat can also be to work on a big project from start to finish. Plan a mix of social and business activities. Day one can be planning the budget for next year; day two can be spent on the golf course. A retreat can be used to write a mission statement or set goals for the next year. Pick any project that requires focus and is hard to accomplish around the interruptions and demands of the office. More administrative work will get completed during a two-day retreat than a whole month in the office.

Couples Retreats

If it's a couples retreat, there shouldn't be as much work unless there is an activity planned for the spouses and partners while the managers are setting goals, planning budgets, or writing a mission statement. The guests can be taken on a sightseeing trip for the day then return to the retreat site for dinner. The spouses and partners will get a chance to know one another and develop friendships outside the office.

ESSENTIAL

The budget for a couples retreat that includes all employees can be prohibitive if the company has a large staff. To include some nonmanagement employees, have a selection process that includes reaching goals as the criteria for attending; make it a treat that has to be earned. Sales departments do this often for their top performers.

Activities

Here are some fun activities to do at a retreat:

- Everyone brings a copy of their baby picture and tries to guess who is who
- Invite a motivational speaker to pump up the attendees
- Hire a chef to teach a cooking class
- Listen to a life coach encourage everyone to pursue their dreams
- Bring a color consultant to teach everyone their best wardrobe colors

Outings

An outing is a little less structured than a retreat. It can be planned for the whole company or just a department. If you're going somewhere far, charter a bus so that everyone can ride together. It will be less expensive than reimbursing everyone for gas, too. Go out to dinner, to an amusement park, miniature golfing, the beach, bowling, etc.

A retreat or outing is not something that employers are expected to do—it's not a standard benefit like medical insurance and vacation pay—it's a nice gesture that will help bring a sense of family to the workplace. And best of all, they are fun!

CHAPTER 9

Workers' Compensation

Where there are people there will be accidents and injuries. Some accidents are caused by employer negligence, employee carelessness, and by circumstance. This chapter will tell you about workers' compensation insurance to cover employees who are injured at work. You'll learn what you need to know to file a claim and about the care that injured workers are entitled to. Smart companies take measures to minimize injuries in the workplace. Take the time and expense needed to provide a safe environment and your efforts will be well spent.

Insurance

Workers' compensation insurance can easily be one of your biggest operation expenses. It is a form of no-fault insurance that pays for medical treatment, lost wages, and monetary awards when a disability occurs. If an injured employee is unable to return to work, it provides vocational rehabilitation to train the worker in a new profession. In the unfortunate situation of a workplace fatality, the policy may pay out a death benefit to survivors and cover burial expenses.

Workers' compensation laws are complex and your insurance provider is a good resource to turn to for guidance, but don't stop there. Like most everything you will read about in this book, laws vary by state and change often. Your state's workers' compensation board is another place to turn to for assistance with getting and staying in compliance.

FACT

More than half of the states require that employers provide workers' compensation insurance regardless of the number of employees. The remaining states that require it do so when there are a specific number of employees on staff, and this may be as low as three or four employees. Whether or not it is required, it is a wise choice to purchase it to protect company liability.

Most states require coverage that provides full medical benefits, but a few have limits. Lost wages are generally reimbursed at a rate of two-thirds of the employee's salary, but there is a cap that varies greatly from one state to another. For instance, there may be a cap of $500 per week, which would mean that an employee is paid for two-thirds of her wages up to $500 dollars. If two-thirds of her salary is $650, she would receive only $500. In addition, there is a waiting period before wage benefits become effective, and the employee must be off work for a specific period of time or be hospitalized. Employers are usually required to continue to provide medical coverage for the employee at the rate it was covered before the accident.

Injured Employees

The procedure for reporting work-related injuries should be included in your employee handbook. You can also distribute a printed copy of the policy to each employee and place a signed receipt in the personnel file. The burden of reporting an injury is on the employee because if the employer doesn't know about it, medical care will not be authorized, a claim will not be started, and bills for services may be denied. All work-related injuries should be reported, no matter how minor. This doesn't mean that a claim will be opened each time an injury is reported, because minor injuries usually don't require medical attention or lost time from work. However, one of these injuries could flare up a few days later. An employee may pull a muscle, for example, but the pain gets worse as the days progress, and he then needs to see a doctor.

There should be a contact person for all employee injuries, with a few alternates in case that person is unavailable when an injury occurs. Companies that operate in the evenings or on weekends need to have people authorized and trained to handle workers' compensation injuries during those shifts. Accidents are not limited to normal business hours.

Labor law postings are covered in Chapter 11. Workers' compensation posters should include the address and phone number of the medical facility where work-related injuries are treated, with an alternate location for after-hour visits. If an employee cannot reach a manager to authorize an emergency visit, he should know where to go for treatment.

An injured worker may request to see a physician even if you feel that medical care is not necessary. It's probably a good idea to go ahead and authorize the trip to the doctor. An employee who requests medical attention should not be denied if the injury is questionable. The reverse may happen as well; an employee may decline medical attention but you, the employer, feel that it is necessary. In this case, send the employee to your medical provider. If he refuses to go, get something from him in writing stating that he is not accepting your recommendation or find someone to witness his refusal and notify the insurance company immediately. If you do not feel that it is safe for him to work, send him home. Call a taxi or arrange for an escort if you feel that he should not drive. The safety of the injured employee and those around him should be your first concern.

Keep the lines of communication open with an injured employee and follow up with him regularly. He may be anxious about his medical bills being paid, lost wages, or if the injury will affect his performance at work. Keep him informed from one phase to the next and don't let his only means of communication about the accident be with the insurance company. He shouldn't feel isolated or inapproachable during this period. Yet, don't put too much emphasis on the injury. Show your concern and check in periodically to make sure that the claim is being handled to his satisfaction.

If you receive a bill from a physician's office that treated an employee who claims to have been injured at work, do not pay it if a workers' compensation claim was not filed by the employee on or before the date of service. Ask the employee if he has a work-related injury to report and go through the usual procedure from there. Forward the bill to the insurance company. Since the charges occurred before the claim was filed, the bill may be denied by the insurance company. Your company may not be obligated to pay a medical bill for unauthorized treatment.

Required Paperwork

Contact your workers' compensation insurance carrier and state labor board to find out what forms are required to file a claim. In addition to an incident report, this may include a claim form, a booklet explaining how workers' compensation insurance works, and a written explanation of the employee's rights. It is important that all paperwork is distributed, completed, and processed in a timely manner. Most workers' compensation insurance carriers require that they are contacted within twenty-four hours of an injury.

FACT

You may be required to maintain an OSHA 300 Log, which is a tracking of all work-related injuries categorized by whether or not modified duty or missed time from work occurred. Chapter 11 includes a section about this federal requirement that may apply to your company.

Have a system in place to ensure that medical care is authorized by the company. Part of your workers' compensation paperwork packet should include a medical authorization form that must be signed by an authorized representative of the company. A hospital or physician's office should not be billing a company for medical services based solely on an employee's instruction to do so. If billing is to be sent directly to the insurance carrier, include the following on the authorization:

- Company name and address
- Name of insurance company
- Billing address of insurance company
- Telephone number of insurance company
- Policy number

If an employee is seen by a doctor, a First Report of Injury form will be prepared by the physician. This is an important document and a copy (or the original) is to be forwarded to the insurance company. It will give an evaluation of the employee's injury, treatment, follow up, and indicate if the employee may return to work and under what conditions.

Incident Reports

An incident report should be kept on file for every work-related injury. The treatment can be as simple as giving the employee a bandage or ice pack, but the injury should still be recorded on paper. It is helpful to have a supply of preprinted forms to be filled in when an incident occurs. Here are some things that should be included:

- Employee's name and social security number
- Date and time of incident
- Location of the injury
- What the employee was doing when injured
- How the injury occurred
- Body part affected
- Description of the injury
- Treatment given to employee
- Names and statements of witnesses
- Signature lines for employee and manager

If the injury endangers the life of an employee, puts him at risk for losing a limb or ability to function, or involves heavy bleeding or intense pain, transport him to a medical facility immediately. Every second counts, and the paperwork can wait until he is stabilized. Do what you can to start the claim with the insurance company in the meantime, even if it's just a phone call with the employee's name to let them know that there has been an injury. If the employee's condition enables him to answer questions for the incident report and complete paperwork, do this before he is sent for medical treatment. When a minor injury occurs that does not involve outside medical care, complete an incident report and file it appropriately. This is known as a nonmedical incident and may not need to be reported to your insurance company unless the employee has complications later. Ask your insurance company if nonmedical incidents should be reported.

If you have doubts about an employee's ability to drive herself to a medical provider for treatment, do not let her operate her own vehicle. If this is the case, call a taxi or have a member of management drive her. If the employee does drives herself, she may be eligible for mileage reimbursement from the insurance carrier.

When filling out an incident report, be very specific about the injury. If an arm was injured, indicate whether it was the right or left arm and if it was the forearm, bicep, or other area. Witnesses should be interviewed to report what they saw. If equipment was used, report whether or not it was used properly. If the employee is at fault for the injury, she will still receive benefits, but for documentation, training, and possible discipline purposes, you'll want to know if the employee caused her own injury.

Files

Paperwork from a work-related injury should not be filed in the employee's personnel file or medical file. Ideally, these forms and reports are filed in a separate workers' compensation file that is set up with the employee's name and date of injury. Like other files for employees, it should be kept in a locked area and treated with confidentiality.

Incident reports for nonmedical injuries can be kept in one file. Store the incident reports in order by last name or date of injury. One file for the entire year is sufficient.

Medical Care

Employers have the right to choose a medical-care provider to treat work-related injuries in some states. Find out what the laws are in your state. There may be a time limit on how long the company has control, such as for thirty days. In some instances, employees may have the right to choose their own doctor if a request to do so is in writing and placed in their personnel file before an injury occurs.

An occupational-health medical facility is most commonly used to treat work-related injuries. Some offices have extended office hours to cover evening and weekend shifts. If the facility is not open during hours when your company operates, have a back-up plan to treat injuries, such as an urgent-care clinic or emergency room.

If your company conducts pre-employment physicals or drug screens, the same facility may be able to treat your injured employees. Before choosing a doctor to provide this service for your company, find out what their procedures are for authorizing medical visits and billing the insurance company. The physician's viewpoint on treating injured workers should be that the employee's health is top priority, while working with you to ensure that he can return to work safely. A doctor who is too quick to excuse employees from work for minor injuries is not working in the best interest of the company or the employee. Likewise, a physician who releases workers to return to work before they are ready can also cause harm to both parties.

As the employer of an injured worker, you have the right to follow up and ensure that the employee isn't missing his doctor appointments. You should always be informed when the next appointment will be. Tell the employee to call the doctor's office directly if he has to change the date or time of an appointment and ask him to keep you updated. Confer with the employee or physician afterward about the new status of his condition.

Bills for medical services after a work-related injury should not be sent to an employee's house, but sometimes an error occurs. Let employees know that if a bill is inadvertently sent to their home it should be forwarded to the human resources office.

Prescriptions

Try to make arrangements with a pharmacy that will bill your workers' compensation insurance company whenever an injured employee needs a prescription. It can be a financial hardship and a disadvantage for employees to pay in advance for prescriptions and wait to be reimbursed.

However, there needs to be a procedure to ensure that only legitimate prescription expenses are billed to your insurance carrier. The pharmacy should be instructed to fill only prescriptions that are authorized by an approved company representative or upon receipt of the employee giving a copy of a claim form for workers' compensation benefits of First Report of Injury.

Modified Duty

An employee may be put on modified duty by a physician after an injury at work. Modified duty is also referred to as light duty or restricted duty. It places limitations on what the employee can do and will sometimes affect parts of her usual job duties. Give the physician a copy of the employee's job description to aid him in pointing out things that should be avoided. It is best for the employee and the company if the employee continues to work, and modified duty may make this possible. Think twice before sending the employee home to receive only about two-thirds of her salary from the insurance company instead of working.

FACT

You may temporarily change an employee's job duties or put her in a new position that meets the work restrictions while recovering from an injury. The employee's pay must remain the same and the work schedule should be similar to what she was previously working.

A note from a doctor putting an employee on modified duty must be specific. If it is not, call the doctor's office to clarify what the limitations are and ask for something in writing. For instance, "light duty" doesn't tell you what the employee can do or needs to avoid. Even "no heavy lifting" is too vague. "No lifting over fifteen pounds" is more in line with what you need. Written instructions that an employee cannot stand for extended periods of time needs to spell out what is considered an extended period of time. A note that says that an employee cannot stand consistently for more than ninety minutes tells you what you need to know. You will also know how long the employee will need to be off her feet before she can stand again. These are just two examples to show how specific orders for modified duty should be. Detailed instructions will protect both you and the employee. The employee will not further aggravate her injury, and you will not be responsible for assigning tasks that the employee should not perform.

If the employee does not want to fulfill the modified-duty assignment, you may be able to offer a leave of absence through the Family Medical Leave Act (FMLA) if the employee is eligible. FMLA is the topic of Chapter 12. Check the laws in your state with the workers' compensation board because some states may require the employee to work modified duty if it is available. But if the employee goes on FMLA leave, it is unlikely that she will collect wage benefits from workers' compensation insurance since there is paid work available that meets her restrictions.

Employees Unable to Work

The treating physician may tell the employee that he should not work after getting hurt on the job. A note from a doctor stating that an employee cannot work must be honored, even if the employee wants to work. The document must indicate how long the employee is to remain off work. If you receive a note without an ending date, you or the employee will need to contact the doctor's office and get a date. This date is usually the employee's next doctor visit. At that time, he will be examined again and the doctor will determine whether or not he may return to work. If he is able to return, you will receive a work release indicating the date he may return to work and if there are restrictions. Do not return an employee to full duty unless it is specified on the work release.

ESSENTIAL

Keep track of the dates when an injured employee is off work and their next doctor appointment. You should hear from the employee after this appointment with an update on his work status. If not, call him or the doctor. Workers' compensation wages end the day an employee is able to return to work, and this must be communicated to the insurance company.

Check in with an injured employee periodically by telephone and with handwritten notes or cards. Ask how he is doing and if he is satisfied with the care he is receiving. Someone who is unable to work is limited to what he should be doing in his personal life, too, and should be taking care of himself. If you have a hard time reaching him on the telephone, he may be out doing things that he is not supposed to be doing. A person cannot properly recover from an injury if they are not at home taking care of themselves. This doesn't mean that they can never leave the house. Just be on the alert for someone who may be doing something to further aggravate his condition. Contact your insurance company if you have any suspicions.

Employees who are unable to work should be put on FMLA leave if this is allowed in your state after a work-related injury. Follow the standard procedures for initiating the leave. If the employee is still unable to work when the twelve weeks of leave is exhausted, he will remain employed and continue his workers' compensation leave. The two leaves can run concurrently.

Litigated Cases

An employee may retain an attorney and sue the company after a work-related injury. If this happens, you may not be required to forward any information to the attorney's office without a summons or court order. Notify the insurance company if you are informed in writing of a lawsuit. From this point on, it's best to leave future correspondence about the claim between the insurance company and the attorney. You will probably be advised not to discuss the case with the employee.

Permanent Disability

An employee may have a permanent disability as a result of the injury. This disability will be rated by a percentage. For instance, an employee may have a 10 percent permanent disability in his shoulder or a 60 percent disability in hearing. The time to determine a permanent disability is lengthy. First, the employee will have undergone treatment with a physician to the point where it is determined that the condition is no longer improving. Next, the employee may be referred to a Qualified Medical Examiner (QME) to determine the final status of the disability. A QME is a physician approved by the state's workers' compensation board to determine the percentage of disability suffered by an injured worker, among other things.

QUESTION?

What happens after a permanent disability has been determined?
If the employee will no longer be able to perform his usual job, the company should place him in another position that meets his skills and physical abilities. If a suitable position is not available, the employment may be terminated, and the employee will start vocational rehabilitation, paid for by the insurance company.

Be very careful about coming to your own conclusion that an employee will not be returning to work and separating him from your payroll records.

Workers may be protected against this in your state and must remain on a leave of absence on your personnel records until a final determination has been made by the insurance company. In the event of a long-term leave from work, this puts employers in a difficult situation because someone needs to be hired and trained to do the work on a temporary basis. If you hire a temporary employee to cover for the injured worker, make it clear from the beginning that the position is temporary, you do not know how long employment will continue, and you cannot guarantee a permanent position.

Uncooperative Employees

It is important to treat injured workers carefully. However, if someone has been hurt at work this does not mean that she is exempt from the company's policies. Just make sure that she is not singled out or being discriminated against because of the injury. It's an unfortunate thing to realize, but some employees will try to use the injury to their advantage by wrongfully thinking that they may now do whatever they want. They may think that they will not be disciplined since they can try to sue the company for the injury. You will cause a lot of problems by treating an employee who is injured on the job differently than one who was injured at home or experiencing any other medical condition. Remember that consistency is the key to fair employment practices.

Employees Who Refuse Work

It is common after a work-related injury for an employee to refuse to accept accommodations for modified duty. This was mentioned briefly earlier in this chapter. If your state gives employees the right to refuse modified duty, there is not much you can do. Otherwise, when this happens, discipline the employee for insubordination as you would anyone else who refuses a reasonable request from management. If they do not report to work, start your usual job-abandonment procedures.

ALERT!

If you feel that an employee has been wrongly sent back to work by a physician, ask that she be re-evaluated. Everyone makes mistakes and the doctor's evaluation could be wrong. Returning to work too early can cause the employee's injury to flare up or cause her to become a liability to the company.

A similar situation may arise with an employee who is released to return to full duty by a physician, but refuses to comply. Treat this scenario as you would any employee who will not perform her job or does not show up for work. Discipline can be up to and including employment termination. Without written orders for modified duty or a work release from a doctor, employees are expected to report to work and perform their usual duties.

Lack of Follow Up

Once an employee has filed a claim for workers' compensation benefits, she has an obligation to respond to correspondence from the employer and the insurance company. Additionally, she is responsible for showing up for doctor appointments and participating in physical therapy or any other treatment prescribed by the doctor. Failure to do so may result in a denial of the employee's claim. Advise your workers' compensation carrier if an employee does not play an active role in her recovery and efforts to return to work.

Workers' Compensation Fraud

Workers' compensation fraud has been on the upswing for several years and some states now have reform initiatives to crack down on offenders. This includes giving employers control over who provides medical care for injured employees and stricter penalties for everyone involved in taking advantage of the system.

Beware of employees who try to open a fraudulent workers' compensation claim because they feel that their employment is going to be terminated for cause. This is one reason why it is important to have a written procedure for reporting work-related injuries immediately, no matter how small. Every employee's personnel file should contain a signed acknowledgment of these procedures. A person who has been disciplined for poor performance, poor attendance, or insubordination may suddenly claim that they hurt themselves on the job ninety days ago and are now unable to work. But what a surprise—this is the first that you have heard of the injury. Having a policy in place may allow you to further discipline the employee for not reporting the injury ninety days ago and make a workers' compensation claim invalid.

Disgruntled former employees are no longer able to file workers' compensation claims after the termination of employment in some states. Before responding to correspondence from or on behalf of a former employee about a work-related injury that was not reported, contact your insurance company. The employee may have no basis for a claim.

Safety Programs

The best way to keep workers' compensation costs under control is to initiate a safety program. Back injuries are one of the most common in the workplace. All employees should be trained about the proper way to lift heavy items, which is to squat first and use your legs, not your back, when you lift something off the floor. A back brace should be issued to every employee who lifts items and they should be required to use it. There are braces on the market with shoulder straps so that the employee can release the belt when they don't need it, yet keep it handy for when they do.

Purchase a DVD about safety in the workplace and require all new employees to watch it before starting work. Choose a program based on the hazards that are prevalent in the workplace. This may include heavy equipment, lifting, climbing, use of chemicals, and other occupational hazards.

If your staff is large enough, put together a safety committee. The committee should meet monthly to discuss new and existing safety issues. Members should be assigned to make periodic safety inspections of all workstations, address violations, and take note of areas that need improvement. Minutes of the meetings should be prepared and kept on file to show a paper trail of the committee's effectiveness.

Here are a few common things in the workplace that are likely to cause an injury:

- Drawers and cabinets that are left open
- Liquid spills on the floor
- Mats and rugs that do not lay flat
- Exposed wires
- Careless storage of chemicals
- Overloaded electrical outlets
- Hot items with no warning notices

Safety-awareness programs can help your company keep injuries to a minimum. Offer an incentive to employees who spot and report a hazard in the workplace. Keep track of accident-free days on a large announcement board and have a celebration when goals are achieved. For instance, for every 100 days that the office or facility is accident free, provide lunch for the entire staff and raffle off prizes. This may encourage employees to watch out for themselves and their coworkers as well.

Managers and human resource representatives should set a good example. Don't ask someone to clean up water on the floor—do it yourself. Intercept when you see someone picking up a box improperly or walking forward while talking to someone and paying no attention to the person coming in the other direction with a heavy cart. Be visible and aware of the conditions in which the employees are working. Your responsibility and concern to provide a safe environment will be noticed and appreciated.

CHAPTER 10

Last Tick of the Time Clock

It's inevitable: Despite a comfortable work environment and generous benefits package, some employees will pack up their desk or locker and journey into a world where they will receive a paycheck with another company's logo printed on the top. Sometimes the employee initiates the change; at other times the parting is dictated by the employer. Regardless of how or why an associate's employment ends, the company is responsible for a smooth transition in the interest of both the employer and employee.

Separation/Release of Employment

Telling an employee that the company is ending his employment is one of the hardest things an employer has to do, especially if he is not at fault. The events leading up to an employment separation can be frustrating for both the employee and the employer when an inability to perform the job is the reason. A good employer will make every effort to train the employee and give him a chance to succeed; however, sometimes a worker is simply not a good match for a job.

Employee insubordination makes a manager's job difficult and causes hardship for the company as well as other employees who are affected. Although an involuntary termination of the employee's job is best for the company, this doesn't make it any easier to deal with.

ESSENTIAL

Prepare a printout for employees that tells them what they need to know about pay and benefits at the time of separation. Advise them of the ending dates of medical, dental, and life insurance, options for retirement-plan rollovers, and when they will receive their final paycheck if your state does not require that it be given upon separation.

Layoffs

Informing an employee of a layoff is probably the toughest of all terminations. The employee being released may be one in good standing with many years of seniority. But if downsizing is necessary to keep a company in business, people are let go as positions are eliminated.

Employees who are laid off due to no fault of their own are eligible for unemployment insurance wages. This will not replace their former salary and may not be enough to cover household expenses while they look for another job. Severance pay will be very helpful to the employee at this time. Most companies that offer a severance benefit base the payout on a percentage of the worker's salary and the length of time they were with the company.

FACT

Remind the employee that W-2 forms will be mailed out after the end of the year and to advise you if his address changes before then. Since the document will include his social security number, he will want to take steps to ensure that it is not mailed to his former address if he moves.

Involuntary Employment Terminations

Employee discipline is discussed in Chapter 15, but corrective action isn't always successful, or the employee has no motivation to remain employed, and it's a lost cause. An involuntary termination of employment is the next and final step in discipline.

To help avoid wrongful-termination lawsuits and keep your unemployment insurance costs down, document events that lead to employment separations thoroughly. Include the date and details about what happened along with counseling or retraining given to the employee. The last incident that leads to separation should be a strong one. For example, if an employee is terminated for excessive tardiness, don't end his employment because he was thirty minutes late to work due to a flat tire. But if he was sixty minutes late because he stayed out late last night and forgot to set his alarm clock, you can justify the termination. If it is a behavior issue, have the documentation that shows he was counseled, retrained, and given a fair chance to improve. Then, when a customer calls you to complain that he was rude and unhelpful, you have good reason to process his final paycheck if this is the third time it's happened.

Only in extreme cases like theft or workplace violence should someone be released without warning that continuing the behavior will result in termination. See Chapter 15 about verbal and written warnings.

Should I ever tell an employee that he's fired?
Don't tell an employee that he is being fired. There are better ways to say it, although the meaning is the same. Refer to it as being released from employment, separated from the company, or that the employment has been ended or terminated. When an employee has been released, all the other workers need to know is that the person no longer works there.

Be quick and direct when informing an employee that the company has made a decision to release him. The topic is not up for discussion and there is no reason for it to drag on. He will want to leave your office and be on his way just as eagerly as you will be to end the conversation. If you think that he may become angry or violent, have another manager with you when you tell him. Escort him to empty his locker or desk only if you feel that it is necessary. If he becomes hostile, you have the right to ask him to leave immediately and tell him that he is not allowed to return to the premises. In most circumstances, the employee will collect his things and leave quietly.

Resignations

Change happens. Just when a department is fully staffed with trained people and everyone has a fresh supply of business cards, someone will submit a letter of resignation. In an ideal world, every associate who resigns will provide her employer with a two-week notice, which is an unwritten rule in the world of business. Two weeks doesn't give an employer enough time to hire and train a replacement, but it can still help with the transition.

An unhappy or hostile employee may quit with just a moment's notice. Don't let such a hasty exit negate the usual practice of getting a letter of resignation. Ask for something in writing stating that the employee is resigning from their position. If you receive no cooperation and there is no witness to the verbal resignation, call a witness into the room. This is to protect the company from an employee who may claim that she was the victim of a wrongful termination or who wants to file a claim for wages through unemployment insurance.

The witness should be a manager or other exempt-status employee. In the presence of the resigning employee and your witness, indicate the employee's intentions, and that your request for a letter of resignation has been denied. Record the conversation in writing, then sign the document in the presence of the employee (if she is still in the room) and ask your witness to do the same. It is unlikely that the departing employee will sign the document, but the signature and attendance of your witness is sufficient backup for your files.

If an employee quits and refuses to give you a letter of resignation, call someone into the room (preferably another manager) to witness that the employee has resigned. Get a statement in writing from the witness about the verbal resignation. Proper documentation of a resignation is important and worth this step when necessary.

When an employee who is an asset to the company resigns, you won't want to see them leave, especially if they are going to work at another company. They probably feel that the new job is a better opportunity for them or it may be a career change into something that they really want to do. Wish them well and work with them to finish up projects that are still pending, and train coworkers to take over job duties until a replacement is hired. It is in everyone's best interest that the employee leaves on good terms.

Letter of Reference

If you are involuntarily releasing an employee from the company, do not agree to submit a letter of reference. If you feel that the employee's performance was not adequate enough to remain on your payroll, raving about him to a prospective employer could cause problems down the road if the employee tries to challenge the separation. You can give the employee a letter on company letterhead that indicates the dates of employment and position.

When you have to lay off an employee due to no fault of his own, you'll want to help him find another job as best you can. Give him a letter of reference that highlights his attendance, dependability, behavior, positive attitude, and skills. Mention any significant accomplishments, and go ahead and indicate that the layoff was due to cutbacks or whatever the situation may be.

An employee may request copies of things from his personnel file that will help him get another job. He may want a copy of his performance appraisal, commendation forms, awards, or training certificates.

Employee Who Does Not Return Property

Employers are prohibited from withholding an employee's final paycheck in most states if she does not return company property at the time employment ends. This may apply to the following items:

- Keys to the building
- Uniforms
- Company credit card
- Electronic equipment
- Locker keys
- Tools and equipment

Find out what the laws are in your state by contacting your labor board or employment office. If an employee doesn't return a locker key, cut the lock or call a locksmith to open it and mail the contents to the employee. It is unfortunate when an employer has to rekey an entire building because a former employee does not return a key, but this has been known to happen. Company credit cards can be cancelled to prevent unauthorized charges.

ALERT!

Do not withhold a former employee's paycheck as punishment or an incentive to return company property. This may work against you in accordance with laws in your state about paying employees in a timely manner. There are usually specific timeframes in which separating employees must be paid.

To collect valuable property such as laptop computers, tools, and equipment, check and see if the police department is able to help you. Since the items were taken to the employee's home with permission, they may not be able to assist you. The refusal to return items may be considered a civil issue. You can also send the employee a certified letter asking her to return the items by a specific date. If she does not return the property, send a second letter by certified mail and indicate that you will have no choice but to take her to court to get the items back or be reimbursed for the value. Give her a final deadline to return the property and follow through with your promise to sue if she does not return them.

If your company has a written cash-handling policy and the employee signed a receipt of acknowledgment, you may be able to deduct any discrepancies from the employee's cash drawer from the final paycheck. Someone who works as a cashier or other position where they are given a cash drawer to balance each day should be subject to a cash-handling policy. If her drawer is short when she turns it in at the time of termination, you can act according to what the policy dictates. The policy would need to specifically state that cash shortages will be deducted from final pay in order to do this.

Exit Interview

You will read about giving your employees constructive feedback in Chapter 15. When an employee decides to leave, it's a good time to ask him for feedback because he is likely to be open and honest and tell you everything. You can do this during an exit interview. The purpose of exit interviews is to find out why people decide to leave the company. If there is a pattern of workers leaving for better pay or benefits, then it may be time to re-evaluate your compensation package. Opportunities for advancement may not be something that you can increase due to staffing needs. When employees reveal that they are unhappy with the work environment, find out the source of the frustration. Is it all about supervisors who do not communicate with the staff or managers who micromanage? Maybe the problem is a lack of morale in the workplace. All of these things can bring a person down.

The exit interview may be verbal or written. People are more likely to open up during a written questionnaire, but a verbal one offers the opportunity to ask for specifics. The person conducting a verbal interview should not be a supervisor of the employee; a neutral third party is most effective. This person should have good listening skills and the ability to react to answers that need further elaboration.

You can give an employee a written exit-interview questionnaire before he departs, or give it to him at the end of his last day to take home and return in a self-addressed, postage-paid envelope. You will receive more responses if you ask employees to complete and turn them in during normal work hours.

Questions that are asked during a verbal or written exit interview should cover the following areas:

- Pay
- Benefits
- Training
- Recognition
- Work environment
- Job satisfaction
- Fairness
- Quality of supervisors
- Company morale

Do not use a verbal exit interview as an opportunity to try to sway a departing employee to stay. If you want to try to convince someone to withdraw his resignation, do this in a face-to-face conversation and ask what it would take to make him reconsider. A person who wants more money or needs to work a different schedule may look for another job that offers what they want instead of asking their current employer. A resignation can encourage someone to open up, but don't ask what it will take to change his mind unless you are able to consider a reasonable request.

The results of exit interviews should be shared with owners, managers, human resources, and supervisors. Some respondents may have unrealistic expectations, but if you see a consistent dissatisfaction in the same areas, put the interviews to good use and implement a plan to turn things around. After all, the purpose of an exit interview is to improve job satisfaction and lower the rate of employee resignations.

Final Paycheck

Find out when employers are required to distribute final paychecks in your state. The timeframe may vary based on whether the employment separation is voluntary or involuntary. If the employee resigned, whether or not they gave an advance notice will make a difference, too. Obviously, if an employee quits on the spot and walks out the door, you won't be expected to hand her a paycheck on her way out. Find out when you need to pay employees in each situation.

If your paid-leave policy pays out accrual balances at the time of separation, this should be included in the final paycheck. If you are required to pay employees who give ample notice in full on their last day, you may have to process the check before their last day of work if you use a third party for payroll processing. In this case, pay the employee for the hours on the schedule and let her know to follow the schedule exactly for her last few days. If she ends up working even fifteen minutes over, you will have to process a separate check for that time.

When an employee receives her final paycheck, remember to ask her to turn in company property such as keys, cell phones, company credit cards, and her ID badge. If she had network computer access, delete her login information and passwords. If she was authorized to make purchases and bill them to the company, remove her name from the vendor's records.

FACT

If an employee's final paycheck is sent after her last day, send it certified mail with a return receipt request or ask her to pick it up and sign for it in accordance with your paycheck distribution policy. If employees do not sign for their paychecks, you may want to consider a new procedure policy for final paychecks that includes a signed receipt.

Unclaimed paychecks should be handled in a responsible manner. Secure them in a safe place. If an employee says that she will pick up her check but does not show up after several days, give her a call. If you can't reach her, leave a message that the check will be sent by certified mail. If the envelope is returned by the post office because she moved or was not available to sign the envelope, put the unopened envelope in her personnel file or store it with the payroll records for that pay period. It is important that you have proof that you made an attempt to pay her.

COBRA

If your company employed twenty or more people consecutively on any day over the past year and offers medical, dental, or vision insurance, COBRA provisions will apply. COBRA is the Consolidated Omnibus Budget Reconciliation Act that went into effect in 1985. It provides separating employees with the option to continue medical, dental, and life insurance coverage at the group rates that the employer pays. If the employee is leaving to work for another company and insurance does not start right away, he may enroll in COBRA coverage to cover the period between the end of one policy and the start of another. If the new job does not provide insurance, COBRA will allow him and/or his dependents to pay for and keep his current plan for eighteen months. If another qualifying event occurs during this eighteen-month period, eligibility may be extended for another eighteen months.

When an employee leaves a company for any reason other than gross misconduct, they are eligible to enroll in COBRA. Gross misconduct is defined as something criminally serious. Poor performance, unsatisfactory attendance, and insubordination are not considered gross misconduct.

Therefore, even if someone is involuntarily terminated, they are still eligible in most situations.

Are COBRA rates the same as the employee's usual payroll deduction for insurance?
No. Under coverage through COBRA, the employee pays the group rates that the employer pays. An employee's medical coverage may be $450 per month, in which the employer pays $400 and the employee contributes $50 through payroll deductions. Under COBRA, the employee would pay the entire $450 per month. This group rate is lower than what the employee would be charged through private insurance.

Employers are required to send COBRA notification to the insured parties of medical plans within fourteen days of employment termination. The paperwork can be hand delivered to the employee, and it is in your best interest to get a signed receipt. Send a COBRA notification letter and COBRA enrollment form via certified mail addressed to both the employee and spouse, if there is one. If the employee has a covered adult dependent child that lives at another address (a full-time college student), send a separate enrollment packet to that person. The reason that eligible adults need to be notified is that they are eligible for enrollment even if the former employee chooses not to sign up. The enrollment papers must be filled out within sixty days of the date the medical insurance ends or of receiving the notification, whichever is later. The first payment must be made within forty-five days of enrollment.

The COBRA notification that you send to employees should provide the following information:

- Date medical/dental/vision insurance will end
- Deadline to enroll in COBRA
- Where and when to send payments
- Cost of coverage
- Name and contact information for plan administrator
- COBRA enrollment form

FACT

Leaving a company is only one of a few qualifying events for COBRA coverage eligibility. A reduction in hours that makes the employee ineligible for insurance is also a qualifying event. If there is a divorce, the employee's spouse can enroll in COBRA. Children who are no longer dependents due to a change in custodian or passing the age of eligibility may enroll as well.

COBRA is a complex issue under IRC Section 4980B. In a nutshell, it means that departing employees who currently have insurance are eligible to retain coverage at their expense. This is an easy way to explain it to employees and you shouldn't assume that they know what COBRA is. Let them know the importance of the enrollment paperwork that you provide to them. You can learn more about COBRA on the U.S. Department of Labor's Web site.

Verification of Past Employment Inquiries

You are free to give a glowing reference for a former employee if a prospective employer calls. Of course, this should only be done if the employee is worthy of a recommendation, and most people are. Even moderately adequate employees have fine traits or you wouldn't have continued their employment. However, be honest. It would be unfair to tell another company that an employee never missed a day of work when in reality she rarely showed up and was terminated for poor attendance. You will look bad in the eyes of the person calling if you say things that are not true.

On the other end of the spectrum, employers are afraid to give honest feedback when an employee is not an ideal candidate. Many businesses have a policy of answering only a minimum amount of questions, such as when the employee was hired, when she left, and what position she held. Therefore, you will usually be asked only these three questions. Additionally, employers are afraid of being sued for defamation of character by revealing unfavorable information that may cause someone to be passed over for a job. The unfortunate thing about this is that what may prevent someone from being hired is their demonstrated behavior. That is the cause of losing out on a job opportunity, not the fact that someone spoke the truth.

There are Job Reference Immunity Statutes (JRIS) that have been passed in forty states as of 2006, and that number is expected to rise. These statutes allow employers to reveal unfavorable information about employees provided that the information is true and documented. Additionally, in some states you don't want to get caught hiding potentially dangerous information about a former employee. Your company can be sued if, for instance, you terminate an employee for bringing a gun to work and she shoots somebody at her next place of employment. To protect itself from a negligence-hiring lawsuit, that company may trace the gun incident back to your company and you could be held liable for not warning the other company, thus putting their employees at risk.

Find out if your state provides employers with a JRIS. Whether or not they do, it is important to know what you can reveal during a reference check. It varies greatly by state. There may be some provisions that allow you to answer certain questions only with permission in writing from the former employee. Others may allow employers to answer questions about performance issues only. Yet others protect employers from defamation of character lawsuits when revealing criminal behavior that occurred in the workplace.

CHAPTER 11

Records and Posting Requirements

People who think that we'll live in a paperless world someday have never worked in human resources! For every chemical at the work site, there is paperwork. When an employee is injured on the job, a file is generated. Some documents are kept under lock and key, yet others are displayed as required by law. And one of these is displayed for only three months out of the year. Do you know which one? If not, keep reading and you will soon find out.

Material Safety Data Sheets (MSDS)

In accordance with the Occupational Safety and Health Administration's (OSHA) Right to Know law, employers are required to ensure that information about workplace hazards and safety issues is made easily available to employees. If there are hazardous chemicals in the workplace, a written hazard communication program must be in place. Manufacturers and distributors of hazardous chemicals are required to produce a Material Safety Data Sheet (MSDS) for every chemical that contains hazardous ingredients. The MSDS sheets are distributed to customers who purchase the product. There are over 650,000 hazardous chemicals in workplaces, and an MSDS for each one.

An MSDS identifies the ingredients of dangerous materials and instructs employees about the safe handling, use, storage, and first-aid measures to take if there is an incident with the chemical. Employers are required to keep an MSDS readily available for each hazardous chemical in the workplace. The documents should be kept in bright binders that cannot be removed from the area. Typically, the binders are secured to a holder or shelf with a chain or cable to ensure that they are not misplaced. You can purchase brightly labeled binders that are specifically for MSDSs. A binder should be kept by the employee time clock and/or the employee bulletin board where legal postings are kept, and also within close vicinity of areas where the chemicals are stored. If your company is very small, one binder may be sufficient. One of the important things about the whereabouts of the MSDSs is that an employee has quick access to a binder when it is needed. Keep this in mind as you decide where to place it.

FACT

The Right to Know law is OSHA's Hazard Communication Standard (HCS). This standard is based on the simple concept that employees have both a need and a right to know the hazards and the identity of the chemicals they are exposed to when working. You can find out more about the standard and training resources at *www.osha.gov*.

Place several copies of each MSDS in your binder so that if an employee has to leave the building for medical attention, he can take a MSDS for the chemical with him to the treating facility. Keep them in alphabetical order with tabs to easily identify the chemical name—clear pocket dividers come in handy for this.

Previously, chemical manufacturers did not follow a specific format for reporting information on the MSDSs. This made it more difficult to find information since there was no consistency from one MSDS to the next. For instance, one chemical may have the instructions for addressing skin exposure in the top section of the MSDS, but another may have it at the end. The Chemical Manufacturers Association's (now known as the American Chemistry Council) MSDS work group established a format for MSDSs. This developed into the American National Standards Institute (ANSI) standard Z400.2, which is a voluntary standard in MSDS preparation, but most chemical companies are expected to follow the format, making MSDS information quicker to access.

Perform an audit of your MSDS binder(s) frequently. If there is only one copy left of an MSDS, make more copies so that someone doesn't take the last one, leaving you with none. When you receive newly revised MSDSs, discard the old ones and place copies of the new revision in your binder. Also, make sure that you have an MSDS for every chemical on the property. Discard the MSDS forms for chemicals that you no longer use.

State and Federal Compliance

Some states have OSHA-approved safety and health programs with their own specific compliance procedures that may be more stringent than federal regulations. Check with state authorities for additional information you may need to know. These states are Alaska, Arizona, California, Connecticut, Hawaii, Indiana, Iowa, Kentucky, Maryland, Michigan, Minnesota, Nevada, New Mexico, New York (state and municipal employees only), North Carolina, Oregon, Puerto Rico, South Carolina, Tennessee, Utah, Vermont, Virgin Islands, Virginia, Washington, and Wyoming.

ALERT!

Employees who do not use chemicals on the job but have access to them are also covered by the Right to Know law. They have a right to know about the potential dangers, the proper use and storage, and what to do if a spill or exposure occurs.

There are two types of hazardous chemicals covered by the HCS. Physical hazards are those that have the potential for flammability or explosions. Health hazards apply to chemicals with acute and chronic effects if employees inhale them or are exposed to them. Proper enforcement of the HCS will help decrease workplace incidents and injuries caused by chemicals, which will help reduce the number of workers' compensation injuries and illnesses.

Get Your HCS in Writing

The federal HCS is your requirement to inform and train workers about the hazards in the workplace, retain warning labels on containers and drums, and ensure that workers know the whereabouts of MSDSs. A written plan that details the HCS should be kept on file and include the following:

- A list of all chemicals kept on site
- Who is responsible for maintaining MSDSs
- How employees will be informed and trained
- Which employees will use chemicals and for what purpose
- Where the MSDS binders will be located
- Who is responsible for ensuring that chemicals are properly labeled
- What to do in the event of chemical spill or emergency

A written HCS policy is not needed if employee contact with chemicals is limited to sealed containers. This may apply to retail, warehouse, or transport industries. However, employees need to be trained on what to do in the event of a chemical spill or emergency.

OSHA 300 Log

Employers are required to maintain a record of work-related injuries on two separate forms. One is OSHA 300, Log of Occupational Injuries and Illnesses. The other is OSHA 300A, Summary of Occupational Injuries and Illnesses. Another OSHA requirement, Form 301, is the First Report of Injury form that is filled out by the attending physician. This form is discussed in Chapter 9.

Injuries that are reportable on Log 300 are ones that include the following:

- Death
- Medical treatment beyond first aid
- Loss of consciousness
- Significant injury or illness
- Missed days of work
- Days of restricted work
- Transfer to another job

When reporting an injury or illness that qualifies as a privacy case, do not indicate the employee's name on the OSHA 300 Log. Instead, refer to the employee as "Privacy Case" and log the employee's identity elsewhere in a confidential file. A few of the incidents that qualify as a privacy case are sexual assaults, injuries to private parts of the body, and communicable diseases.

If an employee has a minor injury that needs only first aid, such as a bandage or ice pack, the injury does not need to be reported on the 300 Log. This applies to first aid that takes place at the work site or a medical facility. Refer to Chapter 9 for record-keeping procedures for minor injuries. All other injuries that happen to employees who are under the supervision of the employer—which includes temporary and contract workers—must be entered on OSHA Log 300 within seven days of the fatality, injury, or illness.

If you question whether or not an employee should see a doctor, send him to be on the safe side. For instance, if a cut looks like it might need stitches, send the employee to your workers' compensation physician. If he doesn't need stitches, the injury will still be considered a first-aid non-reportable injury if he receives only first-aid treatment.

Keep a first-aid kit stocked with basic first-aid supplies such as bandages, antiseptic wipes, gauze, etc. for first-aid treatments that can be administered in the workplace. Following is a list of a few treatments recognized as first aid by OSHA. You can find a complete list by visiting *www.osha.gov* and typing "1904.7" in the search area.

- Hot or cold therapy
- Use of bandages, elastic bandages, or finger guards during first visit
- Treatment of first-degree burns
- Need for hot or cold therapy
- Use of nonprescription medications
- Easy removal of splinters or other foreign matters
- Negative X-ray diagnosis
- Physician observation of minor injury

Reportable Restricted Work

Restricted work after an injury occurs when an employee cannot perform one or more of his routine duties, or is unable to work a full workday. Therefore, if an employee is able to return to work but is unable to stand for more than an hour at a time and must sit down during part of the workday, he is on restricted duty if this is something he normally would not do. If an employee can perform all functions of his job but for a shorter period of time, this is considered a restriction as well. These restricted duties are reportable on OSHA Log 300.

Reportable Missed Work

When an employee misses one or more days of work, the time off is reportable starting with the first day after the injury. If an employee is initially taken off work for six days, and the physician extends the time off, update the extra days off as you are notified. Do not start a new entry if an employee's time off from work is extended. You should start a new entry for the employee only if he has another injury in the future.

QUESTION?

When is it required to report an accident to OSHA?
Report a workplace fatality or an injury or illness that requires three or more days of hospitalization to OSHA within eight hours of notification. You can visit the nearest OSHA office or call the OSHA hotline at 1-800-321-OSHA. There is an exception for some vehicular or public-transportation accidents.

When calculating days off, include weekends, holidays, and any other days that the employee was not scheduled to work. This is because the recordable days are those in which an employee is unable to work and does not take into consideration whether or not he would be scheduled to work. There is a limit to the number of days away from work that must be recorded. Once an employee has missed 180 calendar days of work, you are not required to keep track of additional days off work. The total number of days missed for that employee will be reported as 180. This will be the number recorded in the total column.

Nonreportable Incidents

Not every employee incident is reportable, even if it occurs on company property or while the employee is on the clock. Here are a few examples:

- An injury that occurs while on property as a customer or visitor during nonwork hours
- Involvement in a vehicle accident on the way to or from work, including those that take place in the company parking lot

- Injuries or illnesses that result during personal functions such as eating, taking medications, or grooming
- Delayed symptoms from nonwork-related injuries or illnesses that happened earlier in the day or week
- Injuries or illnesses that occur while an employee is clocked out for lunch during the workday

Summary and Posting Requirements

After the end of the year, review the OSHA 300 Log for completeness and transfer the information to the 300A Summary Form. This log must be posted in a common area for employees that cannot be accessed by the general public, from February 1 through April 30 of the following year (e.g., the OSHA 300A Form for the year ended December 31, 2008 must be posted from February 1, 2009 through April 30, 2009). Once the summary is removed from the posting area, it must be kept on file for five years.

Federal, State, and Local Postings

Federal, state, and local law requires employers to post notices of labor laws in an area commonly visited by all employees. Typically, this would be a break room, lunchroom, locker room, or time-clock area. To determine the federal requirements, log on to *www.dol.gov* and do a search for "workplace poster requirements." You will also need to check with your state labor board to determine your state and local requirements. Some requirements may be based on the number of employees you have or the industry in which you do business.

ALERT!

Federal, state, and local posting requirements change from time to time, and this may occur midyear as well as at year-end. It is important to stay informed about posting requirements on all levels. Sometimes, one regulation will have a change in the wording on the posting, thus making it necessary to purchase a new poster.

Most vendors that sell labor-law posters carry an all–in-one version for both federal and state requirements. Depending on the requirements for your state, you may be able to purchase one large poster that covers everything. Laminated posters are available and worth the extra expense. Some employers display posters under a locked glass display case to avoid alterations. If the posters are defaced and unreadable, they will have to be replaced.

Records Retention Schedule

Earlier in this chapter, you read about the OSHA 300 Log and 300A Summary Form and that the documents must remain on file for five years after the summary has been displayed. Most of the files in your office must be kept for a specific period of time, and there are both federal and state requirements. When they differ, the longer requirement supersedes. This section does not address the retention requirements since most of them are state specific, but it will give you some things to consider about some of the files that you need to keep. It is recommended that you find out how long these files need to be kept. If an employee leaves the company or it is year-end, this doesn't necessarily mean that files can be discarded.

When purging files (which is to take them from your active files and put them in storage), write the discard date of the contents on the box. By doing this, when the contents are ready to be discarded or shredded, it can be done at once; there will be no need to sort through the contents of the box.

The time required to keep workers' compensation files may vary based on whether or not the employee missed time from work due to the injury, and if the claim was litigated. In the event of an unfortunate fatality, it is likely that the file will have to be kept permanently. Ask your workers' compensation insurance carrier how long workers' compensation files must be kept.

Employment applications for unsuccessful applicants must be kept after you have filled the position. How long may be determined by whether or not you interviewed the applicant. Additionally, you may be required to keep advertisements for employment. Generally, this will be regulated by the EEOC, but your state may require you to keep the files longer.

Payroll records include timecards or time-clock reports, the calculation of salary, hours worked, and taxes, and other deductions that are withheld. Payroll tax forms are also considered payroll records. The wage and hour laws in your state will determine how long payroll records must be maintained.

An employee's personnel file is kept through the duration of employment. After she leaves the company, it cannot be discarded immediately. If an employee retires, you may need to keep the file indefinitely if you have a company-sponsored retirement plan. Again, don't toss the file until you know for sure.

FACT

The Fair Credit Report Act (FCRA) regulates how reports received during pre-employment credit checks must be destroyed. The Health Insurance Portability and Accountability Act (HIPAA) mandates the confidentiality of employee records before, during, and after employment. There have been many changes in privacy laws over the past few years.

If your company has a self-funded medical plan, an employee's medical file may need to be kept for several years after she has left the company. This is due to the company's role as plan administrator. There may also be requirements in your state for other files related to self-funded and third-party benefits.

Protection of Confidential Information

The confidentiality of employee records has been brought up on several occasions throughout this book, and it doesn't stop when it comes to purging or discarding personnel files and other employment records. Files that contain personal and identifying information about employees are kept under lock and key when the files are active. When they are purged and sent back into a storage room, confidentiality issues still apply. Just because the employee is no longer employed does not mean that other employees may have access to their records. For instance, if the personnel files of former employees are kept in a storage room that others have access to by using a key, there will be a violation of privacy issues. If there are only one, two, or a few people at the company who have access to the personnel files of current employees, then these are the only people who should have access to the files of former employees. This pertains to payroll files, workers' compensation files, and all other employment records as well.

EEOC Compliance

The Equal Employment Opportunity Commission (EEOC) makes it illegal to discriminate against job applicants and employees. Your employment applications, advertisements for employment, and hiring practices must adhere to EEOC regulations.

Here are the types of discrimination that are covered:

- Age
- Disability
- Equal pay
- National origin
- Pregnancy
- Race
- Religion
- Retaliation
- Sex
- Sexual harassment

Contact your local EEOC office and ask for a copy of the EEOC Compliance Manual. The manual interprets the law for all forms of discrimination and gives examples of unlawful practices. The manual is not available electronically, but recent changes can be found online at *www.eeoc.gov*.

CHAPTER 12

Family and Medical Leave Act (FMLA)

Work can get in the way of life when someone is seriously ill or a child joins the family. The federal Family and Medical Leave Act has helped millions of employees since it was initiated in 1993. It gives people the comfort of knowing that they can take a leave of absence for up to twelve weeks during a qualifying event. The employer's role in this is to process the paperwork, confirm that the reason for the leave qualifies as FMLA, then help the employee transition back to work.

Provisions for Compliance

Employers with seventy-five or more employees within a fifty-mile radius must comply with the federal Family and Medical Leave Act (FMLA) of 1993. At press time, there is federal legislation pending to change the employer criteria to those with twenty-five or more employees. If this may affect your company, check for updates before assuming that you do not need to comply. FMLA provides unpaid, job-protected leave for up to twelve weeks for any of the following events:

- Birth or adoption of a child
- Care of a biological or adopted child under the age of twelve months
- Placement of foster child in the home
- Employee's own serious medical condition
- Care of a spouse, child, or parent with a serious health condition

The job-protected leave that is provided under the Act means that employees are to return to the same or equivalent job when returning to work. An equivalent job is one with the same pay, benefits, and work hours with the same or similar duties.

Employee Eligibility

Employees who have worked at least 1,250 hours in a twelve-month period are eligible for FMLA leave. These 1,250 hours of service are based on federal FLSA principles for determining compensable hours of work. Therefore, paid time off for vacation, holidays, or sick leave may be calculated into the hours. Time spent on a paid or unpaid leave of absence may not count. State provisions may apply.

The twelve-month period may be a fixed one, such as a calendar, fiscal, or anniversary year, or a rolling one. However, your state may dictate which twelve-month period you have to use. If you have the option to choose and make a change, give employees a written sixty-day notice before the effective date of the new twelve-month period measurement.

A rolling twelve-month period is determined by going forward after an employee has taken any FMLA leave. Therefore, if an employee started FMLA leave on March 1 and returned on June 1, he would not be able to start FMLA leave again until June 1 of the following year.

Unclear Eligibility Issues

The criteria for employee eligibility can have a few challenges. Determining if there are seventy-five employees within a fifty-mile radius can be tricky. For example, if a salesperson works out of a small office with a support staff of three people in Austin, Texas, but reports to a supervisor at the corporate office in Detroit, Michigan where 600 people work, is he eligible for FMLA? He is one of four people at the office in Austin and the closest other office is in Detroit, but it is over fifty miles away. Is he employed out of the Detroit office where his supervisor assigns his duties or his Austin office? If his employer considers him to be employed in the Austin office, he would not be eligible for FMLA. But is this the case? His employer would need to find the answer.

The 1,250 hour requirement isn't always as clear as it may seem. Generally, the employee must work at least 1,250 hours in a twelve-month period, but is working 1,250 hours considered actually performing duties, or being paid? Therefore, if an employee is paid sick leave or holiday pay during the twelve-month period, do these hours count? If an employee is full time, they will have long surpassed 1,250 hours of service in a twelve-month period. But when the timing is close, an employee can challenge eligibility and in some states, rulings have concluded that employees are eligible when the employer felt otherwise. These are just examples of some things to think about and look into if you are not sure if an employee is eligible.

FACT

Although the FMLA is a federal law, there are some state statutes that overrule because they are more generous to the employee. Check with your state labor board about the FMLA compliance rules in your state. In addition, there may be state disability laws that run concurrently with FMLA, and ones that extend afterward, such as PDL and CFRA in the state of California.

Two Employees in the Same Household

In most states, two married employees with the same employer cannot take FMLA leave at the same time. In this case, if one employee is out on FMLA leave for his own serious illness, his wife (if also an employee at the same company) may not be able to take FMLA leave to take care of him. This can cause hardship for a family, so check into the laws in your state carefully before you deny FMLA leave to the employee who is the spouse. Although you may not be required to grant FMLA leave to both of them at the same time, you may have the option to do so if you choose. In some states, two married employees can take FMLA leave at the same time, but have to split the twelve weeks between the two of them.

If two employees have a baby together or have a biological child who is seriously ill, only one of them may be able to take leave at a time. If there is a critically ill or injured child in the family, it is unlikely that either parent will be in an emotional state to work. As mentioned above, contact your state labor board and find out if you can grant FMLA leave to both parents.

Covered Family Members

Employees may take FMLA leave during the serious illness of qualified family members, of which there are three: spouse, child, or parent. In the approximately fifteen states that acknowledge common-law marriage, a common-law spouse is a qualified family member for FMLA purposes. Unmarried domestic partners are usually not qualified, but registered domestic partners may be covered in some states.

A covered child is a biological or adopted child, or a foster child who was placed in the home by the state. A foster child transferred to the home through a private arrangement does not qualify. However, a child placed in the home through a private adoption does qualify.

QUESTION?

What is considered a serious illness for FMLA purposes?
A serious illness is one in which a person cannot work or requires the care of another person. The illness must be recognized as such by a health care provider who fills out a Form WH 380, Certification of Health Care Provider. This form is explained in more detail further in this chapter.

In order for a parent to be a covered family member under FMLA, the person must be the employee's biological, adopted, or stepparent. In-laws are not covered. If the employee was adopted by a grandparent or other relative, the relationship counts as an adopted parent.

Qualified Events

The birth of a child is a qualified event for FMLA leave. The reason for the leave is twofold: The mother is recovering from childbirth, which is a qualifying medical condition. In addition, FMLA allows time to care for and bond with the newborn. Fathers may take FMLA leave also, for the purpose of bonding with the child. Since the leave does not need to be taken right away, a mother may take FMLA leave for the first twelve weeks of the infant's life, and the father may take it at any time before the child is twelve months old. Of course, the parents may both take it together if they wish (and are not employed at the same company). The benefit of the parents taking the leave one after the other is that the infant will stay home longer and start daycare at a later age.

Parents may take FMLA leave when a child joins the family through adoption. This is generally taken as soon as the child enters the home, for bonding purposes and making the transition easier for the child. The child does not have to be an infant to qualify. Leave must be taken within twelve months of placement.

Foster children qualify in the same way that adopted children do. The leave must be taken within twelve months of placement and the child does not need to be an infant.

The above situations are the family-leave part of FMLA. The medical-leave part of the Act provides time off for the employee's own recovery or that of a family member. FMLA draws the most attention from women going on maternity leave, but this is by no means the main purpose of the leave.

The term Family and Medical Leave Act may make employees think that they have to have a family event and medical issue combined in order to be eligible. Make sure that your employees know that FMLA leave is available when they or an immediate qualifying family member is seriously ill.

If you are concerned about an employee's health and know that he has a serious illness (which you will usually know only if he tells you or the symptoms are visible), you can require that he sees his physician for an evaluation and starts FMLA leave if he has a qualifying condition. If he is as ill as you perceive, the doctor will sign the certification paperwork. An employee who is seriously ill is a hazard in the workforce. His illness may be contagious or he could become injured or further aggravate his condition. Continuing to work instead of taking care of himself may result in a longer recovery period. You should have a vested interest in the health and well-being of your employees. Sometimes it is necessary to step in and encourage them to do what is best for themselves.

Official FMLA Notice

Have a packet of forms available to distribute when an employee requests leave. This should include an Employee's Request for Family and Medical Leave form. The purpose of this form is for the employee to indicate the type of FMLA leave she is requesting, when it will begin, and when she expects to return. You are also required to give the employee a copy of the company's FMLA policy and an FMLA Employer Response to Employee

Request for FMLA. The fourth and last form, the Certificate of Health Care Provider form, is explained in more detail below. Employers are required by law to distribute these forms to employees within two days of a verbal request for leave. Not all leaves are foreseeable, such as a sudden illness or accident of the employee or a qualifying family member. If the employee has no advance notice of the leave, give him the paperwork as soon as you receive his verbal request. Sample copies of these forms may be found in Appendix A.

The FMLA Employer Response to Employee Request for FMLA form mentioned above serves as the employee's notice of rights, obligations, and what is expected of him. If you choose, you may download and use Form MH-381 from the U.S. Department of Labor Web site listed in Appendix C to notify the employee. You may also use the information on the form to develop your own form. Some of the information on the form may need to be altered to reflect state regulations.

Employees do not need to specifically ask for leave to qualify for FMLA. Distribute the FMLA paperwork packet to any employee who requests leave and gives a reason that may qualify as FMLA leave. An example of a leave that would not qualify is if an employee requests a personal leave of absence to spend the summer abroad, to help an adult child get settled into a new city for college, or to pursue a personal project or hobby.

ALERT!

If the employee is requesting FMLA leave for his own serious illness, he cannot be paid for both sick leave and disability leave concurrently; he will need to choose between the two. If he will be filing a disability claim, he will need a separate set of paperwork for that because FMLA does not generate disability payments.

Employees are expected to give at least a thirty-day advance notice when an FMLA leave is foreseeable. If the employee has no control over the start of the leave, such as in the event of an accident, sudden illness, or premature birth of a baby, you should be notified within forty-eight hours. Since the employee may not be in a condition to inform you in person, this notification may be made by telephone, e-mail, fax, or by a family member. Once you have been notified of the leave, prepare and mail an FMLA request form to the employee's home and a Certification of Health Care Provider form. Even if the leave is not due to the employee's own serious illness, the form is needed to confirm that a family member has a qualifying event.

Certification of Health Care Provider

A Certification of Health Care Provider form (WH-380) may be found on the U.S. Department of Labor's Web site. The health care provider fills it out to confirm that there is a qualifying medical condition. It should include the date of onset of the condition and the expected recovery date. Ideally, as in the case of a thirty-day notice, the form will be filled out prior to the start of the leave. In the event of a sudden leave, the employee has fifteen days to return the completed form to you in order for the leave to be designated as FMLA. In all fairness to the employee, forward this form to him as soon as possible so that he has a chance to get it back to you before the fifteen-day deadline.

Most doctors work within large medical groups and there may be a central office that handles disability and FMLA paperwork. This could cause a delay in the completion, but office personnel should know that the employee needs it back within fifteen days. Mark your calendar fifteen days from the date you gave him the form. Notify him if you have not yet received it by that date. Some medical groups send the form directly to the employer, yet others send it back to the employee.

Most medical offices charge a fee to fill out FMLA paperwork. This fee is usually about $10. This expense belongs to the employee and should not be eligible for reimbursement. As the employer, you should receive the original document once it is completed. File it in the employee's medical file and give a copy to the employee.

The human resources department is sometimes the last to know about employee happenings. Train all supervisors and managers to inform you right away when an employee has an off-work note or a pending leave of absence. You can't get the paperwork started if you don't know that a leave is in the employee's future. If the reason you found out that an employee started an FMLA leave is because you noticed that he hasn't received a paycheck in two weeks, there is a problem to address. If this does happen, the employee cannot be penalized for not getting his paperwork in on time. He will still be eligible for the leave, just do what you can to get the paperwork started and completed as quickly as possible.

After the employee's request for FMLA and medical-certification forms have been received, determine if the leave is designated as FMLA. Send or give the employee a letter to advise him of the status of his request. A copy of a sample FMLA approval letter may be found in Appendix A. The letter should specifically state that the leave is designated as FMLA if it has been approved. Give him instructions for paying his usual medical-benefit premiums, if applicable, and the procedures for returning early from the leave or asking for an extension. Keep a copy of the letter in the employee's medical file. If the leave is due to a family member's serious illness, correspondence should still be kept in the medical file.

Continuation of Medical Benefits

The FMLA requires that the employee's group health-insurance benefits be maintained in the same manner they were before the leave. If the company pays 100 percent of the coverage, this remains the same. Otherwise, the amount the employer pays and the amount the employee pays remains the same. The only change may be the addition of a child due to birth or adoption. This may cause an increase in both the employer's and employee's contributions.

If the leave is due to the birth or placement of a child, go to Chapter 14 to read about adding a newborn to the employee's medical-insurance policy. A delay in enrollment can result in a denial of coverage until open enrollment. It is the employee's responsibility to enroll the child, but she will appreciate you following up.

It is obvious that payroll deductions stop when there is no paycheck. When employees are on FMLA leave without pay, have them issue a check to the company each month to pay their usual deductions for medical, dental, and life insurance, as well as other benefits that are affected. Employers are required to continue their usual contribution, too. If an employee is on FMLA leave due to the birth or placement of a baby in the home, the new family member may result in an increased medical-insurance premium. If the employee is sending in a check for her contribution, advise her of the new amount.

Employees Returning to Work

When an employee returns to work after a leave due to his own medical condition, you should insist on a medical release. A note from a doctor stating that he may return to work will help protect both of you. You will also need to know if he may return to full duty or if he has any work restrictions. When a woman has a baby, she will usually be released to return to work after her six-week postpartum checkup; however, she may continue her FMLA leave. Since she is allowed twelve weeks off work after the birth of the baby, she is free to remain at home if she requested this time off with her FMLA request.

Keep track of when employees are expected to return to work so that you are prepared for their return and can act quickly to deal with employees who do not return.

Employees Who Do Not Return to Work

Your first sign that somebody may not return from FMLA leave is that he did not call and speak with you or his supervisor to confirm that he will be returning to work on schedule. Then the big day arrives and he doesn't clock in.

The first thing to do is to call the employee. This call can be made by either the human resource department or the employee's supervisor. If he is reached on the telephone, tell him that his FMLA leave ended today and he was expected back to work. If he has not used the full twelve weeks of leave, ask him if he is going to request an extension. Although ideally the employee would have requested an extension before the date he was supposed to return to work, you generally can't deny his request if he is still entitled to more time off.

If you are unable to reach the employee within twenty-four hours, send a certified letter to his home. The letter should indicate what date he was scheduled to return to work and that you are concerned and worried that you did not hear from him. Tell him that it is crucial that he contact the company at once, or the procedures for job abandonment will be started, and explain what these procedures are. For instance, if an employee is considered to have abandoned his job after three consecutive no-call and no-shows, state this in the letter. Indicate the date he will have been considered to have abandoned his job, and end the letter saying that you hope to hear from him at his earliest convenience.

This is a time to show concern for an employee if he was on leave for his own or a family member's serious medical condition; the condition could have become worse. Make every possible attempt to get ahold of the employee before starting job-abandonment procedures.

CHAPTER 13

Sensitive Issues

Where there are people, there will be situations that require awareness, an unbiased look at diversity, and a commitment to avoid discrimination due to a disability, religious beliefs, or personal problems that an employee may be facing. As a human resource professional or small business owner, you will sometimes find out more about people than you care to know, but this is part of the job. This chapter takes a look at a few sensitive topics that will show you what human resources is all about.

Request for Reasonable Accommodations

Employers have a legal requirement to accommodate workers with disabilities under the Americans with Disabilities Act (ADA), which applies to companies that employ at least fifteen people. An individual with a disability is a person who has a physical or mental impairment that substantially limits one or more major life activities. A person with only a record of a qualifying impairment is also protected by the ADA. An example would be someone with a history of major depression disorder who is now in recovery. The person cannot be discriminated against because of her medical history. Additionally, persons who may be regarded as having a disability are covered by the ADA, such as in the case of the person above who has recovered from major depression. An employer cannot discriminate against this employee with the assumption that the condition will return and affect her attendance or behavior. Nor can an employer just assume a person has a disability (through a rumor, losing or gaining weight, etc.) because the employee may be discriminated against even though they may not have a disability.

All applicants and employees who are covered under the ADA may be of any status, such as full time, part time, permanent, temporary, per diem, hourly, salaried, or probationary. They may have been employed for one minute, one year, or fifty years. To learn more about the ADA, download a copy of the brochure *ADA Guide for Small Businesses* and the video *10 Small Business Mistakes* at *www.ada.gov.* The brochure introduces tax credits and deductions that may help businesses that employ disabled workers.

Before the Job Offer

During the interviewing process, you may not ask an applicant if he has a disability, even if one is apparent. This means that if an applicant uses a walker, for example, you may not ask why or how long he has needed assistance. Since a disability is visible in this applicant, you may ask him if he is able to perform the essential duties of the job with or without reasonable accommodation. Describe the essential (important, critical) duties of the job to him so that he can give you an accurate answer based on his abilities. An applicant who uses a walker may say something like, "I am able to perform the job with the use of my walker any time I need to walk more than ten feet" or "I can perform this job if I am able to keep the walker with me at all times."

ALERT!

If a disability is not apparent in an applicant, ask him if he is able to perform the essential duties of the job and show him a job description or verbally tell him what the duties are. Do not ask whether or not a reasonable accommodation is needed because it's not appropriate in this situation.

A disability does not give an applicant an advantage over a nondisabled candidate. All persons considered for a position should meet the basic requirements for the job and be able to perform its fundamental duties, with or without a reasonable accommodation. Whether or not a disability is present plays no role in the selection process, and in the event of an unseen impairment, you wouldn't know about it anyway. Therefore, all questions asked during an interview should be identical for each applicant and focus on job skills, demonstrated work ability, education, and training as mentioned in Chapter 2.

You may not ask an applicant questions about disabilities or his medical history during a job interview. Here are some examples of illegal questions:

- What medications are you taking?
- Have you ever filed a workers' compensation claim?
- Do you sleep well at night?
- Have you ever had a mental breakdown?
- What medical conditions run in your family?

The ADA protects only qualified applicants against hiring discrimination. If a candidate with a disability does not meet the requirements for the position, he is to be disqualified from consideration with the same criteria that a nondisabled candidate would be. The ADA's purpose is to provide an equal opportunity for employment for disabled persons; it is not meant to encourage employers to give preferential treatment to a disabled applicant.

Focus your questions on the ability to perform a job while avoiding ones about medical impairments. Although you may not ask an applicant if he suffers from insomnia, you may ask, "This job requires that you are alert and ready to start promptly at 6:00 A.M. each workday. Are you able to do this?"

You may not arrange for an applicant to have a pre-employment physical solely because of a visible disability. If the company has a written, consistent policy to conduct pre-employment physicals, a disabled applicant is to be examined under the same circumstances and in the same manner as one who is not disabled. The purpose of the exam for all applicants is to determine if they are physically able to perform the essential duties of the job. A job offer that is contingent on the results of a pre-employment physical must apply to all applicants for every position that has the requirement. You may not make an exception and signal out those who appear to have a disability or if you suspect there may be one. Remember that in regards to your hiring practices, consistency is critical.

After the Job Offer

The ADA strictly limits inquiries about perceived disabilities after an employee is hired, and an employee does not have to disclose this information. An employee may choose to bring a medical condition to your attention because she needs a reasonable accommodation in order to perform her job, or a pre-employment physical may determine that one is necessary. A reasonable accommodation is an adjustment in the way a job is performed, the hours that are worked, or other criteria in order to enable someone to perform the essential duties. But first there are steps to formally implement a reasonable accommodation, and this is called the interactive process.

ADA Interactive Process—Step One

The first step in the interactive process is for the employee to bring to your attention the need for a reasonable accommodation due to a disability. She may volunteer to share the information—most people with a disability are aware that they are expected to inform their employer if they require an accommodation. She may inform you verbally; it does not need to be in writing. However, if she can perform the essential functions of the job without an accommodation, she does not have to inform you of a medical condition. If you have observed performance issues that would indicate a need for accommodation due to performance or safety concerns, you may ask her about the need for an accommodation. Again, you may initiate this conversation only after you have witnessed something that causes concern; do not ask based on an assumption or rumor.

FACT

The purpose of the interactive process is to identify an ADA recognized disability; learn about the employee's work restrictions; and determine if there is a mutually agreed-upon accommodation that will allow the employee to perform her job safely without the reasonable accommodation causing undue hardship to the company.

Confirm the disability with written verification from the employee's physician that an ADA disability exists. This can be difficult since not all conditions are covered. You will also need written instructions from the physician that describe the employee's limitations and restrictions. A restriction that indicates "No heavy lifting" is incomplete. However, "No lifting more than fifteen pounds above shoulder level" is the kind of detailed restriction you need. Be aware of other vague limitations such as "Light duty" and "No prolonged standing." These examples do not tell you what light duty is considered to be or how much time is considered prolonged. Detailed restrictions will protect both the company and the employee. The employee will probably know what her limitations are, but you want to be sure that there is no misunderstanding about what she can and cannot do. Your job is to protect the employee's health and the company's liability. Remember that an employee does not get to pick and choose the reasonable accommodation. If an employer has a reasonable accommodation that will allow the employee to perform the essential functions, they have met their burden with the ADA.

Due to privacy laws, there may be a limit to how much information the doctor can give you about the employee's condition. However, you should receive enough information to help you determine if the employee has a disability as defined by the ADA. Most physicians will cooperate when assigning restrictions based upon the condition. Doctors should be very familiar with ADA regulations, work restrictions, and the paperwork that goes along with helping their patients communicate adequately with employers.

QUESTION?

What determines if a medical condition qualifies as a disability?
If a person is substantially limited in her ability to perform manual tasks, walk, see, hear, communicate, learn, breathe, or work, she may be defined as disabled. It's not only the condition that determines whether or not there is a disability; the person's limitations and restrictions play an important role, too.

It is not up to the employer to determine whether or not an employee is disabled. Many qualifying conditions are not apparent, and some may be obvious only during an incident, such as someone with epilepsy having a seizure. You can't tell by looking at a person if she has HIV, cancer, rheumatoid arthritis, kidney disease, diabetes, high blood pressure, alcoholism, mental illness, or any of the many other illnesses and conditions that may qualify for ADA protection.

ADA Interactive Process—Step Two

The second step in the interactive process is to determine if the employee will be able to perform the essential duties of the job with or without reasonable accommodation, while causing no undue hardship to the company. It is important to determine the essential duties of the job during this step. Here are some things to consider:

- Amount of time spent performing the task
- Employer's perception of the essential duties
- Relevance of the task as indicated on the job description

- Hardship suffered by the company if the employee is unable to perform
- Work experience needed to perform the job

Once the essential duties have been identified, both you and the employee should offer your suggestions for reasonable accommodations. The goal of the interactive process is to negotiate an accommodation that is suitable for both parties; one that gives the employee the opportunity to perform her job safely at a production level acceptable to the company. You and the employee may agree on an accommodation quickly and easily. Other times, the conversation may go back and forth until a viable solution is agreed upon. Give the employee ample time to explain why she feels an accommodation may or may not work. You are able to have your say as well, making your viewpoint clear to the employee from a business point of view.

Turn to the EEOC's policy entitled *Reasonable Accommodation and Undue Hardship Under the Americans with Disabilities Act* for more information. This seventy-page document may be found at *www.eeoc.org*. The Job Accommodation Network, *www.jan.wvu.edu*, offers examples of accommodations that have been offered in employment, arranged in order by the disease or health condition and the type of accommodation needed.

There are several ways to reasonably accommodate an employee's disability. Some of these ideas are to purchase or modify equipment, reassign duties, change the way a job is performed (allow an employee to sit instead of stand), offer an alternative work schedule, or transfer the employee to another position. Employers are not required to purchase personal items for employees such as hearing aids or a special type of shoe that the employee must wear. Contact your state's Department of Rehabilitative Services or equivalent office. They are an excellent resource and can either fund or find funding for accommodations, as well as do onsite evaluations of what could be a reasonable accommodation for the job.

The EEOC recognizes telecommuting (telework) as a reasonable accommodation. President George W. Bush's New Freedom Initiative emphasizes the value of today's technological advancements that have made it possible for many disabled workers to work from home. Not all jobs can be performed at home, and the ADA does not require employers to offer telecommuting as a reasonable accommodation. However, if telework is offered for some positions, employees with disabilities who work in those positions must be allowed to participate. You may have to modify the telework policy, such as waiving a rule that dictates how long an employee must work for the company before being allowed to telecommute. Additionally, if the company does not permit employees to telecommute, it may still be used as a way to reasonably accommodate an employee with a disability. In other words, you may make an exception for a disabled employee if it will give her the ability to perform her job.

You are under a legal obligation to transfer the employee to another position if there is one available—or soon to be available—that meets her qualifications and skills. If there is no position available, you are not expected to create a new position, nor are you expected to bump an employee from an existing position in order to make room for the disabled worker. Additionally, the need for accommodation should not be used as a reason to promote an employee into a new position.

If an exception is made for an employee with a temporary disability, discontinue the accommodation as soon as you receive written orders from the employee's physician that she may return to her usual work duties. Work restrictions issued by a doctor should always be designated as permanent, or have an ending date which may be extended.

When an exception is given to an employee, another worker may complain. It is unlawful for you to share any information about a disabled employee to another worker. Simply inform the employee who complained that the company has granted a reasonable accommodation as allowed by law and that you are not permitted to disclose the reasons behind it. Assure her that the company is not participating in selective preferential treatment. The employee with the disability is free to disclose her condition if she so chooses, but do not encourage or suggest that anyone ask her about it. It is recommended that you include training about privacy issues and disabilities in the workforce to all new hires.

ADA *Interactive Process—Step Three*

The third step is to put the reasonable accommodation into action or, unfortunately, inform the employee that an accommodation is not possible. An employer is not required to grant an accommodation if it will result in undue hardship. An undue hardship is one that may incur an unreasonable expense or an unsatisfactory level in performance or production. The size of an employer, its resources, and the nature of the business are determining factors in considering a hardship as well.

The employee may be the one to feel that there is no viable option for accommodations. You may offer a reasonable accommodation within the employee's work restrictions, but the employee may refuse to accept it. You cannot force an employee to report to work, nor can you allow him to work against his doctor's restrictions. If the disability is temporary, you may offer a leave of absence (LOA) or you may be required to allow a LOA under FMLA, if applicable (see Chapter 12 for more about FMLA). If the employee's disability is permanent and she does not accept your offer for a reasonable accommodation, your only option may be to end the employment. You are well within your rights to terminate an employee the same as you would any other employee who refuses to report to work. If you are a manager or business owner and have a human resources department, consult with them before taking action. You may have to turn to legal counsel, but this is not necessary most of the time.

ADA *Interactive Process—Step Four*

The fourth step in the interactive process is documenting. A detailed, written synopsis of the verbal communication will help ensure that both parties have an understanding of the employee's work restrictions and whether or not a reasonable accommodation is available. Here is what you want to include:

- When and where the discussion was held and who attended
- The date you were informed of the employee's work restrictions

- A description of the work restrictions
- The essential duties of the job that will be affected by the restrictions
- The accommodations that were suggested, and by whom
- Input from both parties regarding the suggested accommodations
- A description of the reasonable accommodation (if applicable)
- The duration of the reasonable accommodation (if applicable)
- Notification that a reasonable accommodation is not possible (if applicable)

Ask the employee to review a draft of the written documentation before asking her to sign it. The document should be signed by everyone who attended the discussion. Give the employee a copy for her files. Your copy is to be kept in the employee's medical file. If a follow-up meeting occurs, document the event in the same manner. Check with the employee periodically to inquire if the working conditions are comfortable for her or if she has any questions or concerns. If there is a change in supervisory structure of that employee, make sure that the new supervisor is informed of the agreed-upon accommodation. Keeping the lines of communication open will increase the chances of a successful work arrangement.

HIV in the Workplace

Persons with Human Immunodeficiency Virus (HIV) are protected by the ADA during all stages of the disease. Discriminatory protection is provided during the application process, interviewing, hiring, salary and benefit compensation, promotions, leave of absences, and all other workforce activities.

FACT

An HIV-negative applicant or employee who has a relationship of any kind with a person who is HIV positive is also protected from discrimination by the ADA. This includes a spouse, relative, domestic partner, or roommate, among others. An employee who refuses to work with a person with HIV should be subjected to the usual discipline for insubordination.

A person who tests HIV positive may appear to be perfectly healthy and experience no complications. Others may have advanced into Acquired Immune Deficiency Syndrome (AIDS) and suffer from symptoms such as skin lesions, weight loss, excessive diarrhea, headaches, or neurological disorders, to name a few. HIV and AIDS are communicable diseases with potentially fatal outcomes, although the Centers for Disease Control reports that HIV infection doesn't always lead to AIDS. Couple this with a twenty-year epidemic and the result is an alarmist situation fueled by people who have been poorly educated about the disease.

Employers may not inform other employees if a coworker is HIV positive. However, whether or not there is a person known to be HIV positive in the workplace, precautions should be made to deter contact with the disease. HIV infection may occur during physical intimate penetration, a poke with an infected needle, or direct exposure of contaminated blood into an open wound. Therefore, employees should be trained on how to keep themselves and others free from needle contamination and blood exposure while at work.

Workers who empty trashcans must wear protective gloves and be trained about how to avoid needles that may have been disposed of improperly. These needles may come from an intravenous drug user who tossed them in a trashcan or a person with a medical condition, such as diabetes, who uses needles for a legitimate reason. Most people with diabetes know how to properly dispose of needles, but carelessness happens and everyone should be on guard.

Everyone should be trained about blood-borne pathogens and how to handle injuries of their own or a coworker's that involve blood. Exposure to blood-borne pathogens may be a cause of HIV infection, as well as hepatitis B, hepatitis C, and over a dozen other illnesses, of which many may be fatal. Personnel in the health-care field are especially prone to this danger and should receive thorough training on prevention. Nonhealth-care employees should receive training consistent with the risks on the job. Be proactive and initiate this training before an HIV-positive employee joins your team.

Education on HIV and AIDS is a helpful tool to avoid having infected employees treated unfairly by coworkers. As an employer, you may not allow HIV-positive persons, or anyone with a disability, to be treated unfairly by your staff. The biggest problem is an employee who thinks that he is in danger of exposure by working with a person who tests positive.

This is not true. Sharing food, a workspace, toilet seat, office equipment, or oxygen with a person who is HIV positive cannot infect someone. Additionally, casual direct contact will not put anyone in danger, nor will the cough or sneeze of an infected person.

Religious Accommodations

Title VII of the Civil Rights Act of 1964 prohibits employers from the unfair treatment of an employee because of her religious practices. An applicant or employee may ask to take time off for a holiday observed by her religion. She may observe a day other than Sunday as the Sabbath, or her religion may recognize holidays different than those commonly observed in the United States. Federal law requires employers to make a reasonable effort to accommodate religious observances of holidays unless doing so will cause an undue hardship to the company. The EEOC will answer complaints from workers who feel that there is biased behavior toward them for religious reasons.

To honor these religious accommodations, many employers approve vacation or personal time off for the observance of religious holidays that are not part of the company's paid holiday package, or allow the employee to swap holidays. Arranging flex time during the week of a religious holiday is another option.

Your dress-code policy may include exemptions to accommodate clothing or appearance that is united with an employee's religious beliefs, such as a head covering. Religious-diversity training for all employees will help keep harmony in the workplace and ward off feelings that some associates are receiving special treatment because of their religion.

Employee Assistance Programs

An employee assistance program (EAP) is a benefit paid for by employers to help alleviate the personal problems of employees that affect workforce productivity. This includes but is not limited to financial, alcohol, drug, legal, stress, emotional, marital, or parental problems. An EAP will not solve an employee's problems, but can point them in the right direction to get help or offer short-term counseling services.

Employers can contract with an in-house EAP professional, but this is feasible only for very large companies. For the smaller business sector, an off-site professional or vendor can provide services on an as-needed basis. Ask about the cost, which may be calculated by the number of employees on staff rather than the actual instances of assistance. Employees in need of services may self-refer themselves or be referred by their supervisor.

FACT

Most medical-insurance plans, including HMOs, offer referrals for counseling services. The policy's standard copayments will apply, and this should be paid by the employee if there is no formal EAP in place. Encourage employees to see what options are available through their medical plan if they bring a personal problem to your attention.

You can find an employee assistance program professional by contacting the Employee Assistance Professionals Association (EAPA) at *www .eap-association.org.* The association offers a Certified Employee Assistance Professional (CEAP) credential through the Employee Assistance Certification Commission. An accredited professional can be located through the Employee Assistance Society of North America (EASNA) at *www.easna .org.* Additionally, there may be a state Licensed Clinical Social Worker (LCSW) in your area available to provide assistance. Before consulting with an individual or service, verify that the proper insurance, licensing, and credentials are in place and that federal and state privacy laws will be adhered to. Although your company may be paying for services, this does not mean that you may have access to any personal information other than what the employee chooses to share with you. Also, your company should be released from EAP liability.

Restraining Orders

If an employee has a court-issued restraining order against an individual, that person cannot contact her or come within a specified distance in person. This includes contact with the employee at work as well as at home and in public. Therefore, an employee may inform you that she has had a restraining order issued to someone and that person knows where she works.

The employee is not required to tell you why the order has been issued, so do not ask. She may choose to volunteer the information, which is fine. Ideally, she will give you the name and a description of the person and a copy of the restraining order to help in your efforts to keep the person away from the workplace. If the company has a switchboard operator or receptionist, ask the employee for permission to advise these workers as well since they may be the ones to have initial contact with callers and visitors seeking out the employee. If the employee shared information about why the restraining order was issued, you may not forward this information to anyone else on staff.

Wage Garnishments

Wage garnishments are briefly mentioned in Chapter 6. If you are served a wage garnishment for an employee, you may not ask him the reason for the garnishment. Your job as the employer is to simply adhere to the orders of the garnishment and maintain proper recordkeeping. The only other employee at the company who has reason to know about the garnishment is the person who processes payroll. If the employee has a supervisor other than you, this person is not to be informed because the employee's legal issues should have nothing to do with his performance on the job.

A wage garnishment is a personal financial issue of the employee and is not to be made public by management. As with other sensitive issues, if the employee chooses to share the information with coworkers, he is free to do so. When you are served with a wage-garnishment order, you should give a copy to the employee as a way to inform him that the payroll deductions will start. This is the only communication you need to have with him on the matter.

CHAPTER 14

Pregnancy in the Workplace

Smart employers know that the happiest employees are the ones who are taken care of. This includes taking care of an employee's family—or growing family. Women make up a big part of the workforce, and taking time out to have a baby is just a temporary interruption. This chapter will tell you about ways to help women safely work through a pregnancy, receive fair treatment, and make the transition from working woman to working mother.

Performing Job Duties

A healthy pregnancy is not a disability until shortly before birth and several weeks after, or when dictated by the woman's physician. Usually, normal work duties can be performed during the duration of the pregnancy. However, the pregnant employee may be unable to perform her usual job duties if the work is physically challenging. Everyone's situation and physical condition are unique and should be treated as such. For example, one woman may be able to work until the day she gives birth, yet another may not be able to perform any of the work past the fifth month of pregnancy. Someone else may be able to work through the pregnancy if her job duties are modified. Maybe she can vacuum and clean the bathroom and kitchen sinks, but can't stoop down to make beds or clean the bathtub. Splitting the duties or working with a partner may allow her to continue working.

Pregnancy is a temporary condition and restrictions should be accommodated, if possible, the same as they would for a nonpregnant person. If the employee wants to continue working and there is a way to make it happen, employers are expected to make a reasonable effort to comply. You may receive some slack from another employee who feels that the pregnant worker is not pulling her fair share. This uncompassionate view of the situation is unfortunate, but don't let the person sway you. Let her know that if she ever has the need for modified work duties due to a medical condition, she will be taken care of, too. This may be a good time for a talk about the meaning of teamwork.

When an employee announces her pregnancy, treat it as the happy time that it really is. You may immediately start to wonder who will take over her job duties when she is on maternity leave, but this is not an issue to consider right now. Celebrate the joy with her.

This doesn't mean that if accommodating a pregnancy is impossible you must come up with a Plan B. Sometimes there is no option for Plan B. If the employee says that she cannot physically perform a modified version of the job and there is no other work available, she may have to start a leave of absence early.

It should be up to the employee whether or not she is capable of working while pregnant. If a pregnant employee says that she is unable to work, send her to her health-care provider with a copy of her job description for the protection of both you and the employee. Let her and her doctor decide together if she should be excused from work. If this is the case, get it in writing to help avoid a discrimination complaint. Your concern is for the safety of the employee and the baby, but you want to back up the reason she has stopped working as well. If her time away from work will be lengthy and you are unable to hold a job open for her, consult with legal counsel or the Equal Employment Opportunity Commission (EEOC) before terminating the employment if she does not resign.

ALERT!

If a pregnant employee is visibly struggling and you have concerns about her health and safety, you have the right to ask for a note from her doctor detailing what she is able to do. Get specifics on things like how much she may lift and how long she may be on her feet.

Women who work at desk jobs may need help getting through the day, too. Sitting all day can be difficult and uncomfortable for a pregnant woman. She may need additional back support for her chair. A backrest can be purchased at an office supply store for her comfort. Sometimes, bringing a pillow from home to support the lower back will do the trick. Many pregnant women have a problem with their feet swelling by the end of the day. Using a stool throughout the day to keep knees elevated usually helps, or she may need to prop up her legs under her desk. She should be encouraged to get up and down throughout the day to keep circulation flowing. These are simple, inexpensive solutions to help keep a woman comfortable during the last few months of pregnancy.

The beginning of a pregnancy can be the biggest challenge for some women. If morning sickness is severe, the dehydration and dizziness associated with the excessive nausea is something that she should see her doctor about. Be compassionate and ask her what she needs from you to get through this difficult time. This period is usually short-lived, although in rare cases a woman may feel ill during the entire pregnancy. In extreme cases, hospitalization may occur in the early weeks of pregnancy due to dehydration or excessive weight loss, or she may simply need some time off work.

If a woman's pregnancy has a difficult start, this doesn't mean that she will have problems throughout her pregnancy. The first and last trimesters are the most difficult for some women. Take it day by day, and remember that the health of the mother and baby are what is most important.

Potential Discrimination Issues

Pregnant women are protected from discrimination through the federal Pregnancy Discrimination Act (PDA). The PDA was enacted in 1978 as an amendment to Title VII of the Civil Rights Act of 1964. A pregnant woman can't be passed up for a job, raise, or promotion because of her condition. Performance issues should be dealt with carefully. Being pregnant doesn't warrant any special privileges, but you cannot be unreasonable, either. She is not exempt from discipline because she is pregnant, but be very careful about addressing a discipline issue that started before she announced that she was pregnant. For instance, if she had a problem with tardiness before she announced that she was pregnant and you didn't address the issue then, you could be accused of discrimination if you discipline her about it after she announces a pregnancy. This is why performance and behavior issues should always be addressed as soon as they start. If you are proactive about all performance issues, you won't have to worry about unresolved issues being perceived as discrimination later.

If a pregnant woman applies for a transfer or new position, you better have some very valid reasons and the documentation to back up the company if the position is not given to her. However, don't be scared into giving her the position simply because she is pregnant. If you give the position to the person who is best qualified for the job and that person is the pregnant employee, you should offer her the position. The pregnancy should not factor for or against the decision.

Don't assume that your supervisors and managers know about the potential for discrimination claims. Fill them in on the legalities or better yet, send them to a training class. Illegal mistakes by management must be avoided at all costs. The liability associated with an untrained manager can be costly.

The EEOC has seen a rise in the number of pregnancy-discrimination claims, surpassing sexual harassment and gender discrimination. Do not make any decisions or changes that can be perceived as unfavorable toward a pregnant worker. Additionally, inappropriate comments by anybody about pregnancy and childbirth should not be allowed at work because they are a form of harassment.

Employers who feel that once a woman becomes a mother she will no longer value her job and her attendance will suffer are not only wrong, they are setting themselves up for a lawsuit. Let the woman be the one to decide if it's time to step down from a position, ask for a demotion, or reduce her hours at work. Hundreds of thousands of women work full-time jobs while raising children. She wouldn't be there if she didn't want and need her job.

States with Laws That Supersede FMLA

You read about the federal Family Medical Leave Act in Chapter 12. Eleven states must abide by their own provisions that supersede FMLA because they are more generous on behalf of the employee. These states are California, Connecticut, Hawaii, Maine, Minnesota, New Jersey, Oregon, Rhode Island, Vermont, Washington, Wisconsin, and Washington, D.C.

State laws change often. If your state isn't one that currently has laws that supersede FMLA, don't assume that this will always be the case. Check for updates at least once a year. Attending local labor-law update seminars is a reliable way to find out about changes before they take place.

California and Oregon have family leave and disability laws that add to the number of weeks a woman can take off work with job protection as allowed by FMLA. Washington, D.C., has its own disability law that increases time off, too. Therefore, in some cases, a pregnant woman can take more than the twelve weeks off work granted by FMLA.

Here are some of the most common areas of FMLA that may be overruled by more generous state regulations:

- The criteria for the company to qualify for state-law compliance. The number of employees may be lower than the requirement for FMLA.
- Whether or not leave may be taken intermittently throughout the qualifying period. This means that it may not have to be taken all at once.
- Leave is allowed annually each year to take the child to medical and dental checkups and for the parent to attend school functions.
- How long the employer must continue to pay their portion of the employee's insurance benefits.
- The amount of time the employee must be employed and how many hours worked in order to be eligible for protected leave.
- Who does not qualify for leave beyond the disability period due to the nature and status of the job.

To find out if your state has any regulations that overrule FMLA regulations, visit the Department of Labor Web site at *www.dol.gov* and do a search for "Federal vs. State Family and Medical Leave Laws."

Baby Shower Etiquette

It is customary for a company to host a baby shower for an employee who is pregnant or adopting a baby or perhaps another worker who is close to the expectant mother may want to throw a shower. Regardless of who hosts it, it can take place at work, in a home, or in a public area such as a restaurant or park.

As a business owner, manager, or human resource professional, socializing with employees outside the course of the normal workday is something that you should limit. Getting too friendly can cause problems later if there is a discipline issue with someone that you see outside of work. Also, you could be accused of playing favorites. However, your attendance at a baby shower is expected and you will leave a negative impression if you do not attend. If you make it a policy to attend showers, be consistent; do not pick and choose whose baby shower you will attend. Attend everyone's, or attend none. If you regularly attend showers but have to miss one due to a previous engagement, send a gift with your congratulations.

FACT

A group gift may be purchased and the price divided amongst the employees who contribute. This helps the mother with expensive items such as a crib, stroller, or car seat. Ask her what she needs and for the style and model number of things she likes. She may have registered her choices at a store, so ask about that, too.

If the shower is held on company property, it's easier to treat it as an office event and the socializing outside the office rules don't apply. If it's held in someone's home or at a restaurant, leave early if people start drinking alcohol. Employees may have too much to drink and let their guard down, telling you things that they shouldn't, and you'll have to deal with it later. If the company is sponsoring the event, skip the alcohol. You don't need the liability of serving alcohol to people who may get behind the wheel of a vehicle.

From Working Woman to Working Mother

Returning to work after a maternity leave can be a difficult transition for a new mother. It is a lot of work to care for an infant and some women lack sleep during this period. She may still have some hormonal adjustments to deal with as well, so it can be a very emotional time. Even if her intentions have always been to return to work, when the time comes she will realize that it is harder than she thought it would be.

Help her transition back into the workforce by coming back midweek instead of on a Monday. This will give her a few days to work before having a break during the weekend.

Why is my employee crying on her first day back from maternity leave?
She is probably crying because she misses her baby, so don't think that it's because she doesn't like her job any longer or doesn't want to be there. Her time off work was probably spent 24/7 with her infant and now they are suddenly apart. It is a difficult adjustment. Each day will get easier for her.

Chapter 19 talks about the importance of a balance between work and family life. Some women end up not returning from a maternity leave because they want to stay home with their baby. This will always be an issue and will never change. Others may want to stay home but can't afford it. You can take a step above and beyond the work-life balance issues in Chapter 19 and do a few things to encourage women to return to work.

Don't just offer a reduced workweek or flexible scheduling. Decrease the number of hours that are required to work in order to be eligible for benefits. Instead of requiring a forty-hour workweek to qualify, reduce it to thirty-six and continue to offer paid time off for vacation, sick leave, and holidays.

FMLA offers twelve weeks of protected job leave when a baby joins the family, but you don't have to stop there. You can offer an unpaid leave-of-absence program for as long as you wish. If you find that women aren't coming back to work after a twelve-week maternity leave, offer a longer leave period of nine or twelve months. Hire a temporary worker to cover while the new mother is at home with her baby. If she still decides not to return to work, you'll have someone already trained to take over the job permanently. If she does come back, you may not want to part with the temp, and find a way to hold on to that person, too.

Accommodating Nursing Mothers (Breastfeeding Legislation)

The American Academy of Pediatrics recommends breastfeeding for at least the first twelve months of life. Since most women return to work before their infants are a year old, this means that there are a lot of lactating women in the workforce. Not every woman decides to breastfeed; it's a very personal choice and can be controversial.

A recent survey reports that 29 percent of new mothers who stop breastfeeding their baby before he is twelve months old quit because of work issues. Fifty-seven percent of them stop because they have nowhere at work to express milk.

A woman who works full time may be away from her baby for as long as nine or ten hours a day once you factor in travel time to and from work and a lunch break. She will need to express breastmilk at least once during the day, but preferably twice or maybe even three times—it will depend on how much milk her body produces. Engorgement from not expressing milk is very uncomfortable and can contribute to clogged ducts and infections.

There are several high-quality breast pumps on the market that allow a woman to express milk quickly and quietly. They may be rented or purchased and come with an attractive carrying case that resembles a briefcase. Once the mother learns how to use it, she can finish the job in fifteen minutes—including cleanup.

The Talk

A woman returning to work from maternity leave may be apprehensive about telling her supervisor that she will need to express breastmilk during her breaks. Breastfeeding mothers are not ashamed of how they feed their babies—in fact, the opposite is true—but bringing up the subject of breasts and bodily functions with someone that you have a business relationship with may be awkward. You don't need to bring it up, but you can open the door to the topic by saying, "Is there anything that you will need from us once you return to work?"

Most women will bring up the subject while they are on maternity leave by saying that they will need a private place to express breastmilk after they return to work. This is your cue to arrange for a place for them to do this, and the place should not be a restroom stall. You can ask for thier input on where they would feel comfortable and they may have some ideas of their own.

Employer Obligations

Currently, twelve states have breastfeeding legislation that applies to employers. These states are California, Connecticut, Georgia, Hawaii, Illinois, Minnesota, New Mexico, Oklahoma, Rhode Island, Tennessee, Texas, and Washington. Coincidently, half of these states also have state maternity laws that are more generous than federal law.

FACT

State breastfeeding laws vary from requiring an employer to provide a private, sanitary area for mothers to express milk to encouraging employers to make a reasonable effort to do so. Most indicate that employers should not expect women to express milk in a restroom stall.

To find out about breastfeeding legislation in your state, visit the Web site for the National Conference of State Legislatures at *www.ncsl.org* and do a search for breastfeeding. You can also turn to La Leche League International at *www.lalecheleague.org* and type "legislation" in the search box.

If a woman's only option is to express milk in a restroom, supply a chair near the sinks. She should not be expected to sit on a toilet seat. Would you want to prepare a meal for your child there?

A private office is another place to express milk. There may not be running water, which is convenient for cleaning out equipment, but the environment is private and the door can be locked. Tape a "Do Not Disturb" sign on the door. A woman needs to be relaxed to express milk and the interruption of a knock on the door can delay getting things started.

Giving her the time and space she needs to continue to provide breastmilk for her baby while working is a gesture a new mother will never forget.

CHAPTER 15

Employee Discipline

Don't turn your back on performance and behavior issues. The longer you let a problem hang around, the harder it is to correct. Sometimes the issue is minor and can be resolved with a little constructive feedback. It may be a training issue and the employee needs to be shown one more time how to do something. Other times, the problem may be more serious and a written warning is in order. In this chapter, you'll learn about different levels of discipline that do not result in employment termination.

Constructive Feedback

As an employer or human resource professional, one of your goals should be to see people succeed at work. The reason for this is twofold. First, it's the makings of a great manager. Your management skills are only as successful as the people who work with you. They want to feel valuable to the company. To many, it's much more than just receiving a steady paycheck; it's about job satisfaction and achieving goals. Work is like a second family because people who are employed full time spend more hours with their coworkers than their spouse, children, or pets. The security of a job is important because there are household bills to pay and financial stress can harm a person's health and relationships. In addition, benefits like insurance and paid time off enhance livelihood. Employees look to their managers to help them succeed because there is a lot at stake. Do this for them and they will take good care of your customers, and happy customers will help your business succeed, too. It's a win-win situation.

Second, a lot of time and money is spent interviewing, selecting, hiring, and training employees. A valuable employee is an asset to your company. Some studies estimate that the cost to replace an hourly associate is about $6,000. This includes the time spent getting a replacement up to speed. It is a good financial move to put in the effort to address and correct performance issues. One way to do this is with constructive feedback, which differs from constructive criticism.

Don't Criticize

To criticize is to make someone feel incompetent or unprofessional. Here are some examples of criticizing statements:

- The silverware is rolled loosely and the tables look sloppy.
- You are behind in filing paperwork and I can't find the balance report.
- John did not get paid today because you did not process his check.
- You used the last ink cartridge and did not order a new one.
- I heard you tell the bellperson that an old lady needed help with her luggage.

Can you see how each statement is a negative one? By turning the negative statement into a constructive one, you can still get the message across, fix the problem, and encourage the employee to do a better job next time around. It will also make addressing future problems easier for both you and the employee.

Offer Feedback

Ask an employee if you may help correct an issue by saying something like, "May I offer you some feedback about something that I have noticed?" The employee should welcome the opportunity to discuss it. If not, deliver the feedback anyway (and look to page 114 on how to handle uncooperative employees).

QUESTION?

Why should I ask permission to correct an employee's performance?
Asking permission to deliver feedback shows respect for the employee's time and feelings. Nobody likes to be told that they are doing something wrong, but it has to be done because employees are paid to do the job right. You can show compassion while correcting a problem and still make your expectations clear.

To turn around the negative comment above about the silverware that was rolled loosely and made the tables look sloppy, do this: Tell him that the overall appearance of the table will impress the diners if the silverware is rolled tight, and that this is the image the restaurant wants. Instead of pointing out how poor the table looked, you are telling him how he is expected to do it. Then show him tips to roll the silverware tightly. Next, give him a turn to show you how he does it. If it's still too loose, work with him until he gets it right. He may not have been shown how to do it properly in the first place, or he may have been rushing through his work, causing the quality to suffer.

To address the problem with the worker who is continually behind with filing paperwork, tell him that in order for the office to run efficiently, the filing needs to be done daily. Ask him to file everything away now and to give you the balance report when he finds it. Then, ask him how he plans to keep up with it. If he doesn't know, give him the option to file everything as soon as it crosses his desk, or to spend the last fifteen minutes of each day filing before he goes home.

Constructive feedback takes longer than dictating orders, but it is time well spent. By telling employees how and why something is to be done and what the outcome will be, there is a better understanding about the reasons for job expectations. However, this doesn't mean that the employee has the option whether or not to comply.

Next, let's figure out why John didn't receive a paycheck. It is not necessary to say to your payroll clerk, "You didn't process John's paycheck." If it's his job to input the paychecks and someone was skipped, he already knows that the error is his. Tell him that John did not receive a paycheck and ask if the procedure to make sure that everyone receives a check on payday is effective. Either the procedure was not followed or there is a flaw and John's check was skipped and it wasn't noticed. Together, decide what will be done to ensure that it doesn't happen again. But first, ask the payroll clerk to issue a check for John right away.

Instead of saying, "You used the last ink cartridge and did not order a new one," say, "We no longer have a spare ink cartridge since the last one is now in your printer. Did you order a new one yet?" The hotel employee who referred to the guest as an old lady can be asked, "Can you think of another description for the woman that doesn't describe her age?"

To offer feedback is to work together for better results. Put the ball in the employee's court to correct the problem and guide them only when necessary. A little initiative can go a long way.

ALERT!

After you deliver constructive feedback to an employee, make a note of the date and what was said in your supervisor's file. Hopefully, the incident will not come up again, but if it does, you may need to give the employee a verbal warning. Therefore, it's important to show that you have already brought up the problem once.

Feedback can go both ways. You'll be listened to more carefully if employees know that they can speak, too. Although they don't set the rules, take their comments and suggestions seriously. Sometimes the people out there actually doing the work have the best ideas for performing the job more efficiently. Hear them out and give their ideas a chance if they are feasible.

Effective Documentation

There is an unwritten rule that if it isn't documented, it didn't happen. This is where the supervisor's file described in Chapter 5 comes in. The purpose of documentation is to back up and justify discipline up to and including employment termination if there is a problem with an employee that cannot be resolved.

In the example above about the employee who doesn't file paperwork in a timely manner, the first step in addressing the issue is to give constructive feedback and document the date of the discussion in the supervisor's file (some managers may call it a confidential file); it should not be documented in the personnel file. At this point, it's not a personnel-file issue and the hope is that it doesn't get to that point.

Any incident that has the potential to result in disciplinary action if it continues should be documented. Some examples are being late to work, violating the personal phone call policy, performing inadequate work after being trained properly, etc.

FACT

Be specific when documenting something. If someone is late to work, do not just write down that she was late to work on March 21. Instead, state that on March 21, she was scheduled to report to work at 8:00 A.M., but did not arrive until 8:20 A.M. and did not call to say that she would be late.

When something serious happens, such as swearing at a coworker or refusing to perform a reasonable request, jump right into a verbal or written warning. The warning itself is the documentation and this should be placed in the personnel file.

Verbal Warnings

The purpose of a verbal warning or verbal counseling is to give someone another chance. Depending on the nature of what happened, this may be the best course of action. Before issuing a verbal warning or documented counseling session, be sure that you are consistent. If one employee was late to work by more than fifteen minutes three times in a one-month period and wasn't warned or counseled, then you shouldn't do it to someone else unless you formally set forth a policy to do so beginning on a specified date.

When someone is given a verbal warning, the meaning is that further occurrences may result in employment termination. This doesn't necessarily mean that if it happens one more time the employment will end, but it can, depending on the seriousness of the incident and what you state in the warning. Again, consistency is the key. If another employee was released from employment after the second time he refused to perform a reasonable request by management, then this should be the result next time, too. Otherwise, you set yourself up for a wrongful-termination lawsuit from the first employee. People talk and coworkers often stay in touch with each other after someone leaves. Don't think that the employee who lost his job won't find out that someone else did the same thing and remained employed.

ESSENTIAL

A verbal warning is usually documented in the personnel file in the form of a memo. The manager who issues it signs or initials the document and gives a copy to the employee. Set a policy of how long a verbal warning is active and if it can ever be removed from the file.

You can release someone from employment without giving a warning. There is no rule that you have to give a second or third chance, but doing so will help keep your wrongful termination claims at a minimum or nonexistent. It will help reduce the number of unemployment insurance claims, too. Remember, your goal is to help people succeed in their position. It's a good idea to give them the opportunity to improve and remain employed unless they've done something serious, like steal company property or assault another person.

To show the seriousness of a warning or counseling, include language in the documentation that makes it clear that further instances may result in additional discipline up to and including employment termination. This will also back up the company if a decision is made to end the employment because the employee was given a warning of the possible consequence. If he chooses not to improve, he is the only one responsible for the outcome.

Written Warnings

Otherwise known as a pink slip or referral, a written warning is a serious discipline measure that may be one step from employment termination, based on company policy and the nature of the incident.

Here is an example of a company trying to give an employee the opportunity to improve his performance. Donald received feedback on January 5th about how to verify that paycheck processing is complete after John didn't receive a check. Two months later, another employee didn't receive a paycheck because Donald (again) didn't verify that a check was processed for each employee. This time, he received a verbal warning reminding him of the proper procedure. He was also warned that if it happens again within twelve months, he would be subject to a written warning. Four months later, another employee did not receive a check due to carelessness on Donald's part. This time, Donald received a written warning.

FACT

Written warnings are common in both large and small companies. Implement a policy that states how long they are valid and if they are ever removed from the personnel file. Many companies do not allow employees to promote or transfer if there is an active written warning on file.

Generally, a written warning is signed by both the manager and the employee. If the employee refuses to sign it, it is still valid. Have another manager witness that the employee refuses to sign and prepare a statement on the warning indicating that it was read to the employee and he refused to sign. After the other manager signs it, a copy is given to the employee. Failure of the employee to sign the document does not make it go away.

When an employee receives a written warning, management and human resources are not to tell other employees. The issue is between the manager, the employee, and human resources only. If the employee chooses to tell coworkers, that is his choice. Employees cannot be disciplined for talking about incidents that happen at work as long as they are true. In most states, they have the right to express their dissatisfaction about policies and procedures as long as they do not disrupt business operations.

Suspensions

If an employee does something that may result in termination, you want to be sure to have all of the facts before taking action. Sometimes, you witness the behavior and there is little to consider. Other times, it takes a few days to investigate, and in the meantime the employee should not be allowed to work. To allow the person to report to work is to imply that what happened isn't so bad and may be excused for a few days. This is not a message that you want to send. When an employee is suspended, she should be asked to temporarily hand over any keys that she has to the offices or building. However, she may keep a key to her locker and shouldn't be asked to remove her things unless employment is terminated at the end of the suspension.

Give the employee a notice in writing informing her that she is being suspended, and put a copy in the personnel file. Include why she is being suspended and how she will be notified when the suspension ends. Normally, employees are notified by telephone and asked to come in to discuss the outcome in person. Your written policy should state whether or not an employee will be paid during the suspension if the employment is not terminated. It is customary to pay employees during the suspension period if they remain employed.

Theft in the Workplace

There are several types of theft in the workplace. Restaurant employees who eat food while on the job are stealing if food is off limits or they are told to pay for it before eating. Someone who puts a box of staples in his briefcase is just as guilty as someone who steals a laptop computer. Placing an order for office supplies and having a box of computer paper shipped home is theft, too. The definition of stealing is to take possession of property without permission. Theft should always be grounds for immediate employment termination, but suspend the employee first if you still need to gather facts. Avoiding a wrongful termination should always be a priority, along with protecting company property.

If an employee comes forward and reports that he witnessed someone steal, ask him for a written statement with his signature. When you confront the employee suspected of taking property, tell her that you have a witness, but you do not have to reveal the name of the person.

A company can conduct an inspection of lockers, purses, briefcases, and backpacks if company property is missing. However, you must have a written policy in place first. The policy should be included in the employee handbook and there should be proof in the personnel files that everyone has received a copy. If personal property such as purses, briefcases, and backpacks are checked, this is generally done when employees exit the building. All inspections should be conducted by two managers, working side by side.

Don't be surprised if you start a search and the missing item suddenly shows up stashed in an odd place. The employee may have realized that he would not be able to leave the building with the item and didn't want to be found with it. If you have your suspicions about who may have done it, there isn't much that you can do without evidence or a witness. Taking an item with the intent to steal is a valid reason to terminate employment.

If you notice that something is missing and you see an employee leaving the building with a bag or something hidden inside their coat, for example, you have the right to stop them and ask what they are carrying. If they refuse, you should not force the item out of their hands.

You may receive an anonymous tip from someone who knows about a theft but is afraid to come forward. This may be in the form of a letter, e-mail, or voicemail message from an unknown voice. Keep the tip and investigate accordingly. Employees have been caught with stolen property at home due to anonymous tips.

FACT

Whether or not stolen property is recovered, file a police report. It will set the precedent that theft will be dealt with aggressively. If employees are questioned, it may deter the thief from doing it again and may result in finding out who did it.

Your employee handbook should state that theft is grounds for immediate termination. There is no second chance, and the company should press criminal charges as well to back up the decision to terminate. If there is enough evidence to end employment, there should be enough evidence for a conviction.

Violence in the Workplace

Violence in the workplace, which includes but is not limited to hitting, is another behavior that should result in immediate termination. This should be spelled out clearly in your employee handbook. As an employer, you have an obligation to provide a safe environment for the staff. People who assault others or become aggressive when angry are a liability to your company. With the rise in the reported number of workplace shootings, this is not an area to consider lightly.

Threats are a legitimate form of intended violence and should be included in the company's written policy against violence and dealt with accordingly. A threat can be in the form of bodily injury or property damage, such as slashing the tires of someone's car in the parking lot. The issue here is that the behavior frightens employees and they feel unsafe.

ALERT!

An employee who becomes angry during a discussion isn't making an immediate threat, but may intimidate employees who overhear. Ask the employee to calm down or leave the conversation. If the behavior continues, send her home and deal with the incident as a disciplinary action the next day.

Violence in the workplace is a very serious issue. It is worth the time and expense to send all managers to a seminar or to view a training webcast on the topic. They will learn how to spot trouble before it arises and how to deal with it if it happens. You will find training options in Chapter 20.

Attendance Problems

Be cautious when addressing excessive absenteeism because some medical conditions are covered under the ADA and are legitimate reasons to miss work, and there are also some conditions covered under the FMLA that you read about in Chapter 12. However, you will find that the majority of people who miss a lot of work do not have valid reasons—they live a lifestyle that causes poor attendance or they are simply unreliable.

Poor attendance results in decreased productivity and profit. Employees with good attendance get burned out or feel resentful toward the workers with unexcused absences, and for good reason. They are the ones who have to work harder when someone isn't there to do his share of the work.

Your company should have a written attendance policy that spells out how many absences are considered excessive within a given period of time. As always, discipline of employees with excessive absenteeism must be consistent. If it's not acceptable for one person to miss four days of work in a six-month period, it's not acceptable for others either. If your company has several departments, it's important that discipline for excessive absenteeism is consistent across the board. This can be a difficult task in human resources— ensuring that policies are addressed consistently amongst all managers.

Unexcused Absences

When an employee misses a lot of work or you have reason to believe that he is not really sick, you have the right to ask for a note from his doctor excusing him from work. For instance, if he often calls in sick on Fridays and you feel that he is doing this to get a three-day weekend, you can require that he bring in a doctor's note on Monday stating that he was too ill to work on Friday. Employees who call-off sick to extend the weekend or a holiday often get themselves caught by talking about the fun they had on their trip or other activities that make it clear that they were not really ill. You may hear them yourself, or the employees who are unhappy about being assigned extra work when they faked the illness may tell you.

The company's written attendance policy should state that a supervisor has the right to ask for a note from a doctor at his discretion. Your role as a company owner or human resource professional is to ensure that a supervisor isn't asking for doctor notes without a valid reason. Don't permit anyone to abuse the policy.

An unexcused absence should result in discipline, usually starting out as a verbal counseling or warning. Here are some absences that may be considered unexcused:

- An absence in which the supervisor requested a doctor's note, but the employee does not have one
- Requested a day off, but the supervisor said no and the employee says that she won't be in anyway—and she doesn't show up
- Any other time an employee says that they will not be reporting to work without permission and without a valid reason
- Sitting in jail. Employees are expected to act responsibly so that they can report to work each day
- Helping a friend with an emergency. Generally, only a family emergency is a legitimate reason to miss work

No Call/No Show

When someone doesn't show up for work and does not call, the first thing to do is become worried. The employee may have experienced a hardship at home or been in an accident on the way to work. Call the employee's house and cell phone and see if you can reach him.

One no call/no show should not be grounds for immediate termination, but it is definitely a serious issue. It would be reasonable to issue a written warning for this the first time it happens. There should be a level of accountability for employees: To decide not to go to work or to forget to check the schedule and miss a day is irresponsible and causes undue hardship for the supervisor who was not prepared for the absence, and the other employees who had to pick up the slack.

QUESTION?

If an employee has a valid reason for a no call/no show, should I excuse it?

If the employee had a family emergency that resulted in him being unable to think about work or make a phone call, or if the employee was hospitalized suddenly and did not have a chance to call, and family members didn't think to ask about it, the absence should be excused.

You will be surprised at some of the reasons you will hear from employees about why they did not show up for work. He slept in until noon and thought that it was too late to call. A friend from out of town flew in for a surprise visit. She had to clean house because company is coming over this weekend.

Consider what your written attendance policy says about no call/no shows and act accordingly. If all employees were given a copy of the employee handbook with the policy when they were hired, there should be no surprises when someone is disciplined because they decided not to show up for work. If someone gets written up, spell out in the warning what the consequences will be if it happens again. Like all policies, it should be consistent. If two no call/no shows within a twelve-month period are cause for employment termination, this must apply to everyone.

CHAPTER 16

Hearings and Appeals

You can follow all the rules and treat every applicant and employee fairly and still be served with a violation complaint or notice to attend a hearing or appeal. If you are proactive and have taken all the steps to protect the company, you have done your job well. However, this will not make the charges or appeal go away. This chapter will tell you why it's important to keep your files intact, document everything, and how to professionally present yourself during formal proceedings.

Unemployment Insurance Appeals

In most states, if an employee loses her job or is laid off from work due to no fault of her own, she is eligible for unemployment insurance benefits while she looks for another job. Her unemployment wages are usually based on how much money she made during the past year, and other criteria may apply as well. The weekly pay will be substantially less than her working wages, but the benefits are a big financial help to the unemployed. Unemployment compensation is a temporary solution for employees who have been in the workforce long enough to qualify for benefits.

Eligibility Determinations

A layoff or job elimination is always qualifying criteria for benefits, but the employee may have to have worked for a specific period of time in the state to be eligible. With each claim, there will be underlying circumstances that have to be considered before a decision is made. Neither the employer nor the employee can determine what the outcome of a claim will be. In some cases, a voluntary resignation due to relocation after a spouse receives a job offer out of town may be a qualifying event. Whether or not the spouse is the primary breadwinner in the family may affect the claim.

If a new employee has made every effort to perform a job and is unable to succeed, she may be eligible. Sometimes a person is simply not a good match for a job and it is hard to determine this until she actually starts working. It's an unfortunate event that is not anyone's fault, and for this reason she may be eligible. As always, there are specific circumstances that will determine if this is the case.

FACT

Unemployment compensation is paid for by employers through FUTA taxes as explained in Chapter 6. These taxes are based on the number of claims paid out against, or on behalf of, an employer. Therefore, one employer may have higher unemployment compensation expenses than another, and the charges fluctuate each year based on the number of active claims.

Another reason a person may be eligible for unemployment compensation is if a company unfairly terminates her employment. If she was not given proper training to perform her job or a fair chance to improve the issue that led to her termination, she may receive benefits after being released. This is why it's important to use the employee discipline tools highlighted in Chapter 15 as a means to resolve performance and behavior issues rather than proceed to termination too quickly.

Even if an employee is released from employment for good cause, the timing of the separation may determine workers' compensation eligibility. For example, if an employee is terminated for excessive absenteeism a week after her last unexcused absence, the fact that she was allowed to continue working after the incident sends the message that the behavior can be tolerated. If you delay releasing an employee from duty until a time when it is convenient for the company (after a deadline has been met or when someone returns from vacation), the result may be an increase in your unemployment insurance expenses once they start collecting benefits.

Lastly, if an employee quits her job for good reason, such as due to a hostile work environment or sexual harassment, the employer may pay the price. Being "run out" of a company may be seen as a valid reason to leave and she may be eligible for unemployment.

Ineligibility Determinations

There are situations when a person is unlikely to be awarded benefits. In most cases, an employee who quits a job without good cause will be ineligible. What is considered without good cause is up to the unemployment board. Quitting a job because the work is boring is an example of what may be seen as ineligibility for unemployment benefits.

ESSENTIAL

You can try to guess the outcome of an employee's unemployment claim, but you will never know for sure until a determination has been made. Don't be too confident that a claim will be denied and slack off in your efforts to protest the claim. The result may be a surprise that will increase your FUTA taxes.

If an employee is terminated from employment for insubordination or a violation of company policy, she will be unlikely to qualify for benefits, but this is not always the case. Each situation will be looked at on a case-by-case basis. The circumstances and steps leading up to the termination will be a key factor in a final decision.

An employee may apply for unemployment benefits even if she is unlikely to qualify. In all cases, the employee files a claim and the employer is given the opportunity to respond to the claim with the company's side of the story. Since employers pay for unemployment benefits, most are quick to request a denial of benefits to former employees who they feel should not receive compensation. The deadline to respond is relatively short, so if you are going to request a denial of benefits, do it as soon as you receive notice of the claim.

FACT

You need to respond to a claim for unemployment benefits only if you protest the charges to your company. There may be times when you feel it is fair for the former employee to receive benefits, such as in the case of an employee who experienced a hardship and had to resign or was unable to pass the introductory period.

If you protest an unemployment claim, be prepared to give a detailed, thorough explanation of the events that led to the separation, including the final incident. For instance, if an employee was released after her third no-call/no-show, show proof that the employee was aware that she needed to call her supervisor if she was unable to report to work. This could be by means of a signature of receipt for the employee handbook that states absences must be reported. Make a copy of the documentation that shows the employee was counseled the first time it happened, as well as a written warning that may have been issued after the second occurrence. If the written warning stated that another no-call/no-show may result in termination, and it happened again, you have your proof that you did everything possible to communicate the policy to the employee and correct the problem. This is the criteria for a fair and reasonable employment termination.

If a former employee's claim is denied, she has the right to an appeal in most states. If this happens, you will receive a notice to attend an appeal hearing. If the employee was released for good cause, you should attend the hearing and fight the appeal. If you do not show up, the employee wins on default.

EEOC Violations

You will be notified by the EEOC if you have been charged with a discrimination violation and there is some basis to believe that a violation has occurred. A representative will be assigned and the commission will start an investigation. The average claim takes about 182 days from start to finish. Many cases are eligible for early resolution through mediation or settlement.

A mediation program is facilitated by an unbiased, third-party mediator in a confidential setting that usually lasts about eighty-four days from start to finish. The meetings are not tape recorded and notes taken by the mediator are discarded. Employer settlement agreements are not considered an admittance of a violation. The program is voluntary and, if successful, will result in the charge being closed. If unsuccessful, the next step will be the start of an investigation.

You may be asked to tell your side of the story through a Statement of Position and to respond to a Request for Information (RFI). This may include the submission of copies of personnel files and policies. An on-site visit may be scheduled and the EEOC investigator may question witnesses.

ALERT!

Provide the EEOC with a prompt response and cooperate with the investigation even if you believe that a charge is frivolous. If you question the need for some of the requested information, advise the investigator. The EEOC has the right to subpoena the information needed but may modify the request in some cases.

If the investigation concludes that there is no reasonable basis to believe that discrimination has occurred, the charging party will receive a Dismissal and Notice of Rights letter. This will tell him that he has a right to file a lawsuit in federal court within ninety days of receipt. The employer will receive a copy of the letter.

A Letter of Determination will be sent to both parties if there is reasonable cause to believe that discrimination did occur. The charging party and the employer will both be invited to seek resolution of the charge through an informal process known as conciliation. It the conciliation is unsuccessful, the EEOC may file a lawsuit in federal court if it so chooses. If not, the charging party will receive a Notice of Right to Sue and may file a lawsuit in federal court within ninety days. This is different than the Dismissal and Notice of Right to Sue letter mentioned earlier in this chapter because at this point, there has been no dismissal by the EEOC.

A conciliation meeting is a discussion between an investigator, the charging party, and the employer to negotiate a solution for the discrimination. This is a voluntary procedure to resolve a charge informally. One of the benefits is that it avoids future litigation that can be time-consuming and costly.

If the conciliation concludes that discrimination has occurred, there are remedies available to the charging party. If the employee was wrongfully terminated or compelled to resign due to the discrimination, he may be entitled to back pay or reinstatement.

QUESTION?

Is a charging party who is reinstated protected from retaliation?
The same laws that prohibit discrimination also prohibit retaliation against persons who report unlawful discrimination or participate in an employment discrimination determination. Employment terminations, unjustified negative performance evaluations, threats, increased surveillance, and the denial of a promotion are a few examples of perceived retaliation.

Reinstatement may include giving the employee seniority or a pay raise that he may have missed during the period from filing the claim to resolution. If an applicant was not hired for a position due to discriminatory reasons, the resolution could be that he is hired. A person discriminated against because of a qualified disability may be offered a reasonable accommodation in order to perform the job. See Chapter 13 for more about reasonable accommodations to avoid this type of EEOC charge.

A finding that discrimination has occurred can be very costly to employers. The charge could result in reimbursement to the charging party for monetary losses, as well as compensation for mental anguish and inconvenience. Charges for punitive damages may be awarded if the employer acted maliciously. Lastly, the employer may be responsible for paying the charging party's attorney fees, court costs, and fees paid to expert witnesses.

Employee Protection

All employers should avoid discriminating against applicants and employees regardless of whether or not protection is provided. Some employers, generally only very small ones, are not covered by all of the statutes. Employers with fifteen or more employees must comply with Title VII of the Civil Rights Act of 1964, which prohibits employment discrimination based on race, color, religion, sex, pregnancy, or national origin. The act also prohibits sexual harassment.

Employers with fifteen or more employees are also covered by the Americans with Disabilities Act (ADA). However, only employers with twenty or more employees are covered by the Age Discrimination in Employment Act (ADEA). Virtually all employers are covered by the Equal Pay Act (EPA), which applies to employers with employees covered by federal wage and hour laws.

Discriminatory Protection Acts

Protection against all areas of discrimination is provided for both job applicants and employees and applies to hiring, separation, promotion, layoff, compensation, benefits, job assignments, and training practices. Additionally, discrimination against individuals who are married to or associated with those of a protected class is also covered.

All hiring and employment practices are to be based on skills and qualifications for the essential duties of the job without regard to race, sex, color, age, religion, national origin, or medical conditions. This means that a manager cannot give preferential treatment to a specific race of people when selecting a new employee, nor can he disqualify a person based on race or pass them up for a promotion if they are the most qualified person. A person's religious preference has no bearing on the hiring process, nor does national origin.

Persons forty years of age or older are protected against discrimination by the Age Discrimination in Employment Act of 1967 (ADEA). Only in very rare circumstances can an age preference or limitation be specified in an advertisement or posting for employment.

Visit *www.eeoc.gov* and read the question and answer segments for ADA compliance for persons with hearing impairments, vision impairments, cancer, diabetes, epilepsy, and intellectual disabilities in the workplace. These are a sampling of medical conditions covered by the ADA if the employee meets the qualifications.

Men and women must receive equal compensation for equal work performed at the same work site in accordance with the Equal Pay Act. The jobs must be substantially similar in terms of content, and the title is irrelevant. This means that an employee cannot be given an enhanced title while doing the same work as a way to rationalize giving a higher salary.

FACT

There may be an exception to the equal pay rule if one person has been employed longer than the other and has passed a timeframe in which a pay increase is awarded. The company's policies for pay increases will be a determining factor in this rule.

If the skill, effort, and responsibility required to perform a job is the same, one gender may not be paid more than another under similar working conditions. The skill needed to perform a job is determined by the experience, ability, education, and training required for doing a job. If one person has a credential that is not part of the required skills, he cannot be paid a higher salary. Effort is measured by the physical or mental exertion needed to perform a job. Working conditions play a role in salary determination also, and exposure to extreme temperatures or hazardous conditions can warrant a pay differential as well.

If one person has a higher amount of responsibility than another, this person may be paid a higher wage than the other. An example would be two people who work as customer-service-center representatives. If one person handles calls about product information and placing orders and another person is assigned to the calls for complaints and resolutions, the second person has a higher level of responsibility and may be paid more. Ideally, his position title will change to reflect the different duties, which may be considered substantial.

Workers' Compensation Board Hearings

If an employee's workers' compensation claim is denied, she may appeal the decision through the workers' compensation appeals board or equivalent in your state, or initiate a lawsuit in court. When the status of a claim has made it to this point, there will be an attorney involved who has been retained by the workers' compensation insurance company.

By the time someone has had a workers' compensation claim denied or the court date for a lawsuit has arrived, a year or more is likely to have passed. You will not be able to remember all of the events surrounding the incident and neither will respective witnesses. This is why it is important to have complete files with everything documented. Do not rely on memory alone.

Effective Witnesses

You may have to ask an employee to accompany you to a hearing or appeal meeting. You cannot force an employee to participate, but in some cases they may be summoned, if not by you, by an attorney or government entity handling the situation. If the employee is scheduled to appear during normal work hours, he is to be paid his usual wages in addition to mileage to travel to and from the hearing site if he drives himself. If it is a court case, he will have been summoned to appear. For a hearing, he may want to send a written, notarized statement in lieu of attending, but this is not effective because the judge cannot cross-examine or ask questions of a piece of paper. The most effective witness you can have is a real person.

ESSENTIAL

Do not tell an employee what to say during a hearing; however, you can collaborate together to discuss the reason for the hearing and review the facts. Thank the employee for his cooperation—he may find it difficult to testify if the claimant is a person that he works with or socializes with outside of the workplace.

An employee may be asked to attend a hearing after witnessing behavior that has led to employment termination or he may have information about an employee with an alleged workers' compensation injury who is trying to defraud the system. No employer wants to get employees involved in issues like these, but it may make the difference between winning or losing a claim.

Behavior and Expectations During a Hearing

A hearing with an appeals board does not take place in a municipal or superior court, but the proceedings are very similar. The person facilitating the hearing may be a retired judge and the decisions made are final. You and your witnesses will be sworn in and expected to tell the truth. Let the judge or mediator set the pace for the proceeding. Speak only when spoken to, or ask for permission if you have something to say. Instead of a court recorder present to transcribe the session, it may be recorded. The dress code is one of professionalism and respect. So that you can speak clearly and be easily understood, do not chew gum. It is appropriate to address the judge as "Your Honor" whether the judge is one who is currently practicing or retired. Any behavior you feel is appropriate in a courtroom should also be displayed at a hearing.

CHAPTER 17

Developing Company Policies

The key to establishing a fair, collaborative workplace is to have consistency. There is no better way to do this than to have policies, but they are worthless if they are not enforced. So if you have a rule that says employees may not come to work with pink braids, you'll need to say something to someone who does. This chapter will give you some insight on a few of the most common policies that companies develop and (hopefully) enforce.

Dress Code

Your dress code should be practical and project the image the company wants to deliver, from head to toe. It should also be in writing, with a copy given to each employee. Get a signed receipt in return or include it in your employee handbook; you can't enforce a dress code if the employees are not informed. Make sure that you are consistent in enforcing the dress code. If one employee is counseled or sent home to change for violating the dress code, you must act accordingly when another employee does the same.

Hair and Grooming

For both men and women, you can require that hair is kept out of the eyes, neatly trimmed, and washed. Wigs and hairpieces may be allowed if the style and color are conservative and follow the contour of the employee's head. You don't need to specifically spell out that pink braids are prohibited—this will not prevent people from coming to work with blue or green braids. Instead, indicate that hair must be of a color that is natural to the human race, or that hairstyles must not be extreme or attention getting.

Grooming habits can, and should be, included in your dress code. Most people bathe, brush their teeth, and use deodorant each day, but there are a few who need to be reminded that this is expected. The wording in your dress code can say something like, "It is a common courtesy to bathe, brush your teeth, and use deodorant each day before reporting to work."

You may prohibit employees from chewing gum as part of the dress code for those who verbally communicate with the public. It is reasonable to ask that employees who use the telephone or talk to customers in person refrain from chewing gum. It can be difficult to understand or hear someone while they are chewing, and gum isn't an ideal thing for housekeeping issues, either.

If men are allowed to have facial hair, specify the length and condition permitted for sideburns, mustaches, and beards. Men with long hair may be required to keep it in a ponytail during work hours.

Tattoos and Piercings

You may require that individuals keep tattoos covered while at work, especially if they are employees who are in public view. For back-of-the-house employees, you may choose to allow tattoos to be visible.

It is reasonable to prohibit employees from wearing pierced objects anywhere that can be seen other than the ears. Additionally, you can limit the number of earrings that may be worn at one time.

Clothes and Shoes

You can specify the length of skirts and dresses for women and require that shirts and blouses are long enough to cover backs and fronts. Slacks may be permitted but denim jeans not allowed, or if jeans are allowed, make it clear if faded, ripped jeans should be kept at home. T-shirts with lewd statements are inappropriate for work.

Backless and open-toed shoes and flip-flops are not only too casual for the workplace, they can promote trips and falls and injured toes. Help keep your workers' compensation claims down by requiring safer shoes.

Internet and E-mail Usage

A growing number of companies are implementing Internet and e-mail policies. Some companies will allow a moderate use of company e-mail for personal use, just as they do the telephone, as long as it does not distract the employee from work. Others strictly prohibit the use of company e-mail and the Internet, and this is a good idea since it cuts into productivity and company profits. If employees who have their own desk and computer are not allowed to use e-mail or the Internet for personal use, then supervisors and managers should set a good example and stay away, too.

FACT

If employees are allowed to use the Internet or e-mail, have a policy against the distribution of jokes, pictures, or slogans that may be offensive to other employees. A good rule of thumb is to avoid sharing anything that wouldn't be appropriate to hang on the wall at work.

Employees may be under the misconception that since they have to use a login ID and password to access company e-mail, that their correspondence is private. This is not the case. All communications, even those that have been deleted, are detectible on the company's computer network. Let the employees know this so that they are aware that there is no confidentiality with their e-mail and Internet usage. This will also give them a fair chance to stop the Internet and e-mail usage before they are caught.

Call-Off-Sick Policy

Consider how and when employees who are too sick to work are to report that they will be absent. If the company opens at 8:00 A.M. and an employee is scheduled to report to work at that time, is it okay to call off sick then or should she call her supervisor at home an hour or two before? If the employee works a service-type job where her absence will affect business (she is one of two food servers scheduled to work the breakfast shift), the sooner the manager knows the better. Make it clear to employees if they are to contact their supervisor before the start of their shift if they are ill.

Hiring Family Members

Most companies that have policies about hiring family members limit it to prohibiting someone from supervising her own family member, as it can be seen as a conflict of interest to do so. This doesn't mean that a relative of a supervisor or manager cannot work elsewhere in the company. The key is that the two do not work in the same department with one supervising the other. It is common for relatives of anyone in human resources or who has access to payroll and personnel records to be ineligible for employment at the same company.

Tardiness Policy

Your tardiness policy should indicate at what point someone is considered tardy. Are they tardy if they show up more than five minutes after they were scheduled to report to work? Do they need to be in uniform and at their workstation on the dot? At what point does someone need to call in to say that they are running late? Also, indicate how many tardies in a thirty-day period are considered excessive and what the consequences will be.

If an employee has a problem getting to work on time on a regular basis, give the employee some counseling and advice. The tips for getting to work on time may sound simple to you, but another person may struggle with them. Recommend that she go to bed in time for her to wake up easily and refreshed in the morning. If she brings a lunch to work, she should pack it the night before. Suggest she set the alarm clock and have a back up, such as the cell phone alarm, in case the first alarm malfunctions. She should give herself ample time in the morning to eat a healthy breakfast, get dressed, and arrive to work on time.

On Property After Work Hours

Hourly employees should not be permitted to perform work on business property during nonwork hours. This is illegal! In addition, if he is injured, he will not be covered by workers' compensation insurance and this will create a whole new set of problems. You may allow him to visit the workplace as a customer or guest, and it is reasonable to require him to behave in the same professional manner as he would while working. Customers may recognize him, and his demeanor is a reflection on the company.

Breaks and Meals

Employees who are paid by the hour are required by law to take an off-the-clock meal break when they are scheduled for a specified number of hours. Check with your state regulations to see what the requirements are. Also, paid breaks of ten to fifteen minutes may be mandatory as well. Managers should make every effort to ensure that hourly employees have the opportunity to take a break each day.

Dating Coworkers

Implementing a policy against dating coworkers is hard to enforce and having such a policy may not be worth the effort. The reason behind the policy is to alleviate problems that may come up in the future if the couple breaks up or one party sees the other flirting with another person. The best way to handle it may be to discourage public displays of affection, which should not be allowed in the workplace anyway.

Sexual-Harassment Awareness

Perhaps the most important policy in place should be your policy against sexual harassment. Sexual and other forms of harassment provide a hostile work environment and there should be zero tolerance for it. Sexual harassment is a form of sex discrimination that violates Title VII of the Civil Rights Act of 1964. The Act applies to employers with fifteen or more employees. If you are a small business with less than fifteen employees, this doesn't mean that sexual harassment should be allowed!

QUESTION?

What is sexual harassment?
Unwelcome sexual advances, requests for sexual favors, and other verbal or physical conduct of a sexual nature. When this behavior interferes with a person's work performance and creates an intimidating, hostile, or offensive work environment, it is considered harassment. The behavior doesn't have to be directed at someone for it to be offensive to them.

Defining Sexual Harassment

Some forms of sexual harassment are obvious, such as one person making lewd comments to another, or touching an inappropriate area of another person's body. But other forms may not be as obvious. The important thing to know is that what is seen as harassment can vary from person to person. For instance, an employee who overhears two people laughing at a dirty joke may be offended. Therefore, something that a third party overhears may be considered sexual harassment. Here are some other examples of sexual harassment:

- Eyeing somebody up and down while saying something suggestive
- Passing around a dirty joke that somebody printed from the Internet
- Sharing details about your sex life in public
- Purposely rubbing against someone while walking by
- Asking personal questions

Some forms of sexual harassment are obvious, while others may be more subtle. What is important is to recognize that it's someone's perception of what harassment is that is important. What may be offensive to one person may not offend another person in the room. If an employee is feeling uncomfortable, then sexual harassment is taking place.

Sexual harassment, or any other harassment complaints, must be taken extremely seriously. All employers should conduct sexual-harassment awareness training, and some states may even require it. Additionally, you may be required to facilitate refresher courses after a specific period of time.

Men and Women Alike

One of the most commonly talked about forms of sexual harassment is *Quid pro quo* harassment. *Quid pro quo* is a Latin term that means "this for that." This type of sexual harassment refers to when a supervisor offers a raise or promotion to an employee in exchange for sexual favors.

Sexual harassment is not limited to supervisor and subordinate relationships. It can occur between any two people in the workplace of the same or opposite sex. They may both be employees or one may be a vendor or customer.

FACT

Women are not the only victims of sexual harassment. Of the 12,025 charges of sexual harassment filed with the EEOC in fiscal year 2006, 15.4 were filed by males. The offenders were a mix of both females and males. Educating employees about the consequences of sexual harassment is a step toward prevention.

All employees should be trained about what to do if they are harassed. The first step is to let the offender know that their behavior is inappropriate and ask them to stop. If it continues even just one more time, report the person to a supervisor. In the event of a serious, blatant action, such as a request for sex in exchange for a favor or touching an inappropriate part of the body, report the incident to a supervisor immediately.

How to Stop It

Touching someone excessively in a nonsexual way may be perceived as sexual harassment to an individual. If an employee likes to hug everyone and somebody doesn't want to be hugged, that person should let the other employee know. Although hugging may not be meant as a form of sexual harassment, it can be perceived that way by someone. Remember, it's the perception of the behavior that determines whether or not it is harassing. The person who wants the hugging to stop should say something like, "I do not want you to hug me. Please stop it" or "It makes me uncomfortable when you do that. Please stop." The offender should be told two things—that the behavior is unwanted and that it needs to stop.

Another example of sexual harassment occurs when an employee asks another employee out on a date, the employee says "no," but the employee who asked continues to ask on a regular basis. The employee who is being asked out should say, "Do not ask me out again," and from that point on, the requests for dates should stop. If they do not, then you need to know about it because an employee is being harassed. A similar situation would occur if an employee leaves cards and flowers on an employee's car or by her locker. If he is asked to stop and does not, a few flowers and a supply of note cards is now a form of sexual harassment.

By training your employees about what sexual harassment is, and what to do if it happens, you are sending the message that the behavior will not be tolerated. Additionally, employees need to know that some of the things they do can be offensive to other people. Many instances of sexual harassment are things that the offender doesn't realize are offensive. Unless he is told, he may never know that some people can perceive his behavior as harassment.

Employees should also be educated about body language and to respect the nonverbal messages they receive from people. The person above that likes to hug everyone should be able to sense someone tense up and not hug back. This is a cue not to hug them again. Also, anyone who isn't reciprocating with sharing jokes or laughing at them is probably someone who doesn't want to hear them.

Formal Complaint

Complaints made by employees about alleged sexual harassment are to be taken very seriously. Do not make the mistake of being an employer who doesn't act on an employee's report that they are feeling harassed. There can be harsh financial and legal consequences as a result. Supervisors, managers, and human resources personnel can be held personally liable for ignoring an employee's report of sexual harassment.

If you receive a complaint from an employee, inquire if he asked the offender to stop. Document everything the employee tells you and ask him to give you a signed statement in writing. If the act was serious, you should talk to the offending employee immediately. Find out if there were any witnesses and speak to them as well, and get written statements if they are willing to cooperate. The discipline administered to the offending employee will be based on the outcome of the investigation. If it is inconclusive, the offending employee should receive a warning, possibly a written warning, which indicates that further incidents may result in discipline up to and including employment termination. If there is proof that a very serious act of sexual harassment occurred, employment termination may be the necessary outcome.

If the act of harassment wasn't too severe, and the reporting party asked the other person to stop, and the behavior did cease, decide with the employee what the next step should be. Since he asked that the behavior stop and it did, he may not want you to confront the other employee. He did the right thing by reporting the incident. Keep the documentation in your files and tell the employee that if the behavior happens again, to let you know immediately. An employee needs to tell another employee only once that his behavior is inappropriate and must stop. If it happens again, management needs to know right away.

Let employees know that sexual harassment from customers, clients, and vendors will not be tolerated. These incidents should be reported to a manager or the human resources department, and in turn, reported by the manager or H.R. representative to the supervisor of the person who harassed the employee. You can request that the worker does not visit your company again. If this is not possible, and the offense was not one of a very serious nature, make it clear that the offender is not to approach or speak to the employee in the future. If the offense was one of a very serious nature, strictly prohibit the worker from entering the property again, even if it means ending the business relationship with the customer or vendor.

Employees will know that you care if you take the time to train them about sexual-harassment awareness. They need to know what it is and what to do about it if it happens. Have all employees sign a copy of your written policy that prohibits sexual harassment in the workplace. Document the names of employees who have received proper training by asking employees to sign an attendance sheet during all training sessions. An awareness that sexual harassment will not be allowed in the workplace is the first step in preventing it.

CHAPTER 18

Employee Retention

A lot of time and expense is put into hiring employees, so you'll want to keep the ones you have, and especially those that are an asset to your company. If you don't take good care of them, they will find someone else who will. This chapter will focus on employee development, which is to nurture and enhance the careers of others. Some ways to do this are through mentorships, recognition programs, empowerment, and promoting from within whenever possible.

The Cost of Employee Turnover

The rate at which employees come and go is called turnover. Ideally, the majority will come and stay. Realistically, this may not be the case. It is impressive when a company has a high number of employees who have been there for ten or more years. If the majority of employees aren't sticking around for their first-year anniversary, it's time to re-evaluate the company's recruiting and hiring practices.

When an employee leaves he needs to be replaced, and there is an expense that goes along with this. The time and investment put into that employee will no longer benefit the company and it's time to start from scratch with someone new. A revolving door is a part of doing business, but it's how fast the employees are traveling through that door that sets the pace for employee retention.

Here are some of the costs of replacing an employee:

- Administrative costs associated with COBRA paperwork, processing a final paycheck to arrive in time, and other separation issues.
- Employment advertisements. This includes the wages paid to the person who writes and places the ad as well as the actual advertisement.
- Time is money. The time spent reviewing applications and interviewing candidates is money spent.
- Background checks and pre-employment screenings are additional expenses if it's part of your hiring practices.
- The wages paid to the employee who trains the new employee and his lost productivity as a result.
- Waiting for the new employee to get up to speed and meet performance expectations. Profits may go down during this period.

This is why employee-retention efforts are so important, but you can never expect a zero turnover rate. Life events come up that cause an employee to leave, such as a family relocation, staying home to raise a new baby, or taking care of a sick relative. And of course, people retire. These things will continue to happen no matter how terrific an employment opportunity you provide, but for the issues you can influence, like employees being dissatisfied and seeking work elsewhere, there are some things you can do.

Hire the Right People

Don't rush through your selection process of applicants. Chapters 1–3 walk you through the steps of finding the best candidates. If you are suddenly in a bind and need someone quick, it's tempting to rush into hiring the first person that comes along. Resist the temptation to do this. Consider hiring a temporary worker from an employment agency to fill gaps while you look for a new employee. You may even end up hiring the temp as a permanent worker.

FACT

Many companies offer an incentive to employees who refer an applicant who is subsequently hired. The employee receives a bonus after the new hire has passed the introductory period or worked a specific period of time as designated in the policy. Go a step further and give the employee another bonus after the new hire reaches his one-year anniversary.

Focus on the training seminars and workshops mentioned in Chapter 20. Sign up for sessions on interviewing and selection skills. Read every book on the topic that you can get your hands on. Conduct research on the Internet. Consider a peer-review system where your current employees are involved in the selection process of new employees. They are the ones who will be working directly with the new hire; their input may be more valuable than you think.

Employee Development

One of the best ways to keep your customers happy is to take good care of your employees first. Guide and encourage them and they will take care of your customers in return. Without satisfied customers to give you repeat business and spread the word about the excellent product or service you provide, you'll be missing the core of a successful business. Therefore, consider your employees your most valuable asset and you'll create a win-win situation for everyone.

Your associates want to enjoy coming to work each day. After all, a full-time employee spends more time at work than she does at home. She wants to have the tools to do a good job through the use of supplies, training, and skills—or a combination of all three. In return, she will expect you to let her know how she is doing and offer recognition for a job well done.

If you develop an employee with the use of training programs, performance evaluations, assessments, and career development, you will increase her chances for success. Your company will only be as successful as the people who work with you, so invest time and money in their careers—it will boost your bottom line in the long run.

Managers are usually so busy with day-to-day business operations that employee development may be pushed aside. As long as the work is getting done and there are no problems, people are taken for granted. It is worth the time and effort to implement an employee development program to increase employee satisfaction.

Some employees like to simply report to work, do a good job, and receive a check on payday. They are complacent to stay where they are, do the job they are paid to perform, and don't want any further responsibilities. There is nothing wrong with this. People have their own individual goals and motivators. Yet even workers who are content with what they are doing need development to keep their skills up to par with changes in the workforce and give them a sense of accomplishment and value. Employee development isn't limited to taking an employee to the next level, it's about feedback, encouragement, praise, teamwork, and letting a person know that they make a difference.

Performance Evaluations

All employees should receive an evaluation or review throughout the course of their employment. Most companies will give one after the first ninety days of employment, which is typically after he has passed an introductory period. This timeframe gives ample time for a fair evaluation. Additionally, it is customary to give a review to everyone at the end of the year, or on the anniversary of each employee's hiring. Preparing reviews during a time of year when business is slow is a good idea. This will give you time to put more focus into the evaluations.

Employees should know when to expect a performance appraisal, and they should be conducted on time. It is frustrating for an employee to anticipate a date when he expects to receive your feedback, only to have the date, then weeks and months, pass by without an evaluation. This sends the message that he is not important to the company and you don't have time for him. Don't make the mistake of giving this perception to your associates.

ALERT!

A performance evaluation is not to be used to inform an employee for the first time that there is an issue with his performance. Problems that require corrective action should be addressed immediately, as discussed in Chapter 15. However, if the problem persists, indicate this in the evaluation as you rate the employee in that particular area.

Use a performance-evaluation form to rate each employee consistently and fairly. There is a sample of one in Appendix A or you can find one on the Internet or through one of the associations that you belong to. A generic form can be used for all positions, but you may find it helpful to use a different format for supervisors and managers since they have different responsibilities and expectations. To ensure that everyone is evaluated fairly, use the same evaluation form for everyone, especially when evaluating people in the same positions. It doesn't mean that you can never change your evaluation form, it just means that there should be consistency. So if you change the form, don't change it just for one person; make the change and stay with it for a while.

Preparing for an evaluation is something that you should be doing at all times. Keep a running log for each employee and jot down things they do that go above and beyond the expectations for the job. Also, keep copies of any commendation forms, awards, or comment cards or letters from customers that mention the employee. Things like this should be acknowledged in a performance review.

Schedule a date and time to give the employee his evaluation and stick with it as you would any important appointment. If your policy is that employees are eligible for a pay increase based on how well they score on their evaluation, this makes it even more important to do the review on time. Receiving a raise is very important to your associates and they have every right to receive it on time. Additionally, giving raises late will result in processing a retroactive pay adjustment, which is more work when payroll is processed. It is much more effective and sends a positive message to the employee to give him a performance evaluation on time and start his new salary on the effective date.

When you sit down with the employee to give him an evaluation, turn off your cell phone and transfer all incoming calls to voicemail to avoid distractions. This is an important meeting and whether an employee is getting a rave review or there are ongoing performance issues to discuss he deserves 100 percent of your attention.

Give him a copy of the completed evaluation form and go over each entry with him individually. He should have the opportunity to give his input as well. However, if there are performance problems addressed in the evaluation and the employee becomes defensive, put a stop to it. This is not the time for a debate, or to let an employee blow off steam. As long as you have evaluated the employee fairly and have documentation and backup to verify performance problems, the score of the evaluation is final. If the employee wants to further discuss any deficiencies, schedule a time to meet in the next day or two to discuss them.

Your evaluation form should have space at the end for the employee to include his input and goals for the future, as well as a signature line. If an employee received an unfavorable review and refuses to sign the document, call in a supervisor or manager as a witness and document with her signature that the employee refused to sign. Give the employee a copy of the review form once all signatures have been obtained. The original should be kept in the personnel file.

Some companies use a self-review program. An employee is given a blank appraisal form and he evaluates himself. The manager also fills out an evaluation form and the two meet to compare ratings and notes. This helps determine if the manager and employee are both on the same track regarding performance.

Mentorship

The purpose of a mentorship program is to match up a manager or other experienced employee with someone new to the company or position. The mentor takes a mentee, or protégé, under her wing and helps groom his professional career. A mentor program can be formal, as in the case of assigning a mentor to a protégé and following specific guidelines for the program, or it can be informal, such as to encourage people to volunteer their services or seek out a mentor and meet on their own terms. A successful mentoring program will not only help retain employees, it will assist your training efforts and help boost employee morale.

A mentorship program will be successful only if both parties want to participate. This is most true for the mentor because she will be doing most of the work. A person with an overloaded calendar who isn't too keen on mentoring somebody will resent the program. This is why it is not a good idea to require mentors to participate. However, if you consider a mentorship program part of your training efforts, it is reasonable to require mentees to take part.

A successful mentor is someone who takes pride in teaching others and has a sincere desire to see a coworker succeed. She is patient of amateur questions and is not judgmental. Her listening, communication, and coaching skills are excellent, and she is able to multitask. Murphy's Law dictates that the times her protégé needs her most will be when she is juggling a few of her own deadlines.

What can cause a mentorship program to fail?
It may fail if it is viewed as a "hand-holding" program, isn't supported by upper management, or if the two people paired up are not a good match. The unwillingness by either party to devote enough time to the program is another obstacle, as is a consensus in the workplace that people chosen to participate are receiving preferential treatment.

The ideal mentee is someone who looks up to people in management or seniority and will respect that person's guidance. She is able to accept constructive feedback well and wants to learn everything she can about her new position and the company she works for. Her time spent with her mentor will be put to good use, as she will implement what she learns into her normal workday.

Formal Mentoring Program

To set up a formal mentoring program, consider the following:

- How will mentors and mentees be nominated or selected?
- Will there be specific criteria required for participation?
- How many hours per week will be put aside for mentorship purposes?
- Will mentors receive an incentive for their work?
- How will the success of the program be measured?
- Will there be a budget for mentoring expenses?
- Who will oversee the program?
- How long will the program last?
- What are the goals of the mentoring program?

To get started, try a test run. Compose a plan in writing and try it out with two people first. Ask them to document what works and what doesn't throughout the program. Troubleshoot any obstacles and make necessary changes, then try again with another pair. The first run may be just what you are looking for or just need a quick fix.

Recognition Programs

Recognition programs that acknowledge exceptional performance, outstanding attendance, or meeting a milestone are fun and relatively inexpensive ways to boost employee morale.

Offer an incentive for each time an employee is praised by a customer verbally or in writing. If a customer sends a letter or e-mail, post a copy on the employee bulletin board for everyone to see. This will not only give the employee well-deserved congratulations from coworkers, it will encourage others to have their name mentioned as well. As a reward, you can add a bonus to his paycheck or give a gift certificate to a local store or restaurant.

Encourage customers to recognize outstanding customer service by distributing comment cards or an e-mail survey. One of the greatest compliments an employee or a team can receive is to be individually recognized by a satisfied customer. Put a copy in the employee's personnel file. If a customer calls to commend an employee, document and file the conversation.

Start an employee-of-the-month program if your staff is large enough. First, decide how the winner will be chosen. Will he be nominated by his peers or selected by management? Can someone win more than once a year? Recognize your employee of the month with a certificate or a plaque to take home. For the business site, you can purchase a large plaque that will give you the room to display the engraved name and month of each employee of the month. Designate a preferred parking spot for the winner, complete with a "Reserved for Employee of the Month" sign. Take the award a step further by designating an employee of the year. This person will typically receive his award at an end–of-the-year holiday party or banquet if one is planned.

Empowerment

To empower an employee is to give her permission to do whatever she thinks is reasonably necessary to satisfy a customer. For example, let's say that you own a clothing store and a customer is unhappy because the pair of slacks that he wants to purchase is missing a button and there is not another pair in stock. You're at the bank making a deposit or out to lunch when the customer comes in. By empowering the employee to do what she feels will please the guest, you are showing your trust and confidence in her business-making decisions. In this case, the employee may give the customer a 20 percent discount on the slacks that will cover the inconvenience of having to replace the missing button. The customer didn't have to wait around for a resolution from management, and the store clerk made the sale.

FACT

Set a limit on how far an employee can negotiate with a customer without management approval. Employees should be comfortable telling you what they did to correct a problem, and they should know to report incidents as they occur. If they are afraid of being reprimanded for giving discounts, they won't feel empowered.

An incident may occur with a customer who is angry and unwilling to accept a discount or other concession that an employee is trying to offer. His voice may get loud and he may start a scene, putting an employee in an uncomfortable position. If you or another manager are not available to rectify the situation, the employee may end up making a decision that you normally would not have approved in order to get the angry, screaming customer out of the building. If this happens, tell the employee that you understand her reasoning for doing what she did and that you support her decision. Give her some suggestions for how far she should have gone with her empowerment privileges and that will help guide her next time she is in the same situation. Again, don't put your employees in a situation where they are afraid to tell you what they had to do to calm an angry customer.

Training

You read about training programs and options for new hires in Chapter 4, but training shouldn't stop there. A recent job-satisfaction survey concluded that many employees are unsatisfied with the amount of training they receive to do their jobs. This can be the quality or quantity of the training or both.

Consider training seminars, webcasts, workshops, and conventions as mentioned in Chapter 20 for everyone on staff. These events aren't limited to human resource training—you'll find topics for every discipline. Look for computer, customer service, and training directly related to the employee's essential functions.

The people chosen to train employees should be patient and thorough in explaining the steps of the job from start to finish, and everything in between. Telling someone why something is done a specific way and what the consequences will be if it's done differently will help workers grasp the concept of a task. They shouldn't just be shown how to do something, but also why it should be done that way.

Many companies set training goals for everyone each year and keep track of the training hours worked. Time spent with a mentor is considered training time, so these hours count, too. Don't set training goals for your employees if you don't intend to follow through and make it happen.

Promoting from Within

One of the many benefits of employee development is that it will give you a good candidate to fill a vacancy. Whether it's a transfer into a department in which the employee has cross-trained or a promotion, you will have someone capable of taking on the new job. Surveys show that opportunities for advancement ranks up there with pay and benefits to most employees. Promote internally whenever you can and your employee retention rates will peak.

ALERT!

Before promoting an employee from within, find out what the job-posting requirements are in your state. You may be required to advertise the position to the public and give both internal and external candidates the opportunity to apply before making an offer. If this is the case, all qualified candidates should be interviewed and considered equally.

To help prepare a current employee for future promotions, assign additional responsibilities to him as you feel he is ready. Make sure that you don't violate any FLSA regulations in the process. Also, ask him to assist with big projects. For instance, a rising managerial candidate can help prepare the monthly profit-and-loss statement or annual budget.

Not all companies are in a position to offer growth and advancement because the company may be too small. Simple things like adding new responsibility and changing a person's title along with a pay raise can do the trick. Some people are very motivated by taking their careers to the next level; do what you can to give them that feeling of accomplishment.

Showing That You Care

There are many ways to show employees that you care about their opinions and that they are valuable to the company. These can be fun and relatively inexpensive:

- All-employee staff meetings to keep everyone informed about things they should know about the company. Include lunch for an added treat.
- Monthly newsletter to announce new hires, service anniversaries, and promotions. Highlight an employee or two each month.
- Suggestion box. Read each suggestion and respond during the staff meetings. If a suggestion cannot be accommodated, explain why or offer an alternative.

- Purchase a big birthday cake on the first of every month to cele-brate everyone who is having a birthday.
- Free car wash for all employees twice a year. The cars are washed by the supervisors and managers in the parking lot.

An employee-satisfaction survey is one way to show your employees that you care about their happiness at work. You can do this informally by distributing survey forms yourself and asking employees to fill out and return them, with or without their name. You can also hire the services of a third party to conduct the survey. This will usually deliver the most accu-rate results since any unhappy employees who are afraid to speak up don't have to worry about their handwriting being recognized. The questions on the survey should ask their opinion about pay, benefits, training, advance-ment opportunities, work environment, fair treatment, and a rating of the supervisory and management staff.

CHAPTER 19

Work and Family Balance

The fact that work gets in the way of life can't be argued, and some employees struggle with this more than others. They are looking for ways to balance their work and personal life and have found alternate work schedules to be the solution. They're making it happen with the help of job sharing, telecommuting, flex time, part-time work, and 4/10 or 9/80 work schedules. Here's what you need to know to help alternative work schedules succeed and understand how they can benefit your company.

How Does the Employer Benefit?

The employer benefits in several ways, one of which is a happy, productive employee. Workers who are given the flexibility to balance their lives have less stress and are generally happier, healthier, and more productive. Time off during the week allows them to schedule appointments without adjusting their work schedule. The result is that they miss less scheduled days of work. They are refreshed and energized on the days that they do work, and it's a win-win situation for everyone.

Alternate work schedules are not an added expense to you, and surveys show that it is the perk that employees want most. Workers who report high levels of job dissatisfaction are frustrated about their work and life balance. Giving an employee the flexibility to manage his life is a big morale booster. Your company will be considered a premier employer if you give workers this valuable benefit.

ESSENTIAL

Reducing hours will usually decrease or eliminate an employee's benefits, based on your company's policy. Employees who want to cut their hours at work should know this and acknowledge it as a fair compromise.

Any change in hours, pay, or benefits should be written up in an agreement and signed by both you and the employee. Employees paid by the hour should maintain their hourly rate. Obviously, those paid on a salary basis will see a cut in their weekly rate. The document should indicate that the schedule change will be a trial period for evaluation—three months is a reasonable amount of time. If it is successful, the arrangement should be up for renewal annually. You may want to indicate that the work agreement can be withdrawn by either party during the year. If you do so, indicate how much advance notice should be given. It would not be fair to an employee to tell him on a Friday that he has to go back to a Monday through Friday, 9:00 A.M.–5:00 P.M. work schedule the following week.

Offering alternate work schedules is a sure way to increase your employee retention. Benefits like this are hard to come by, and for those employees who really value them, they're likely to stay for the long haul. One thing that workers struggle with is finding rewarding work with a non-traditional schedule.

Job Sharing

When two part-time employees share one full-time position, they are job sharing. This arrangement is commonly requested by an employee who has a baby and wants to return to work on a part-time basis. What is keeping her from part-time work is a position with full-time duties. Her other dilemma is that she loves her job and doesn't want to give it up. Mothers with older children may become so burned out over the course of time that they request this as well.

It's not only women who are on the job-sharing bandwagon. Anyone, regardless of gender or family obligations, may request to spend more time at home and less time at work. They may no longer need a full-time income, have elderly parents who need their help, or want to ease into retirement slowly.

Several books and magazine articles have been written on the subject and they all have one common denominator: these work arrangements are requested by employees, not by supervisors. They're an easy sell if the employee puts herself in the shoes of her employer, does the legwork, and prepares a proposal that is hard to turn down.

Job sharing is not covered by the Fair Labor Standards Act, so it's fair game as long as the agreement between you and the employee does not violate any labor laws. The arrangement is likely to be successful if the two people sharing the job also share the ability to:

- Communicate effectively and promptly
- Pick up where another person left off
- Be a team player
- Trust another person to do the job right
- Share the credit for a job well done
- Troubleshoot problems immediately

You can expect the employee to begin the search for a job-sharing partner herself. The candidate may be another current employee who also wants to reduce her hours, or someone from the outside may apply and you will need to interview them and make the final decision. You are under no obligation to consider letting an employee job share unless you think it can be done successfully.

A job-sharing arrangement will work only if the two part-time people can be as productive as one full-time employee. Since employees with flexible work schedules are generally less stressed, employers are likely to be ahead of the game. Two part-time employees can surpass one full-time employee in productivity, especially since failing to do so can end the arrangement.

Other benefits to the employer are:

- Two people are trained to do one position. If one leaves, the remaining person can train the replacement for you.
- Vacations can be coordinated so that one person is always there to cover the other. The job will rarely be left vacant.
- When a job-share partner is sick, the other may be able to cover. This results in full coverage for the job every day.
- A decrease in benefits expenses if part-time employees do not qualify for full-time benefits. This will directly increase your bottom line.

Overall, you'll get better coverage for less money. This is why it's best to have the employees cross-trained instead of splitting the job duties. Both workers should know every task of the job so that you have the same benefit you would get from a full-time worker.

Some of the employee benefits may be split if you, as the employer, agree to do it. Insurance plans can't be split, but vacation, sick leave, and holiday pay can be split between two employees. If employees are given two weeks of vacation pay per year, each would receive one week. If the job-sharing schedule starts midyear, the paid-time-off hours will be adjusted accordingly. Holiday pay would be four hours per holiday for each employee, instead of eight.

Telecommuting

The most recent stats from the Department of Labor estimate that about 15 percent of the workforce has some type of compensated, at-home work schedule. With off-site computer networks, WiFi, cell phones, and e-mail attachments it's a wonder more people don't telecommute. To telecommute is to work from a remote office that is usually in the comfort of the employee's home. With the advances bound to happen in technology over the next few years, telecommuting is estimated to rise.

A telecommuting arrangement may be full or part time and can require the employee to come into the office rarely, occasionally, or frequently. Companies have even gone as far as to set up direct-dial company phone lines in the employee's home and give them access to company databases.

QUESTION?

Which employees make the best telecommute prospects?
Employees who don't rely strongly on the social connections at work and have the self-discipline to get the job done when the comforts of home are just a room away are the best at telecommuting. They have to be trusted 100 percent, be self-motivated, and have excellent verbal and written communication skills.

Telecommuting can work for many positions that do not involve direct personal contact. Since we're slowly becoming a paperless world, more and more positions can be performed remotely. Many payroll clerks now rely on automated timekeeping systems to process checks, so why not let them do it at home? With caller ID, busy executives can screen their own phone calls, while their executive assistants perform some duties from home while alternating days in the office with a coworker.

The ability to work from home is a benefit that does not cost you extra money, but rewards the employee by providing a financial advantage. In essence, you're giving the employee more money in his pocket by reducing the money he spends on gasoline, vehicle maintenance, or public transportation. Car insurance rates for people who do not drive to work every day go down, too.

Flex Time

Flex time is all about "when." This arrangement gives employees the option to come and go as they please, as long as they don't miss deadlines and agree to be at their workstations on the days requested by management. The employee is given keys to the office so that if he wants to come in on a Sunday morning he can. Again, the issue of trust must be 100 percent.

ALERT!

If a shift differential is paid to workers with traditional schedules for weekend, holiday, or night shifts, the flex-time arrangement should state that this pay rule is waived. The benefit of flexible working hours should not include the ability for employees to pick the highest-paying timeframes in which to get their work done.

Flex time is very popular with parents who want to avoid daycare costs and give their children the benefit of having a parent at home around the clock. Employees are able to work around their spouse's schedule and the savings in daycare expenses equals extra cash in the hands of the employee. The employee will look at it as a pay raise, at no cost to you.

Like job sharing, parents aren't the only ones to benefit from flex time. People whose biological clock dreads the 9:00 A.M.–5:00 P.M. workday prefer flexible hours. Students juggling school schedules can balance class and homework. People who want to pursue interests that are not limited to weekends are also likely to enjoy flex time.

Part-Time Schedules

Some people just want to keep it simple and work part time. They like coming into work and want to work normal hours. They just don't want to do it every day or all day.

Reduction to a part-time schedule may ultimately result in a job-sharing situation. If the employee isn't likely to job-share successfully, your best bet is to just hire another part-time worker and divide the job duties.

If a full-time employee asks to have his hours reduced to part time and you decline, there is a good chance that he will seek part-time work elsewhere. He wouldn't ask for a reduction in time and pay if it was not important to him; this is why it is best to make a reasonable effort to accommodate the requests of employees who ask to cut back to part time.

Part-time workers are known to be very productive because they can't always say that they'll finish something tomorrow, or that they have all day to get it done. Keeping their part-time work schedule is dependent on whether or not they can complete their work while maintaining quality and quantity. You are likely to get both from part-time workers if they want to keep the schedule. It's when someone works part time but wants full-time hours that you run into problems.

Special Needs of Parents

Here's a typical morning for a working parent: Wake up before dawn, pack lunches, prepare the diaper bag, find lost shoes, and fight traffic while eating a granola bar to drop one kid off at day care and the other at school. Arrive at work and realize that lunches are still sitting on the kitchen counter. On a good day, the toddler will not have a tantrum in the morning, and there will be no phone call from a crying child who left his homework on the kitchen table.

Whew! It's no wonder that working parents want, and need, flexible work options, but some of them simply can't do it. Their position can't be transitioned into one with alternative schedules or they can't afford to cut down to part-time work. The best thing you can do for them are the little things that will make them and their children happy, and relieve some of the stress.

Fortune magazine publishes a list every year of the top 100 companies to work for. These are large companies, and most likely as a small business owner you are unable to match what they have to offer. Besides an attractive compensation package, one of the things that makes these companies so special is their options for work and life balance, most notably the availability of telecommuting and on-site day care. *Working Mother* puts out an annual list of the 100 most family friendly companies in America. These are the companies with high employee-satisfaction level in work and life balance. To many people, this is just as important, or more important, than their rate of monetary compensation.

FACT

Companies who make the *Fortune* and *Working Mother* lists (and some make both) proudly display this honor, and for good reason. The companies have gone above and beyond what workers in America want and need to take care of themselves while they provide for their families.

If you have enough workers who would take advantage of on-site day care, this is something to consider even if your business is small. You are unlikely to need the large day-care centers that the larger companies have, but an adequate room for on-site child care would be appreciated by many parents. The employees would pay for the service, making this another benefit to employees at no cost to you. However, you will have up-front costs to purchase the items you need to get started. If you don't have the space and would need to add on a room, this could be a major setback, but something that will repay itself in the long run, as you see employee satisfaction and productivity rise and turnover rates decline.

There are many things to consider before offering on-site day care. You will need to prepare a consent form and liability waiver for parents to sign. Your insurance company will need to be notified. Determining if the person who cares for the children will be put on payroll or be considered contract labor will need to be determined. If it's contract labor, find out if the parents will pay the provider directly or if you should pay the child-care provider. Also, look into the legal issues and employment laws in regards to payroll versus contract labor. Once you get started, parents will pay daily, weekly, or monthly for the service, and this should offset any expenses that would come out of your company's pocket.

If you do decide to provide on-site day care, have a backup plan for when the caregiver gets sick. If there are enough kids enrolled to need two or more providers, one of them getting sick could still shut the center down for the day if the child-to-adult ratio is too high. Employees with children being watched can take turns helping during the day or a person may be kept on call to come in and assist when the need arises.

Another option to help working parents is to offer a place for older kids to come after school to do their homework while they wait for their parents to get off work. This is only feasible for children who go to school nearby. A teenager from the local high school can be hired to keep an eye on everyone and help with homework.

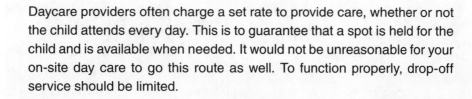

Daycare providers often charge a set rate to provide care, whether or not the child attends every day. This is to guarantee that a spot is held for the child and is available when needed. It would not be unreasonable for your on-site day care to go this route as well. To function properly, drop-off service should be limited.

Parents also want and need the flexibility to leave work to attend parent/teacher conferences, classroom parties, awards ceremonies, and performances at school. They may want to chaperone field trips or become active in PTA events and fundraisers. You'll be known as a compassionate employer if you give them the time to do this. You're not expected to do it on company time; simply allow them to occasionally adjust their schedule or work a few hours less that week when things come up.

You may run into an issue with an employee who does not have children and feels that the working parents aren't contributing fairly because they are out when their kids are sick or miss time from work for school events. Just remind these employees that when something comes up for them, all they have to do is ask for the same privilege. They may have an elderly parent who needs a ride to the doctor, a friend who needs to be dropped off at the airport, or a cat that needs to see the veterinarian.

4/10 and 9/80 Work Schedules

These work schedules offer your employees a weekday off two or four times a month with no cut in pay or benefits. A 4/10 schedule means that the employee works four ten-hour days in the week for a total of forty hours per week. The most common days employees take off are Monday or Friday. If this will leave staffing too thin on these days, you can have a rotating schedule or give these days off to the people with seniority and have the others take Tuesday, Wednesday, or Thursday off. If employees are paid biweekly, a 9/80 work schedule may also be considered. This consists of nine workdays in the two-week pay period. Eight of the nine days are worked at nine hours and one at eight hours for a total of eighty hours. There is one day off every other week.

If you live in a state where overtime applies to any hours over eight that are worked in one day, there are ways to get around this, but you have to be sure to do it legally to avoid stiff penalties and breaking the law. Contact your state employment agency to find out how to do it. You may be required to put the idea up to a vote, with a requirement of two-thirds majority for it to pass. There will be paperwork and employee signatures required before implementing the schedule change and the ability to waive the overtime pay.

CHAPTER 20

Continuing-Education Opportunities

Human resources branches out into many areas and you may find yourself being somewhat of a generalist. You'll be recruiting talent, developing their careers, administering benefits, training, and processing paychecks. The people you hire count on you to stay on top of the constantly changing labor laws, at the state level and federal level. To do this—get the people on board and take care of them on the job—the education never ends. Have fun while learning through conferences, seminars, networking, and even teaching others what you already know.

20

HRCI Certification

You may be familiar with M.D., Ph.D., and L.S.W., but did you know that there are human resource credentials as well? Human resource professionals who have met the standards of the Human Resources Certification Institute (HRCI) advertise their credentialed status by displaying PHR, SPHR, or GPHR after their names. As of January 2007, over 87,000 HR professionals held credentials from HRCI. In the HR world, certification is held in high regard.

There are three levels of certification: Professional in Human Resources (PHR), Senior Professional in Human Resources (SPHR), and Global Professional in Human Resources (GPHR). Job postings for human resource positions often require or prefer a college degree or certification. To many, certification is viewed as highly as having a college degree.

A person with certification has demonstrated a working knowledge of all aspects of human resources. This includes but is not limited to strategic planning, international business issues, compensation, benefits, HR development, employee rights, and emerging HR issues. Certification also shows a commitment to stay educated on new developments in the HR field, and recertification is required.

The GPHR credential is for those professionals with an international HR body of knowledge and is intended for HR professionals who develop and implement global HR strategies, manage HR operations overseas, and those who oversee international-assignment management.

An assessment test may be taken for a fee prior to applying for the exam to become a credentialed human resources professional. It is a good idea to take the assessment test first to get a feel for the questions that will be asked and to help you decide if you are ready to take the exam.

Interested candidates who apply to take the exam must meet the eligibility requirements. Two years of exempt-level human resource work experience is required and must be proven; however, it is recommended that SPHR applicants have six to eight years of experience. The position must be exempt, as defined by the Fair Labor Standards Act (FLSA). This work experience does not need to be current or sequential. The HRCI Web site provides a list of position codes that meet the work-experience requirement.

ALERT!

Workers at an exempt-level status who perform HR duties during at least 51 percent of the workday may qualify to take the exam. Passing the exam isn't easy. In December 2006, 63 percent of entrants for PHR certification passed, 55 percent for SPHR, and 56 percent for GPHR.

Students and recent graduates may qualify to take the PHR exam only. In this category, candidates must not have two years exempt work experience and must take the exam no earlier than twelve months before their graduation date and no later than twelve months after graduation.

In 2007, the nonrefundable application fee to take the exams was $75. Exam fees for members of the Society for Human Resource Management were $175 ($225 for nonmembers) for the PHR exam and $300 ($350 for nonmembers) for SPHR or GPHR. The fee for qualified students taking the PHR exam was $45.

The exams are broken down into the areas of strategic management, human resource development, total rewards (benefits and compensation), employee and labor relations, and workforce planning and development.

Once you are a certified human resource professional, you will be required to apply for recertification every three years after attending sixty credits of qualified HR-related continuing-education classes and/or by documenting professional development activities. Some choose to take the exam again, which is another, less popular, option. Recertification credits are available through online courses, seminars, workshops, and college campuses. To upgrade your certification, (e.g., you have PHR certification and feel ready to upgrade to SPHR certification) it is required that you take the exam for that classification.

Certificate Programs

Not to be confused with the exam certification, there is no previous work experience required to earn a certificate in human resource applications. These programs will teach you a new skill, sharpen your technical knowledge, and keep you up to date with new concepts. Classes may be taken online, through a series of seminars, or at a local college or university. The most common human resource certificate topics are:

- Human Resource Management
- Selection and Staffing
- Performance Management
- Payroll Basics
- ADP Payroll System
- Labor Relations

In some cases, certificate programs may qualify for college credits. Other classes prepare you for the HRCI certifications mentioned at the beginning of this chapter or count as credits toward recertification.

Get an HR Degree Online

If you don't have to take the time to drive to school and sit in a classroom to earn a bachelor's or master's degree in human resources, you can do it online. The first step is to find an online university that offers a degree in human resources management. Check the Elearners.com Web site or contact one of the universities in your area. Many traditional campuses now offer Internet or distance-learning courses.

If the school is a new one to you and you have already taken some college courses, have your transcripts sent over after you register. Next, make a telephone or in-person appointment with a counselor to discuss the path you need to take to reach your goal.

There are several ways to receive your instruction. Most classes use traditional college textbooks that can be purchased online through the campus bookstore. Many bookstores have easy one-step ordering that match the books you will need to the ID number of the class you are taking. You also have the option to purchase used textbooks through the campus bookstore in person or online. Television or CD-ROM broadcasts may also be used. If the campus is near your home, you may be able to watch the broadcasts for free through your cable or satellite station. Otherwise, you can rent CD-ROMs and return them when the course ends.

ESSENTIAL

If you do not have much of a college background, it may be economical to work toward an associate's degree first. If you take the right classes, most of them will transfer to a bachelor's degree. Even if you attended high school a long time ago, get a copy of your transcript if you took college-prep classes.

You will communicate with your instructor via e-mail or telephone, and most courses offer message boards where you can communicate with other students. The course Web site or syllabus is where you will find your lesson plans. Complete them at your own pace and turn them in by the due date. Open-book tests are completed online by logging in with your social security number or student ID number.

There are two ways to take midterms and final exams as a distance-learning student. One is with the assistance of a proctor, which can be a teacher or librarian or other qualified person designated by the school. The campus will send the exam directly to the proctor, who will administer the exam following the school's guidelines. The guidelines generally state that you must show proper ID before taking the exam and that you remain within sight of the proctor while being tested. Expect time restraints for taking the exam just as there are in a classroom. After you finish, you'll give the exam to the proctor, who will sign paperwork stating that she facilitated the exam and send it back to the school. It is customary for you to give her the stamps needed for U.S. mail.

The ideal distance-learning student is someone who likes to work at her own pace and can resist the temptation to slack off. The ability to work independently and meet deadlines is crucial. Since the guidance of face-to-face interactions with a teacher and stimulation from live classroom instruction is missing, self-motivation is a key factor for success.

ALERT!

Midterms and final exams need to be completed within a specific time-frame. Check with your proctor ahead of time to make sure that she received your exam, and set a date and time to take it. Find out whether your deadline for completing the exam is the date it is postmarked or the date it is to be received on campus.

Conferences and Seminars

Take advantage of workshops at conferences and seminars to help you manage your staff better and increase your HR knowledge. These sessions are usually held at hotels or conference centers and you can find them nationwide. Here are some of the companies that can help you update your expertise:

- American Management Association
- Cornell University School of Industrial and Labor Relations
- Council on Education
- Fred Pryor Seminars
- Linkage Incorporated
- Lorman Education Services
- National Business Institute
- National Seminars Group
- Padgett-Thompson
- SkillPath Seminars

Some offer online training, and you'll find webcasts at HR.com. Consider courses and workshops on the following topics:

- Americans with Disabilities Act (ADA) Compliance
- Compensation
- Equal Opportunity Employer (EEO) Compliance

- E-mail and Internet Policy Compliance
- Employment Law
- Fair Hiring Practices
- Interviewing and Recruiting
- Job Analysis
- Surveillance and Privacy in the Workplace
- Training and Development

Attending an annual wage-and-hour-law update seminar every year is one of the wisest investments you can make in your career, whether or not your focus is HR. Take any supervisors you have on staff with you. Wage and hour laws change yearly and are state specific. These courses keep you up to date with what's new for the year.

Many conferences and seminars include lunch with the registration fee. You will also see vendor booths from companies that offer services beneficial to human resource professionals. Bring a stack of business cards with you to distribute as you network with other professionals.

How to Work a Room

Networking is commonly referred to as working a room. Recent research confirms that first impressions are established within thirty seconds of meeting someone. It's easiest to make the right impression the first time, rather than try to repair a poor impression later. Your handshake should be firm and confident, but not too hard. Maintain direct eye contact and speak clearly. Think about the image you want to project, then project it. Be the person that others will want to meet and get to know better.

QUESTION?

How can I start a conversation with a stranger?
Nametags usually indicate where someone works, so you can comment about the company or city. People love to talk about themselves and open-ended questions will encourage them to engage in conversation. Chances are the person you approached is just as nervous about meeting new people as you are and will welcome your initiative.

You may see some of the presenters and speakers while you're mingling in the halls or exhibit areas. Read about their credentials and background in the conference brochure and introduce yourself while impressing them with the knowledge you have about them. You may meet again at another conference and be remembered. This is what networking is all about.

If you see someone who you have met before but can't remember his name, shake hands and introduce yourself. This may prompt him to do the same. If someone is with you, introduce your colleague to the person whose name you forgot, and this may trigger him to introduce himself. There is also nothing wrong with saying, "I'm sorry, but will you please remind me of your name?"

A conference or workshop is a great place to meet a mentor. This may come about when you're talking with another attendee at lunch or between workshops, and be the start to a professional relationship. When someone gives you their business card and says to call if you ever need something, take them up on the offer. A mentor is someone who surpasses you with knowledge and experience and will be a phone call or e-mail away when you come across new HR situations you aren't sure how to handle. He can share great ideas, templates for forms and letters, and a few horror stories with a "Don't let this happen to you" scenario. An effective mentor is motivational, a good listener, provides constructive feedback, and encourages self-confidence while guiding you in the right direction. Like most fields of work, human resources is one where people can learn a lot from each other.

Mentoring is a two-way street. To be the type of person that someone will want to mentor, you need to have goals, the commitment to learn without taking shortcuts, the ability to accept feedback, and the motivation to excel.

Look for Business Opportunities

The person sitting next to you at lunch could be a potential client for your company or refer you to someone who needs your services. Or you may be looking to fill a position, and a qualified person between jobs is sitting in the chair next to you. You never know what opportunities can come from people you meet at conferences. You may be able to do something for someone else, too.

It's not only what you know, but also who you know that can help you and your business. Be prepared to share contact information. Wear an outfit with pockets so that you can quickly whip out your business card without the struggles of a purse or briefcase. Show a genuine interest in getting to know others and you will be sure to reap the benefits.

Society for Human Resource Management

Membership in the Society for Human Resource Management (SHRM) will help you take your HR knowledge to the next level. It is the largest HR association in the world and offers accurate, up-to-date information along with educational opportunities. Free educational webcasts and a monthly subscription to HR magazine are included in the annual membership. You will also receive reports and newsletters about workplace issues, national and state legislative updates, and articles to help you manage your staff legally. Membership and renewals are about $160 per year with a reduced price for students of only about $35 per year. Prices are subject to change.

Membership entitles you to research statistics on issues such as salary surveys, employment outlook, recruiting topics, and emerging issues that may affect the workplace. There are online discussion forums where members share best practices and consult each other for advice and input. Help with human resource questions is available via live chat, telephone, or e-mail.

FACT

The SHRM Annual Conference and Exhibition will mark its sixtieth anniversary in 2008. The conference is held in June of each year. Smaller, statewide conferences are scheduled throughout the year in all fifty states. You do not have to be a member of SHRM to attend, but members receive a discount upon registration.

The annual SHRM conference is the world's largest HR conference. SHRM also organizes an annual Staffing Management Conference and Exposition in the spring of each year. This conference is specifically for HR professionals involved in employment and staffing. The Employment Law and Legislative Conference is usually scheduled sometime in March and will teach you what you need to know about changes in federal compliance. Last, but not least, the October Workplace Diversity Conference and Exhibition will show you how to enhance diversity initiatives within your organization. All conferences span three days.

There are smaller chapters affiliated with SHRM that you can join. Annual dues still apply. PIHRA (Professionals in Human Resources Association) is in the greater Los Angeles area, NCHRA (Northern California Human Resources Association) is in northern California, and NEHRA (New England Human Resources Association) covers six states in the region.

Chamber of Commerce

There are literally thousands of chambers in the United States. There's the U.S. Chamber of Commerce, followed by chambers at the state and local levels. Small business owners find membership to be beneficial for networking opportunities and staying up to date with local, state, and national labor laws through publications and webcasts.

A wealth of information may be found on the U.S. Chamber of Commerce Web site under the "Small Business Toolkits" tab. You'll find links to state-specific information about several of the topics highlighted in this book, such as hiring people, pre-employment screenings, and employer payroll taxes.

Your local chamber of commerce may have a monthly breakfast that is popular in many cities. Chambers also sponsor some of the job fairs mentioned in Chapter 1. From your state chamber, you may be able to purchase updated manuals on labor-law issues specific to your state. Membership is also a good way to get to know the other business professionals in your community.

The Opportunity to Teach Others

A college degree may qualify you to teach a night course at your local community college or university. In most cases, at least a master's degree is required. A trade school or other vocational entity may need someone to teach students how to apply for a job after graduation, and a degree is normally not needed for this. Your role will be to talk to students from the perspective of the person on the other side of the desk. Call it giving the inside scoop, if you will.

In most cases, a degree is not required to teach an adult continuing-education course. Doing so will not only result in extra cash, it will help you develop your public-speaking skills and establish expertise. Monetary compensation varies and can be anywhere from $25–$150 per hour. Teaching is a great credential to add to your accomplishments and many find it to be a rewarding experience. Your local school district or community college may offer community-education courses that do not require degreed instructors, too.

If you do not have a master's degree, look for noncredit classes to teach such as continuing-education or community-education courses taught through your local school district, college, university, civic center, parks and recreation department, or chamber of commerce.

To get hired as an instructor, present yourself as a practitioner and prepare a course outline, including visual materials and handouts. Consider which textbooks you'll use, if applicable. There is a lot of preparation involved, but the curriculum will remain yours and you can use it again at another facility. Some classes will require a minimum number of enrollees, which means that if not enough people sign up you may have to solicit students to help get the class started. New instructors find it easiest to start out with small classes.

Volunteerism

Volunteer work can be rewarding in terms of professional development and intellectual stimulation. As a human resource professional, you can volunteer your time offering job search, interviewing, and resume tips to high school students or for nonprofit organizations that assist recovering drug addicts, battered women, incarcerated persons, or other people transitioning into the workforce.

APPENDIX A

Samples of Written Documents

Contingent Job Offer Letter

Date:

Mr. Hourly Employee
1234 Compensation Lane
New Hire, NH 00223

Dear Hourly:

I am pleased to offer you the position of pastry chef at the ABC Lounge in City, State.

This job offer is contingent upon the successful completion of a pre-employment physical and drug screen. Please take the enclosed paperwork with you to the occupational medicine clinic located at (address, City, State) on Tuesday, June 2, 2008 at 3:30 P.M. The drug screen is a urine test—please be prepared.

Your starting salary will be $10.50 per hour. As a full-time employee, you are eligible for enrollment in our medical, dental, and life insurance plans. Enrollment materials will be sent to you within two weeks of your start date. If you do not receive them in a timely manner, please let me know. You must sign up for benefits within 30 days of hire to be eligible without delay. You will receive a ninety-day performance evaluation on September, 2, 2008. At that time, you may be eligible for a pay increase of 1%–5%.

I will notify you as soon as I receive the results of your drug screen and physical. Please contact me if you have any questions. Your signature below confirms that you understand that this is a contingent offer of employment.

_____	_____
Applicant Signature	Date
_____	_____
Manager Signature	Date

Job Description

Human Resource Clerk II

Non-exempt _____   Exempt _____

Position reports to:

_____

Duties: Process payroll for approximately seventy-five employees on a biweekly payroll schedule. Provide clerical support for Human Resource Manager. Complete any reasonable requests assigned by management.

Essential Functions

Input numeric data quickly and accurately into automated payroll system.

Monitor employee time data on a daily basis. Troubleshoot discrepancies.

Report noncompliance of FLSA hour laws on employee timecards to Human Resource Manager.

Collect employee vacation and sick-leave sheets from department heads in a timely manner.

Meet payroll-processing deadlines at the end of each pay period.

Distribute employee paychecks.

Prepare purchase orders prior to making purchases for office supplies.

Process invoices in accounts payable system.

Enter employment applications in applicant flow log and forward applications to department head for review.

Make appointments for drug screens and pre-employment physicals.

Enter personnel action forms and benefit-enrollment data into HRIS quickly and accurately.

Answer incoming calls and communicate effectively.

Job Description

Human Resource Clerk II
Page Two

<u>Marginal Functions</u>
Maintain supply of new-hire paperwork and benefit-enrollment kits.
File payroll and personnel documents in a timely manner.
Prepare paycheck signature log each payday.
Order office supplies.
Prepare personnel files for new hires.

Employee Signature	Date

Print Employee Name

Supervisor Signature	Date

Print Supervisor Name

Performance Evaluation—Hourly Employee

Employee: Title:
Department: Review Period:
Reviewed By: Date:

Job Title:
Rating Scale: E=Exceeds Standards M=Meets Standards B=Below Standards
*Ratings of B-Below Standards require comment.

Appearance: Adheres to company's written dress code and grooming standards. _____
Comments:

_____

_____

Customer Service: Responds promptly to customer requests. Provides exceptional service.

_____
Comments:

_____

_____

Teamwork: Ability to work with others. Cooperative.   _____
Comments:

_____

_____

Feedback: Accepts suggestions and constructive feedback from supervisor.   _____
Comments:

_____

_____

Attendance and Punctuality: Shows up for work in a timely manner. Reliable.   _____
Comments:

_____

_____

Performance Evaluation—Hourly Employee

Page Two

Quality of Work: Demonstrates competence in required job skills and knowledge. _____

Comments:

_____

_____

Productivity: Work is accomplished timely and accurately. _____

Comments:

_____

_____

Initiative: Accomplishes assigned tasks with limited supervision and direction. _____

Comments:

_____

_____

Proprietary Interest: Displays an interest in the company's success. _____

Comments:

_____

_____

Growth: Has a desire to learn new tasks and take on additional responsibility. _____

_____

_____

Troubleshooting: Uses sound judgment. _____

Comments:

_____

_____

Technology and Equipment: Proficient use of equipment, technology, and tools needed to perform the job. _____

Comments:

_____

_____

Performance Evaluation—Hourly Employee

Page Three

Self-Management: Sets priorities and multitasks when needed. _____
Comments:

_____

_____

Adapts to Change: Adheres to new procedures and fluctuating workloads. _____
Comments:

_____

_____

Innovation: Offers ideas for increasing productivity and effectiveness of departmental
operations. _____
Comments:

_____

_____

Overall Performance Rating: _____

Additional Comments from Supervisor:

_____

_____

Employee Comments:

_____

_____

_____	_____
Employee's Signature	Date
_____	_____
Supervisor's Signature	Date
_____	_____
Manager's Signature	Date

Documentation of Verbal Counseling

Date: June 11, 2008
To:
From:

This memo is to document the conversation we had on Wednesday, June 11, 2008.

On Tuesday, June 10, 2008, you were scheduled to report to work at 8:00 A.M. You called at 9:15 A.M. to report that you were ill and unable to report to work. You left a message with the receptionist and did not ask to speak to me, your supervisor.

On February 15, 2008, you received a copy of our employee handbook, of which there is a receipt in your personnel file indicating you have read and received the handbook. Page 13 of the handbook states the following:

If you are unable to report to work due to an illness or other circumstance, call your supervisor at the first indication that you will be unable to report to work, but no later than the beginning of your shift. If your supervisor is not available at the office or by cell phone, call the switchboard and ask to speak to the manager on duty.

Although you are aware of our call-off policy, you did not call by the start of your shift. Further, when you did call, you left a message with the switchboard operator and made no attempt to contact me directly. This is a violation of our call-off policy as stated on Page 13 of the employee handbook.

The reason I need to be notified in a timely manner if you are unable to report to work is so that I can call in a replacement to cover your station. When the dining room is short-staffed, the service to our guests suffers. Since you didn't call me until 9:15 A.M., this delayed the time it took for another server to arrive and take over your shift.

Next time you are ill and unable to work, you are expected to call me directly no later than the start of your shift. Failure to do so in the future may result in disciplinary action.

If you have any questions about our call-off policy, please contact me and I will be happy to answer your questions.

Written Warning

Date: July 18, 2008
To:
From:

This document is a written warning for violation of our call-off policy on Thursday, July 17, 2008.

This is the second time you violated the company's call-off policy. The first occurrence was on Tuesday, June 10, 2008. You received a verbal counseling about this incident on Wednesday, June 11, 2008.

On July 17, 2008, you were scheduled to report to work at 8:00 A.M. You did not report to work, nor did you call. I called your house at 9:30 A.M. to see if you were okay. Your roommate answered the phone and said that she did not know your whereabouts. I called your cell phone afterward and left a message on your voicemail. You called me back two hours later, at 11:30 A.M. Worried about you, I asked if you were okay. You said that you had a cold. I asked you why you did not call me to report that you were unable to work. Your response was that you forgot to call.

This is the second time you have violated the company's call-off policy within the past six weeks. You are aware of the call-off policy. It was brought to your attention on your first day of work during orientation when you received your employee handbook. Additionally, you were reminded of the policy when you received verbal counseling for violating the policy on June 10, 2008.

If you have any questions about what is expected of you when you are unable to report to work, please contact me. It is important that you remind yourself of the call-off procedures next time you are ill. A further occurrence of an improper call-off may result in additional disciplinary action.

_____   _____
Manager Name   Signature

_____   _____
Employee Name   Signature

Last-Chance Warning

Date: August 26, 2008
To:
From:

This is a last-chance warning that one more violation of the company's call-off policy between now and February 26, 2009 will result in the termination of your employment at the ABC Lounge.

It has been documented that you are aware of the company's call-off policy. However, you violated this policy on Tuesday, June 10, 2008 and again on Thursday, July 17, 2008. On both days, you did not contact me by the beginning of your shift to report that you were ill and unable to report to work.

You received a written warning for the improper call off on July 17, 2008. However, you again violated the call-off policy on Monday, August 25, 2008. You were scheduled to report to work at 5:00 P.M., but you were not at your workstation at that time. At 6:00 P.M., you called the switchboard and left a message reporting that you were ill and unable to report to work. I was in my office and had my cell phone with me. You again made no attempt to contact me directly.

To repeat, one more violation of the company's call-off policy between now and February 26, 2009 will result in the immediate termination of your employment. Please contact me if you have any questions regarding the call-off procedures.

_____   _____
Manager Name   Signature

_____   _____
Employee Name   Signature

Letter of Employment Separation

Date: September 30, 2008
To:
From:

This letter is to inform you that you have been separated from employment at the ABC Lounge effective Tuesday, September 30, 2008.

You violated the company's call-off policy on June 11, 2008, July 17, 2008, and August 25, 2008. On August 26, 2008, you received a last-chance warning indicating that an additional violation of the policy prior to February 26, 2009 would result in the immediate termination of your employment at ABC Lounge.

Despite the warning, you violated the call-off policy today, September 30, 2008. You were scheduled to report to work at 5:00 P.M. I called you at 5:45 P.M. to see if you were okay and where you were. You answered the phone and said that you were ill and unable to come to work. I asked you why you did not call me, and you said that you forgot to call.

Your final paycheck is enclosed. I wish you well in your future endeavors.

Sincerely,

Manager Name

Memorandum to Announce Change in Policy

Date: June 8, 2008
To: All Employees
From:

Page 26 of the employee handbook states that this company observes the following six days as paid holidays:

New Year's Day
Memorial Day
Independence Day
Labor Day
Thanksgiving
Christmas

Effective immediately, two additional days have been added to our holiday paid time-off package. These two holidays are:

Martin Luther King Jr. Day
President's Day

Please sign and return the copy of this amendment to me at your earliest convenience. The original will be placed in your personnel file. The enclosed copy is for your records.

Employee Name	Signature

Sample Letter to Unsuccessful Job Candidate

Date:

Name:
Address:
City/State/Zip:

Dear:

Thank you for your interest in employment at XYZ Company. I enjoyed meeting you during the interview, and I appreciate your taking the time to travel to our offices.

We received applications from several qualified candidates for the position of administrative assistant. We had only one opening, and I regret to inform you that the position was offered to and accepted by another candidate.

Again, I wish to thank you for your interest in the position and I wish you well in your future endeavors.

Respectfully,

Manager Name

Confidential Exit Interview

Employee Name: _____

Department: _____

Position: _____

Supervisor's Name: _____

Last Day of Employment: _____

1. Please rate the following reason/s that has/have been a factor in your decision to leave the company. Use 1 for the main reason, and descending numbers from there until all that apply have been accounted for. Leave choices that do not apply blank.

_____ Salary

_____ Benefits

_____ Scheduling conflicts

_____ Limited opportunities for advancement

_____ Family obligations

_____ Health condition

_____ Drive to work is too far

_____ Dislike work

_____ Pursuing my dream job

_____ Return to school

_____ Graduated from school

_____ Relocation

_____ Self-employment

_____ Inadequate training

_____ Supervisor difficult to work with

_____ Conflict with coworkers

_____ Other _____

Confidential Exit Interview

Page Two

2. If salary was your reason for leaving, what do you think would have been a fair salary for the position? Please explain.

_____

Please answer "yes" or "no" to questions 3–11 and provide an explanation:

3. Do you feel that the employee benefits were adequate?
Yes ❑   No ❑
Please explain:

_____

4. Do you feel that the company's paid time-off policy for holiday, vacation, and sick leave is adequate? Yes ❑   No ❑
Please explain:

_____

5. Is there a sense of teamwork among the managers and staff?
Yes ❑   No ❑
Please explain:

_____

6. Were you ever harassed by a coworker, supervisor, or manager and did not report it?
Yes ❑   No ❑
Please explain:

_____

7. Is the job that you performed what you expected it to be when you were hired?
Yes ❑   No ❑
Please explain:

_____

Confidential Exit Interview

Page Three

8. Do you feel that you were always treated fairly?

Yes ❑   No ❑

Please explain:

_____

9. Do you feel that there was adequate communication among coworkers and other departments?

Yes ❑   No ❑

Please explain:

_____

10. Did you receive recognition for a job well done?

Yes ❑   No ❑

Please explain:

_____

11. Would you ever apply for a job here again in the future?

Yes ❑   No ❑

Please explain:

_____

12. What did you enjoy most about your job?

_____

13. What did you dislike most about your job?

_____

Thank you for taking the time to answer our exit interview. Our employees are our most important asset and when someone decides to leave, it is helpful for us to know why in an effort to properly evaluate our goal of being a preferred employer in the community. We wish you well in your future endeavors and thank you for being part of our team.

Sample FMLA Letter for Employees Who Give Advance Notice

(For your convenience, you may download Forms WH-380 and WH-381 from the Dept. of Labor Web site. Use of the forms is optional, but the relevant information must be given to the employee in a written format.)

Date:
Employee Name:
Address:
City/State/Zip:

Dear _____:

We have received your request dated _____ to take time off from work under circumstances that may qualify for leave under the Family and Medical Leave Act (FMLA). I have enclosed a copy of our FMLA policy along with forms for both you and your health-care provider to fill out and return. An FMLA Employer Response to Employee Request for FMLA Leave (Form WH-381) is also enclosed. This serves as your notice of FMLA regulations, your rights, and the obligations and expectations of you during leave. You will be notified in writing about the status of your leave request.

Please fill out and return the enclosed Employee's Request for Family and Medical Leave form no later than thirty days prior to the first day you are requesting leave. However, if your leave has been foreseeable for less than thirty days, please fill out and return the form immediately.

The Certification of Health Care Provider (WH-380) form is for your health-care provider to complete and return. The form may be returned to you or mailed directly to us. I have enclosed a return envelope for your provider's convenience. Please follow up with us to ensure that we have received the completed form from your health-care provider within fifteen days of the request. If there is a delay, your condition or situation will not be certified and this may result in the discontinuation of your leave. As stated in our enclosed copy of the FMLA policy, your medical-certification paperwork is considered confidential and will be viewed only by the person(s) involved in approving your FMLA leave.

The Notice and the copy of the company's FMLA policy are for you to keep for your records. It is recommended that you make a copy of your FMLA request form or ask us to make a copy for you when you turn it in. All of the information in the Notice is important. However, please pay extra attention to the section about the continuation of your medical benefits and the use of your accrued paid time off.

FMLA Letter

Page Two

FMLA can be complex and I understand if you have questions. Feel free to contact me at any time if I may be of assistance.

Sincerely,

HR Representative Name
Enclosures
cc: Employee medical file

Sample FMLA Letter for Employees Who Did Not Give Advance Notice

(For your convenience, you may download Forms WH-380 and WH-381 from the Dept. of Labor Web site. Use of the forms is optional, but the relevant information must be given to the employee in a written format.)

Date:
Employee Name:
Address:
City/State/Zip:

Dear _____:

You have not reported to work on _____. We became aware that your absence may be due to circumstances that may qualify for leave under the Family and Medical Leave Act (FMLA).

I have enclosed a copy of our FMLA policy along with forms for both you and your health-care provider to fill out and return. An FMLA Employer Response to Employee Request for FMLA Leave (Form WH-381) is also enclosed. This serves as your notice of FMLA regulations, your rights, and the obligations and expectations of you during leave. You will be notified in writing about the status of your leave request.

Please fill out and return the enclosed Employee's Request for Family and Medical Leave at your earliest convenience. This form is to be completed no later than thirty days before the start of a leave that is foreseeable. Since there has been no advance notice of your absence, we ask that you fill it out as soon as possible.

The Certification of Health Care Provider (WH-380) form is for your health-care provider to complete and return. The form may be returned to you or mailed directly to us. I have enclosed a return envelope for your provider's convenience. Please follow up with us to ensure that we have received the completed form from your health-care provider within fifteen days of the request. If there is a delay, your condition or situation will not be certified and this may result in the discontinuation of your leave. As stated in our enclosed copy of the FMLA policy, your medical-certification paperwork is considered confidential and will be viewed only by the person(s) involved in approving your FMLA leave.

FMLA Letter

Page Two

The Notice and the copy of the company's FMLA policy are for you to keep for your records. It is recommended that you make a copy of your FMLA request form or ask us to make a copy for you when you turn it in. All of the information in the Notice is important. However, please pay extra attention to the section about the continuation of your medical benefits and the use of your accrued paid time off.

FMLA can be complex and I understand if you have questions. Feel free to contact me at any time if I may be of assistance.

Sincerely,

HR Representative Name
Enclosures
cc: Employee medical file

Request for FMLA Leave

Employee Information

Name: _____   Date: _____
Position: _____   SSN: _____
Address: _____
Does your spouse work for this company? _____

Type of Leave Request

Estimated Start Date: _____   Estimated Return Date: _____

Reason for the Leave: (please check one)

❏To care for my child after birth.
❏To care for a child placed in my home by adoption or foster care. Please indicate the date of placement: _____ ❏Anticipated ❏Actual (check one)
❏To care for a family member who has a serious health condition. Please indicate relationship of family member: ❏Spouse ❏Child ❏Parent (check one)

Name of family member: _____

(Note to employer: If your state allows leave to be taken intermittently, you may add an option to request this type of leave here.)

I understand that certification from a licensed medical care provider on behalf of myself or an immediate family member is needed for FMLA leave to be approved. I am also aware that the company is required to pay their usual contribution of my medical benefits while I am on leave, and that I am also required to pay my share. Failure to do so may result in discontinuation of my medical benefits due to lack of payment.

_____   _____
Employee Signature   Date

Sample FMLA Leave Approval Letter

(Employers—note that your policy or state regulations may be different than the information provided in this sample.)

Date:

Employee Name:
Address:
City/State/Zip:
(Hand deliver or send certified-mail return-receipt requested)

Dear:

This letter is to inform you that your request for leave has been designated as Family and Medical Leave (FMLA) under the Family and Medical Leave Act of 1993. Your leave begins on MM-DD-YY and ends on MM-DD-YY. This time off will be charged against the twelve weeks of leave that you are entitled to receive in a rolling twelve-month period. The method for calculating the twelve-month period is explained in the written copy of the company's FMLA policy that you received on MM-DD-YY.

According to company policy, you are required to use the balance of your unpaid sick leave at the start of your leave. You currently have (number) hours on record. Your paycheck for this leave will be processed during the normal payroll cycle.

Once your paychecks are discontinued, you are required to pay for your health insurance premiums by the first of each month. Payments will be credited toward the insurance for the month in which they are paid. Premiums are payable by check or money order and may be sent to the company via U.S. mail to the attention of the accounting department. Please be sure to send a note with the payment or indicate on the reference line what the payment is for. The amount due by the first of each month is $264.76.

Your position will be held for you while you are on approved leave. If you do not return at the end of the twelve-week period, your position may no longer be available for you if you return at a later date.

Due to the nature of your leave, you will be required to present a return-to-work authorization from your physician before returning to work. This is for your protection to ensure that you are physically able to perform the essential duties of your job upon return.

FMLA Approval Letter

Page Two

Please be aware that in some circumstances, the FMLA entitles employers for reimbursement of health insurance premiums paid by the employer during leave if the employee does not return from FMLA.

As allowed by section 825.309 of FMLA regulations, please contact your supervisor or the human resource department every four weeks, starting with the beginning of your leave, to give your status and intent to return to work.

If you have any questions about FMLA, your sick leave usage, health insurance premiums, or any other matters, please don't hesitate to contact me at 555-555-5555.

Respectfully,

Supervisor Name
Supervisor Title

Sample FMLA Policy

(Employers—note that your policy or state regulations may be different than the information provided in this sample.)

This written notice highlights the FMLA policy at ABC company.

Employees who have been employed for at least twelve months and worked at least 1,250 hours in that year are entitled to twelve weeks of unpaid leave under the Family and Medical Leave Act of 1993. Time worked is considered hours designated by the Fair Labor Standards Act (FLSA).

FMLA may be requested due to the birth or placement of a child with you for adoption or foster care, during your own serious health condition that makes you unable to perform the essential duties of your job, or during the serious health condition of an immediate family member that requires your care. The immediate family members who qualify are your spouse, child, or parent.

Employees are to notify the company verbally or in writing that they are requesting a leave of absence. If the leave is believed to be one that qualifies for FMLA, the appropriate packet of paperwork will be forwarded to the employee within two days.

You have a right under the FMLA for up to twelve weeks of leave with job protection in a twelve-month period during a qualifying event. This company recognizes a rolling twelve-month period. This means that the company takes the last date of FMLA leave used and counts forward twelve months to determine if unused leave is available.

The job protection provided to employees under the FMLA requires reinstatement into the same job upon return, or a job with substantially similar pay, duties, status, hours, and working conditions.

Our policy requires employees to use accrued sick leave while they are on FMLA. Sick leave is to be used at the beginning of the leave until exhausted. Vacation leave or personal leave may be used at the employee's discretion. The payroll department must be advised of an employee's desire to use accrued vacation or personal leave during this time.

Once an employee's paychecks stop while they are on leave (after the usage of sick leave), employees are required to pay their usual premiums for health insurance. The human resources office will advise employees of the amount due. Payments are due at the first of the month for the month of payment (for example, the insurance due on May 1 is for insurance premiums for the month of May).

Sample FMLA Policy

Page Two

Employees who are granted leave due to their own serious health condition may be required to present a return-to-work authorization from their health-care provider upon returning to work. The work authorization should indicate if the employee is able to return to full duty or if there are restrictions. Work restrictions must be detailed.

If leave granted is for less time than the twelve weeks allowable by law, employees are asked to request an extension within two weeks of the ending date of their approved leave.

Employees who do not wish to return from leave are asked to notify the company in writing as soon as a decision has been made not to return. In some circumstances, employees who do not return from approved FMLA will be liable for reimbursing the company for the company's share of health insurance benefits paid for the employee.

While on leave, employees are asked to contact their supervisor once every four weeks with their intent to return to work. Employers are entitled to this courtesy under section 825.309 of FMLA regulations.

Employees who are a key employee, as described in section 825.217 of the FMLA regulations, may be denied leave. A key employee is a salaried employee who holds a position in the top 10 percent of all salaries within the company. Leave may be denied if an extended absence of the employee will cause undue hardship to the company.

Employees who request FMLA leave are notified in writing of the status of their request upon receipt of medical certification from a health-care provider.

Receipt of Employee Handbook

I, _____ , received a copy of the employee handbook for XYZ Company on _____. I understand that I am expected to read the handbook in a timely manner and that I will be held accountable for obeying the rules and policies printed in the handbook.

If I have any questions about the contents of the handbook, I will contact my supervisor or a human resource representative.

_____

Employee Printed Name

_____   _____

Employee Signature   Date

Glossary of HR Acronyms

AAP
Affirmative Action Plan

ACH
Automatic Clearing House

ADA
Americans with Disabilities Act

ADEA
Age Discrimination in Employment Act

AMA
American Management Association

AOE
Arising Out of Employment

APA
American Payroll Association

BFOQ
Bona Fide Occupational Qualification

CDHP
Consumer Driven Health Plan

CEAP
Certified Employee Assistance Professional

COBRA
Consolidated Omnibus Budget Reconciliation Act

CODA
Cash or Deferred Arrangements

COE
In the Course and Scope of Employment

DFEH
Department of Fair Employment and Housing

DOL
Department of Labor

EACC
Employee Assistance Certification Commission

EAPA
Employee Assistance Professionals Association

EASNA
The Employee Assistance Society of North America

EE
Eligible Employee

EEOC
Equal Employment Opportunity Commission

EEVS
Electronic Employment Verification System

EGTRRA
The Economic Growth and Tax Relief Reconciliation Act of 2001

EPA
Equal Pay Act

EPO
Employment Process Outsourcing

FACTA
Fair and Accurate Credit Transactions Act

FEHA
Fair Employment and Housing Act

FEPA
Fair Employment Practices Agency

FLSA
Fair Labor Standards Act

FMLA
Family and Medical Leave Act

GLB
Gramm-Leach Biley Act

GPHR
Global Professional in Human Resources

HCE
Highly Compensated Employees

HCS
Hazard Communication Standard

HDHP
High Deductible Health Plan

HIPAA
Health Insurance Portability and Accountability Act

HMO
Health Maintenance Organization

HRA
Health Reimbursement Account

HRCI
Human Resource Certification Institute

HSA
Health Savings Account

IRCA
Immigration Reform and Control Act

JRIS
Job Reference Immunity Statutes

JSA
Job Safety Analysis

LCSW
Licensed Clinical Social Worker

LOA
Leave of Absence

MSDS
Material Safety Data Sheet

OSHA
Occupational Safety & Health Administration

OWBPA
Older Workers Benefit Protection Act of 1990

PHI
Protected Health Information

PHR
Professional in Human Resources

PIE
Period of Initial Eligibility

SARBOX
Sarbanes-Oxley Act of 2002

SHRM
Society for Human Resource Management

SOX
Sarbanes-Oxley Act of 2002 (alternate acronym)

SPHR
Senior Professional in Human Resources

SRA
Salary Reduction Agreement

SSA
Social Security Administration

TDA
Tax-Deferred Annuities

TSA
Tax-Sheltered Annuities

WARN
Workers Adjustment and Retraining Notification Act

Online and Print Publications Helpful to HR Professionals

Web sites

American Management Association
✍ *www.amanet.org*

Americans with Disabilities Act
✍ *www.ada.gov*

Employee Assistance Professionals Association
✍ *www.eap-association.org*

Equal Employment Opportunity Commission
✍ *www.eeoc.gov*

HireVetsFirst
✍ *www.hirevetsfirst.gov*

Human Resource Certification Institute
✍ *www.hrci.org*

Internal Revenue Service
✍ *www.irs.gov*

Job Accommodation Network
✍ *www.jan.wvu.edu*

Leadership IQ
✍ *www.leadershipiq.com*

National Conference of State Legislation
✍ *www.ncsl.org*

Profit Sharing Council of America
✍ *www.psca.org*

Society for Human Resource Management
✍ *www.shrm.org*

Society for Industrial and Organizational Psychology, Inc.
✍ *www.siop.org*

U.S. Chamber of Commerce
✍ *www.uschamber.com*

U.S. Citizenship and Immigration Services
✍ *www.uscis.gov*

U.S. Department of Health & Human Services
✍ *www.hhs.gov*

U.S. Department of Labor
✍ *www.dol.gov*

Print Magazines

Many of these magazines also offer free electronic newsletters and publish articles on their Web sites.

Corporate Meetings & Incentives
www.meetingsnet.com

HR Magazine
www.shrm.org/subscribe

Human Resource Executive
www.hreonline.com

Outsourcing Today
www.outsourcingtoday.com

Staffing Management
www.shrm.org/subscribe

Talent Management
www.talentmgmt.com

Workforce Management
www.workforce.com

Electronic Newsletters and Magazines

Employee Benefit News
www.benefitnews.com

HR.com
www.hr.com

Plan Sponsor
www.plansponsor.com

Workforce Management Online
www.workforceonline.com

WorkLife Excel Employee Newsletter
www.bizreport.com

State Employer Tax Offices

Alabama Department of Revenue
www.ador.state.al.us
(334) 242-1170

Alaska Department of Revenue
www.revenue.state.ak.us
(907) 465-2300

Arizona Department of Revenue
www.revenue.state.ax.us
(800) 843-7196

Arkansas Department of Finance and Administration
www.state.ar.us/dfa
(501) 324-9052

California Board of Equalization
www.boe.ca.gov
(800) 400-7115

California Franchise Tax Board
www.ftb.ca.gov
(916) 845-6500

Colorado Department of Revenue
www.revenue.state.co.us
(800) 659-3656

Connecticut Department of Revenue Services
- *www.drs.state.ct.us*
- *(800) 382-9463*

Delaware Division of Revenue
- *www.state.de.us/revenue*
- *(302) 577-8205*

District of Columbia Office of the Chief Financial Officer
- *cfo.dc.gov/main.asp*
- *(202) 727-1000*

Florida Department of Revenue
- *www.state.fl.us/dor*
- *(800) 352-3671*

Georgia Department of Revenue
- *www.etax.dor.ga.gov*
- *(877) 602-8477*

Hawaii Department of Taxation
- *www.state.hi.us*
- *(808) 587-4242*

Idaho State Tax Commission
- *www.state.id.us*
- *(800) 972-7660*

Illinois Department of Revenue
- *www.revenue.state.il.us*
- *(800) 732-8866*

Indiana Department of Revenue
- *www.ai.org/dor*
- *(317) 233-4018*

Iowa Department of Revenue and Finance
- *www.state.ia.us*
- *(800) 367-3388*

Kansas Department of Revenue
- *www.ksrevenue.org*
- *(785) 368-8222*

Kentucky Revenue Cabinet
- *www.revenue.ky.gov*
- *(502) 564-8139*

Louisiana Department of Revenue and Taxation
- *www.rev.state.la.us*
- *(225) 219-7318*

Maine Revenue Services
- *www.state.me.us/revenue*
- *(207) 624-9595*

Maryland Comptroller of the Treasury
- *www.comp.state.md.us*
- *(800) 492-1751*

Massachusetts Department of Revenue
- *www.dor.state.ma.us*
- *(800) 392-6089*

Michigan Department of Treasury
- *www.michigan.gov/treasury*
- *(517) 373-3200*

Minnesota Department of Revenue
- *www.taxes.state.mn.us*
- *(800) 657-3594*

Mississippi State Tax Commission
- *www.mstc.state.ms.us*
- *(601) 923-7000*

Missouri Department of Revenue
- *www.dor.state.mo.us*
- *(888) 751-2863*

Montana Department of Revenue
www.state.mt.us/revenue
(406) 444-6900

Nebraska Department of Revenue
www.revenue.state.ne.us
(800) 742-7474

Nevada Department of Taxation
www.tax.state.nv.us
(775) 684-2000

New Hampshire Department of Revenue
Administration
www.state.nh.us/revenue
(603) 271-2191

New Jersey Division of Taxation
www.state.nj.us/treasury/taxation
(609) 292-6400

New Mexico Taxation and Revenue Department
www.state.nm.us/tax
(505) 827-0700

New York Department of Taxation and Finance
www.tax.state.ny.us
(888) 698-2908

North Carolina Department of Revenue
www.dor.state.nc.us
(919) 733-8510

North Dakota State Tax Department
www.nd.gov./tax
(701) 328-2775

Ohio Department of Taxation
www.state.oh.us/tax
(888) 405-4039

Oklahoma Tax Commission
www.oktax.state.ok.us
(405) 521-3160

Oregon Department of Revenue
www.oregon.gov/dor
(800) 356-4222

Pennsylvania Department of Revenue
www.revenue.state.pa.us
(717) 787-1064

Rhode Island Division of Taxation
www.tax.state.ri.us
(401) 222-1120

South Carolina Department of Revenue
www.sctax.org
(843) 852-3600

South Dakota Department of Revenue
www.state.sd.us
(800) 829-9188

Tennessee Department of Revenue
www.state.tn.us/revenue
(615) 741-2461

Texas Comptroller of Public Accounts
www.cpa.state.tx.us
(877) 662-8373

Utah State Tax Commission
www.tax.utah.gov
(800) 662-4335

Vermont Department of Taxes
www.state.vt.us/tax
(802) 828-5723

Virginia Department of Taxation
www.tax.virginia.gov
(804) 367-8037

Washington Department of Revenue
www.dor.wa.gov
(800) 647-7706

West Virginia State Tax Department
www.state.wv.us/taxdiv
(800) 982-8297

Wisconsin Department of Revenue
www.dor.state.wi.us
(608) 266-2772

Wyoming Department of Revenue
www.revenue.state.wy.us
(307) 777-7961

U.S. Employment Offices

Alabama Department of Labor
www.alalabor.state.al.us
(334) 242-3460

Alaska Department of Labor and Workforce Development
www.labor.state.ak.us
(907) 465-2770

Arizona State Labor Department
www.ica.state.az.us
(602) 542-4411

Arkansas Department of Labor
www.arkansas.gov/labor
(501) 682-4541

California Department of Industrial Relations
www.dir.ca.gov
(415) 703-5050

Colorado Department of Labor and Employment
www.coworkforce.com/lab
(303) 318-8000

Connecticut Department of Labor
www.ct.gov/dol
www.ctdol.state.ct.us
(860) 263-6505

Delaware Secretary of Labor
www.delawareworks.com
(302) 761-8000

District of Columbia Department of Employment Services
www.does.dc.gov
(202) 671-1900

Florida Agency for Workforce Innovation
www.floridajobs.org
www.MyFlorida.com
(850) 245-7105

Georgia Department of Labor
www.dol.state.ga.us
(404) 656-3011

Hawaii Department of Labor & Industrial Relations
www.Hawaii.gov/labor
(808) 586-8842

Idaho Department of Commerce and Labor
www.labor.state.id.us
(208) 332-3579

Illinois Department of Labor
✍ *www.state.il.us/agency/idol*
✆ *(312) 793-1808*

Indiana Department of Labor
✍ *www.in.gov/labor*
✆ *(317) 232-2655*

Iowa Workforce Development
✍ *www.iowaworkforce.org*
✆ *(515) 281-5365*

Kansas Department of Labor
✍ *www.dol.ks.gov*
✆ *(785) 296-4062*

Kentucky Department of Labor
✍ *www.labor.ky.gov*
✆ *(502) 564-3070*

Louisiana Department of Labor
✍ *www.laworks.net*
✆ *(225) 342-3111*

Maine Department of Labor
✍ *www.state.me.us/labor*
✍ *www.maine.gov/labor*
✆ *(207) 287-3787*

Maryland Department of Labor, Licensing and Regulation
✍ *www.dllr.state.md.us*
✆ *(410) 230-6020*

Massachusetts Department of Labor & Work Force Dev.
✍ *www.mass.gov/dlwd*
✍ *www.state.ma.us*
✆ *(617) 626-7122*

Michigan Department of Labor & Economic Growth
✍ *www.michigan.gov/cis*
✆ *(517) 373-3034*

Minnesota Department of Labor and Industry
✍ *www.doli.state.mn.us*
✆ *(651) 284-5010*

Mississippi Department of Employment Security
✍ *www.mdes.ms.gov*
✆ *(601) 321-6100*

Missouri Labor and Industrial Relations
✍ *www.dolir.mo.gov/lirc*
✆ *(573) 751-2461*

Montana Department of Labor and Industry
✍ *www.dli.mt.gov*
✆ *(406) 444-9091*

Nebraska Department of Labor
✍ *www.nebraskaworkforce.com*
✍ *www.dol.state.ne.us*
✆ *(402) 471-3405*

Nevada Department of Business and Industry
✍ *www.laborcommissioner.com*
✍ *www.dbi.state.nv.us*
✆ *(702) 486-2650*

New Hampshire Department of Labor
✍ *www.labor.state.nh.us*
✆ *(603) 271-3171*

New Jersey Department of Labor
✍ *www.state.nj.us/labor*
✆ *(609) 292-2323*

New Mexico Department of Labor
✉ *www.dol.state.nm.us*
✆ *(505) 841-8409*

New York Department of Labor
✉ *www.labor.state.ny.us*
✆ *(518) 457-2741*

North Carolina Department of Labor
✉ *www.nclabor.com*
✆ *(919) 733-0359*

North Dakota Department of Labor
✉ *www.state.nd.us/labor*
✉ *www.state.nd.gov/labor*
✆ *(701) 328-3708*

Ohio Division of Labor and Worker Safety
✉ *www.state.oh.us/ohio/agency.htm*
✉ *www.obg.ohio.gov*
✆ *(614) 644-2239*

Oklahoma Department of Labor
✉ *www.state.ok.us/~okdol*
✆ *(405) 528-1500*

Oregon Bureau of Labor and Industries
✉ *www.oregon.gov/boli*
✆ *(503) 731-4070*

Pennsylvania Department of Labor and Industry
✉ *www.dli.state.pa.us*
✆ *(717) 787-5279*

Rhode Island Department of Labor and Training
✉ *www.dlt.state.ri.us*
✆ *(401) 462-8870*

South Carolina Department of Labor, Licensing & Regulations
✉ *www.llr.state.sc.us*
✆ *(803) 896-4300*

South Dakota Department of Labor
✉ *www.state.sd.us*
✉ *www.sdjobs.org*
✆ *(605) 773-3101*

Tennessee Department of Labor
✉ *www.state.tn.us/labor-wfd*
✆ *(615) 741-6642*

Texas Workforce Commission
✉ *www.twc.state.tx.us*
✆ *(512) 463-2829*

Utah Labor Commission
✉ *www.laborcommission.utah.gov*
✆ *(801) 530-6680*

Vermont Department of Labor
✉ *www.labor.vermont.gov*
✆ *(802) 828-4000*

Virginia Department of Labor and Industry
✉ *www.doli.virginia.gov*
✆ *(804) 786-2377*

Washington Deartment of Labor and Industries
✉ *www.lni.wa.gov*
✆ *(360) 902-4203*

West Virginia Division of Labor
✉ *www.labor.state.wv.us*
✉ *www.wvlabor.org*
✆ *(304) 558-7890*

Wisconsin Dept of Workforce Development
✑ *www.dwd.state.wi.us*
✆ *(608) 267-9692*

Wyoming Department of Employment
✑ *http://wydoe.state.wy.us*
✆ *(307) 777-7672*

Guam Department of Labor
✑ *www.Guamdol.net*
✆ *(671) 475-7012*

Puerto Rico Department of Labor and Human
Resources
✑ *www.dtrh.gobierno.pr (Spanish)*
✑ *www.fortaleza.govpr.org*
✆ *(787) 754-2119*

Virgin Islands Department of Labor
✑ *www.vidol.gov*
✆ *(340) 776-3700*

Index